Warren Quinn was widely regarded as a moral philosopher of remarkable talent. This collection of his most important contributions to moral philosophy and the philosophy of action has been edited for publication by Philippa Foot.

Quinn laid out the foundations for an antiutilitarian moral philosophy that was critical of much contemporary work in ethics, such as the antirealism of Gilbert Harman and the neosubjectivism of Bernard Williams. Quinn's own distinctive moral theory is developed in the discussion of substantial, practical moral issues. For example, there are important pieces here on the permissibility of abortion, the justification (if any) for punishing criminals when no particular good seems likely to result, and on the distinction between killing and allowing to die, a distinction crucial to the subject of euthanasia and other topics in medical ethics. The volume would be ideally suited to upper-level undergraduate courses and graduate seminars on the foundations of ethics.

"Quinn's writings were always the product of lengthy reflection and great care and precision in argument: they are intellectually packed and elegantly written. And they make distinctive contributions at three different levels of moral philosophy: metaethics, moral theory, and applied ethics, . . . I use most of these essays in my own teaching, and they are standard references for those working in the field. Putting them together would create a book of lasting value, which displayed the range and insight of an outstanding moral philosopher."

Thomas Nagel

D0988571

CAMBRIDGE STUDIES IN PHILOSOPHY

Morality and Action

CAMBRIDGE STUDIES IN PHILOSOPHY

General editor ERNEST SOSA

Advisory editors J.E.J. ALTHAM, SIMON BLACKBURN,
GILBERT HARMAN, MARTIN HOLLIS,
FRANK JACKSON, WILLIAM G. LYCAN, JOHN PERRY,
BARRY STROUD, SYDNEY SHOEMAKER

RECENT TITLES

Morality and Action

Warren Quinn

CAMBRIDGE
UNIVERSITY PRESS

Published by the Press Syndicate of the University of Cambridge
The Pitt Building, Trumpington Street, Cambridge CB2 1RP
40 West 20th Street, New York, NY 10011-4211, USA
10 Stamford Road, Oakleigh, Melbourne 3166, Australia

© Cambridge University Press 1993

First published 1993

Printed in the United States of America

Library of Congress Cataloging-in-Publication Data
Quinn, Warren, d. 1991.
Morality and action / Warren Quinn.
p.   cm. – (Cambridge studies in philosophy)
Edited by Philippa Foot.
Includes bibliographical references.
ISBN 0-521-44164-1. – ISBN 0-521-44696-1 (pbk.)
1. Ethics.   2. Act (Philosophy)   I. Foot, Philippa.   II. Title.
III. Series.
BJ1012.Q56   1993
170 – dc20   93-2769
                                                      CIP

A catalog record for this book is available from the British Library.

ISBN 0-521-44164-1 hardback
ISBN 0-521-44696-1 paperback

Contents

Acknowledgments

I am most grateful to friends of Warren Quinn who helped with the proofreading for this volume: Torin Alter, Sean Foran, Amy Kind, Michael Otsuka, Derk Pereboom, Laurie Pieper, and Carol Voeller. And I am especially grateful to Houston Smit for having it in his care.

Philippa Foot

Introduction

In September 1991, at the time of Warren Quinn's sadly early death, he had completed all the papers reprinted in this volume; most had been published and even the last two were at the printers. Earlier, the Cambridge University Press had approached him about a collection of articles, and after his death I suggested that I should edit them. The selection had to be mine, but I think that Quinn himself would have agreed, first in including everything (except book reviews) published from the eighties onward and second in leaving out some earlier papers; these earlier articles show the same excellence of mind, but are not, I judge, of the same enduring interest.

With the exception of essay number 10 (an intriguing contribution to decision theory) the present papers are all on central topics of moral philosophy, and are, in spite of their rigor, such as to be comprehensible to philosophy students and even to nonphilosophers. They fall into four main categories: 1. Essays 1, 5, and 6 are critical pieces expressing Quinn's dissatisfaction with arguments advanced by other philosophers on the topic of the objectivity of moral judgment. 2. Essays 2 and 3 deal, in depth, with substantive moral issues: the first with abortion, the second with punishment. 3. Essays 8 and 9, originally written as a single paper, belong in the very important middle area between philosophical psychology and casuistry, where such concepts as *doing, allowing,* and *intending* are explored. 4. Essays 11 and 12, the most ambitious, and to my mind the most fascinating, of the papers give his own views on the crucial issue of rationality and human goodness. They will surely be the subject of much discussion in time to come; anyone not already familiar with Quinn's work could well begin with these papers.

Taken as a whole, these essays present a formidable challenge to two prevailing doctrines of the past forty or fifty years: first, utilitarianism and other forms of consequentialism, and second, subjectivism. The objections to consequentialism appear especially in his work on the doctrine of double effect and on *doing* and *allowing* (essays 7[1] and 8, 1989), where Quinn gave his own account of the distinction between doing and allowing, and between intending a result and bringing it about as a side effect; arguing, against consequentialists, that both distinctions are directly relevant to questions of moral justification. There is, he says, truth in the doctrine of double effect because of our special *prima facie* right not to be made the tool of other people's purposes. And the need for special justification for doing harm as opposed to allowing it to come about, comes, he thinks, from the special authority that all persons have over the way in which others may act *on* them.

Both these articles show the importance that Quinn saw in *rights;* it was a topic that particularly interested him, and this interest comes out also in "Abortion, Identity and Loss" (essay 2, 1984). Even the earliest abortion is not, he says, morally negligible: the fetus has a certain right to our consideration because, as a human being in the making, it can suffer the loss of the human life that *it* might have had. There is, however, another right – "the right of respect" – which becomes more compelling as the fetus comes closer to full human status. Quinn thus hopes to do justice to both our intuition that even the earliest abortion *matters* and the thought that the objection to abortion becomes stronger as the fetus develops.

In "The Right to Threaten and the Right to Punish" (essay 3, 1985) Quinn sees the problem from the beginning as the problem of the *right* we have actually to carry out punishments even in the absence of utilitarian justification. In this highly idiosyncratic paper Quinn argues that it is the right to threaten punishment that justifies the right to carry it out, rather than, as has been supposed, the other way around. A reply to a critic of this theory ("Reply to Brook," 1988) is printed here as essay 4.

Thus Quinn challenges consequentialism in a number of his papers. But it seems to have been even more important to him, as time went on, to criticize, and find an alternative to, the subjectiv-

---

1 This article was discussed by J. Boyle ("Who is Entitled to Double Effect?") and by Frances M. Kamm ("The Doctrine of Double Effect: Reflections on Theoretical and Practical Issues") in a special issue of *The Journal of Medicine and Philosophy* 16: 1991. Quinn's reply to Boyle and Kamm is reprinted as essay 9.

ism of such moral philosophers as C. L. Stevenson, R. M. Hare, John Mackie, and Bernard Williams. In "Moral and Other Realisms" (essay 1, 1978) he goes no further than to argue the inadequacy of certain arguments to settle the question of objectivity one way or the other. But in his final essays, "Rationality and the Human Good" and "Putting Rationality in its Place" (essays 11 and 12, 1992 and forthcoming, June 1993), he strikes at the root of emotivism and prescriptivism by challenging the neo-Humean theory of rationality on which contemporary subjectivism is so largely based. It has been, and still is, the boast of emotivists, prescriptivists, and their heirs, that they alone can do justice to the *practical* aspect of morality: that only if moral language is seen as expressing feelings, attitudes, or commitments, can its essentially reasongiving aspect be understood. Quinn argues that on the contrary the mere presence of a feeling, attitude, or prior decision cannot in itself give reason for any action, so that these "expressivist" theories are far from being able themselves to give an account of the rationality of acting morally. Moreover the problem of the rationality of moral judgment arises for philosophers such as Richard Hare, John Mackie, and Bernard Williams precisely because they have taken over a broadly Humean theory of practical rationality, in which an independent, neutral Reason acts to coordinate ultimately uncriticizable motivations. Quinn argues (in "Rationality and the Human Good") that a so-called virtue of practical rationality that found itself in such a complaisant position even in the face of shameful desires would have little claim to be the supreme human excellence. There is, he says "something in the moral indifference of neo-Humean rationality that stops it from shining forth in this role," and he himself outlines a neo-Aristotelean view of rationality which gives it a voice in the determination of human goodness extending even to the judgment of our most ultimate ends.

In these final articles Quinn has, therefore, mounted a strong attack on the Humean roots of contemporary moral subjectivism. He had earlier cleared the path by paying critical attention to a new argument against objectivism, originated by Gilbert Harman and also used by Bernard Williams, to the effect that the existence "out there in the world" of objective properties of actions corresponding to our judgments about what we ought morally to do, was suspect, because it could play no part in explaining the fact that we make these judgments. Quinn gives reasons for rejecting this "explanatory requirement," as also for denying the significance placed by Williams in a distinction between "thick" and "thin" moral concepts.

These critical essays, "Truth and Explanation in Ethics" (essay 5, 1985), and "Reflections and the Loss of Moral Knowledge: Williams on Objectivity" (essay 6, 1986) demand a reply. Together, the positive and the critical pieces add up to a contribution to moral philosophy that it will be impossible to ignore. Quinn's work should do much to weaken the widespread prejudice in favor of a Humean theory of practical rationality, and so to call in question contemporary subjectivist theories of moral judgment, which cannot do without its support.

Philippa Foot
April 1992

Warren Quinn

1

Moral and other
realisms: Some initial difficulties

Some very similar problems and disputes arise in ethics, aesthetics, and the philosophy of perception. One of the most basic of these parallel controversies concerns the connection between certain *features* we attribute to objects and certain mental *responses* that somehow or other provide a basis for these attributions.[1] Three examples of such feature–response pairs drawn from ethics, aesthetics, and philosophy of perception respectively are (a) moral goodness and moral approval, (b) funniness and amusement, and (c) something's being red and its looking red. What makes these and many other examples controversial is the fact that one kind of philosopher (the *realist*) finds it plausible to claim first that whether an object possesses one or another of these features is independent of and prior to the question whether it provokes the correlative response and second that the response itself is a genuinely cognitive state of mind in some way directed to the feature as part of its object.[2] While

From A. I. Goldman and J. Kim (eds.), *Values and Morals*, 257–273. Copyright © 1978 by D. Reidel Publishing Company, Dordrecht, Holland. Reprinted by permission of Kluwer Academic Publishers.

1 I mean "feature" to be given a neutral reading according to which, e.g., even a noncognitivist could call moral goodness a "feature" of things. Note that R. Brandt in *Ethical Theory* (Englewood Cliffs: Prentice Hall, 1959), p. 265, correlates ethical features and responses by means of the following principle: "a 'corresponding' attitude is the attitude someone justifiably has if some ethical statement is properly asserted by him." But for present purposes (mainly to avoid begging questions in setting up the problem) I prefer to leave the principles of correlation undefined.

2 Some recent writers in ethics (e.g., S. W. Blackburn in "Moral Realism," J. Casey, ed., *Morality and Moral Reasoning* (London: Methuen, 1971), pp. 101–124) use a weaker sense of "realist" to mark off theories holding that feature-ascribing sentences are true or false in virtue of their correspondence or noncorrespondence with extra-linguistic fact. But my stronger sense of "realist" also implies that the feature is mind-independent in the manner indicated. All naturalistic theories that count as nonrealist in my scheme count as realist in Blackburn's.

another kind of philosopher (the *mentalist*) finds it plausible to deny both these claims and to assert instead that the response has conceptual priority over the feature and that what the realist takes in the response as cognitive of the feature is really some noncognitive attitude, disposition, sensation, or act of will. In other words, the realist regards the response as a response *to* the feature while the mentalist sees the feature as some sort of construction *out of* the response. In considering the dispute it will be convenient to have a way of generalizing over all feature-response pairs that tend to generate this kind of controversy; thus I shall take the liberty of speaking of C-pairs ("*C*" for "Controversial") and, in the context of discussing such pairs, C-features and C-responses.

For the realist, a true occurrence of the C-response necessarily involves the *thought* or tendency to think that the object responded to has the C-feature, perhaps as that thought is embedded in a perception of the thing as having the feature.[3] Implicit in this, of course, is the idea that the feature is objectively present in its objects and therefore that ascriptions of it are objectively true or false. Also implicit is the claim that the concept of the C-feature is *prior* to that of the C-response. The mentalist, reversing the order of things, analyzes the feature into the response and strips the response of any cognitive function vis-à-vis the feature. Of course a mentalist may allow or even insist that the C-response involves any number of genuine cognitions of *other* features of the object if only because some thoughts about the object will be needed to get it in focus as an object of response. A mentalist about color (e.g., a secondary quality theorist like Locke) must admit that in paradigm cases of color experience color sensations are "superimposed" on genuine perceptions of an object's shape qualities.[4] And in ethics, mentalists typically grant thought a more or less prominent role in the composition or formation of ethical attitudes and decisions.[5] The issue

---

3 See Sidgwick, *The Methods of Ethics,* Seventh Edition (London: Macmillan, 1907), p. 27, for a classic statement of the realist view of moral feeling. See also Philippa Foot's arguments in "Moral Beliefs," *Proceedings of the Aristotelian Society,* 59 (1958–59), that moral attitudes are *internally related* to their objects.
4 For Locke's account of the distinction between primary and secondary qualities see *Essay Concerning Human Understanding,* Book II, Chapters viii, 9–26 and xxiii, 9–11; and Book IV, Chapter iii, 11–13 and 28.
5 Stevenson in "The Emotive Conception of Ethics and Its Cognitive Implications," *Facts and Values* (New Haven: Yale University Press, 1963), esp. p. 67, finds an essential role for thought in the formation of ethical attitudes. Frankena, a non-

between the mentalist and realist is thus not whether the C-state is cognitive, but whether it is cognitive *of the C-feature*. Both realism and mentalism come in importantly different varieties. A realist may hold that the C-response is logically separable into some pure cognition of the C-feature on the one hand and some noncognitive concomitant state on the other. But another form of realism denies that it is in this way possible to distill a purely noncognitive component out of the C-response. Furthermore, a realist may or may not hold that a given C-response is, for human beings at least, *the* central epistemic mental state regarding the C-feature, i.e., may or may not hold that it is only because we or someone we depend on is capable of experiencing the C-response that we are able to ascribe the C-feature.[6] When the C-response is intrinsically motivational or affective (as it seems to be in the two examples from ethics and aesthetics) a realist who regards it as both homogeneously cognitive and epistemically central must take the motivation or affect to be in some sense *internal* to ascriptions of the C-feature.[7]

Mentalism also embraces a wide variety of viewpoints. Some mentalists regard C-feature ascriptions as objectively true or false. This means that although they suppose that there are genuine beliefs and/or perceptions directed toward the C-feature, they deny that the C-response is itself among them. For them, the C-response enters the picture at a pre-epistemic stage, serving to constitute the essence rather than the recognition of the C-feature. This may be explained in a number of different ways. Some mentalists define the feature as a disposition to produce the response; others hold that to say that a thing has the feature is to say that the response is a reasonable or appropriate reaction to it.[8] Still others, of course,

cognitivist of a different sort, suggests that ethical assertions imply the thought that others will under certain conditions share the relevant attitude. See *Ethics*, Second Edition (Englewood Cliffs: Prentice Hall, 1973), p. 108.

6 John McDowell drew my attention to David Wiggins' use of the "perspective" metaphor to express a related point. The possession of a range of affective, motivational or sensory responses creates the perspective without which certain features could not be descried. See the "Philosophical Lecture: Truth, Invention and the Meaning of Life," in the *Proceedings of the British Academy*, 62 (1976); reprinted in Wiggins, *Needs, Values, Truth* (Oxford: Basil Blackwell, 1987), pp. 87–137.

7 See Frankena, "Obligation and Motivation in Recent Moral Philosophy," in A. I. Melden, ed., *Essays in Moral Philosophy* (Seattle: University of Washington Press, 1958), pp. 40–81.

8 R. Firth's Ideal Observer Theory is a prominent example of the former view that

deny the externality of the C-feature altogether and with it the idea that there is *any* genuine cognition that takes it as an object. In modern ethical theory this position is held by the emotivists and prescriptivists, who claim that the feature term functions to express, evoke or prescribe the response. Note that a mentalist of this last variety may nevertheless hold that occurrences of the C-response and corresponding C-feature speech acts can be rationally justified or unjustified even though they are neither true nor false.[9]

The noncognitive as a classification of theories of meaning is to be distinguished from the noncognitive as a category of mental state.[10] It is this latter sense of the cognitive-noncognitive distinction that directly concerns us here because it is this sense that generates the distinction between realism and mentalism. With its roots reaching back as far as Plato and Aristotle's division of the psyche into rational and nonrational components, the distinction is meant to capture our natural inclination to draw a line between appetite, feeling, and sensation on the one hand and belief, judgment, perception, and acquaintance on the other. Hume formulates his version of the distinction with typical ingenuous vigor. Some actions of the mind viz. judgments and opinions, having reference to truth and reason, are thereby capable of "agreement or disagreement either to the *real* relations of ideas or to *real* existence and matter of fact." But . . . "our passions, volitions, and actions are not susceptible of any such agreement or disagreement; being original facts and realities, compleat in themselves."[11] It is not my intention here to examine critically or choose between any of the historically important formulations of the distinction between cognitive and noncognitive mental states but simply to note that it is hard to see how philosophy could do without such a distinction and to see how far we can go by appealing to our intuitive sense of it in formulating and attempting to resolve the dispute between realists and mentalists.

The dispute appears to be a real one, clouded no doubt by various

could be modified to fit the latter as well. See "Ethical Absolutism and the Ideal Observer," *Philosophy and Phenomenological Research*, XII (1952), pp. 317–345.

9 Both Brandt (*Ethical Theory*, p. 267) and Frankena (*Ethics*, pp. 110–113) endorse this qualification.

10 For Stevenson, the former clearly derives from the latter. See *Ethics and Language* (New Haven: Yale University Press, 1944), Chapter 3, esp. sections 6–7.

11 *A Treatise of Human Nature*, ed. L. A. Selby-Bigge (Oxford: Clarendon Press, 1888), p. 458. See also pp. 413–418.

confusions but not wholly generated by them. This impression of genuineness is supported by our familiarity with some response-feature pairs that seem to admit only of a mentalist interpretation and others that seem to admit only a realist. Among the former are a) wanting and something's being wanted, b) pain and painfulness and c) fear and fearfulness. Of course these three mentalist paradigms differ in many respects. Wanting and fear take what is wanted and what is fearful as objects, while pain takes no object at all.[12] And while it is natural to think that wanting requires no particular thought about its object (although some would deny this), fear seems to require the thought (however self-consciously irrational) that its object is dangerous. But despite such differences, each response is naturally taken to be conceptually prior to its paired feature. What is wanted is what someone wants. What is painful is what causes or is disposed to cause pain. And the fearful either marks the category of things that tend to arouse fear or the things that are its appropriate objects. Perhaps even some occurrences of the expression "fearful" fit an emotivist interpretation as linguistically suited to express or arouse fear. On the other hand, realist paradigms are even more abundant. Most of us regard the concept of something's looking square as dependent on the prior concept of squareness. The same could be said for being taller than and looking taller than, being a person and seeming to be a person, being a drum and sounding like a drum, etc. A mentalist interpretation of these concept pairs could be warranted only on the assumption of wholesale phenomenalism.

Of course it is one thing for an issue to be genuine (or even partly genuine) and another for it to be easily solved. In the following I will investigate what seem to me to be three promising ways in which one might hope to settle or at least alleviate the controversy. The first attempts to turn interpersonal agreement or disagreement into a criterion by which one may rule out at least some forms of realism or mentalism. The second is a skeptical argument against the realist that appeals to the contingency of the way we map C-features onto the world. And the third is an argument designed to play against the mentalist's alleged inability to provide suitable differentiating accounts of the C-response. The net result will be

---

12 But see G. Pitcher "Pain Perception," *The Philosophical Review*, LXXIX (July 1970), pp. 368–393.

negative – that is I will try to show that each criterion or argument proves in the end either irrelevant or incomplete in ways that are far from easily remedied, and in the conclusion I will indulge in a brief reflection on why in general this should be so.

I

When facing issues having to do with objectivity and subjectivity, it is customary to look for help from some criterion of interpersonal agreement and disagreement.[13] So it seems natural to wonder whether if it were the case that we agreed or disagreed with each other in our C-responses to things, we could as a result rule out certain forms of mentalism or realism. To this end we might try to make something of the common hunch that knowledge and intelligence determine one's *beliefs* far more than they determine one's *attitudes, choices,* or *sensations*. Perhaps some maximal list of cognitive advantages – pieces of knowledge, mental abilities, intellectual virtues, etc. – could be found that would uniquely determine our C-responses were it the case that these responses really were cognitive of the C-feature but would leave them undetermined were this not the case. Of course the list could not contain any item that begged the question against some variety of mentalism or realism that was being tested. So it should not, on pain of offending a mentalist who offers a noncognitivist account of the C-feature, contain such advantages as *knowledge* of which things have the C-feature or *sensitivity* to the C-feature, etc. But let us suppose for the sake of argument that we have some such non-question begging, maximally complete list.

The first question to be asked is whether universal agreement in C-responses (the fact that all would respond and fail to respond to exactly the same things) among the qualified responders who satisfy our list would rule out any form of mentalism. It would certainly not seem to threaten any variety that held that C-feature judgments are empirically true or false; such theories might even *define* the C-feature in terms of the uniform C-responses of qualified responders.[14] But it might seem plausible to think that at least some

13 For a recent discussion of issues related to this criterion, see C. Wellman, "Ethical Disagreement and Objective Truth," *American Philosophical Quarterly*, 12 (July, 1975), 211–221.
14 As Firth does in the Ideal Observer Theory.

forms of agreement among qualified responders would be incompatible with subjectivist varieties of mentalism that allow for relativism among responders at large. Just how plausible this is would depend, I think, on the kind of agreement we had in mind, and especially the modality attached to it. That all qualified responders *in fact* agree in their C-responses should give the subjectivist little cause for alarm, since the agreement could result from common conditioning in contingent noncognitive attitudes. And even that all qualified persons should of *psychological necessity* agree in their C-responses seems at least theoretically compatible with any reasonable form of subjectivism. Thus it seems the only interesting possibility that agreement could be used against the subjectivist depends on whether *logically* or *metaphysically necessary* agreement would be incompatible with his theory.

In facing this question one is likely to confuse two different issues. It is true that many contemporary subjectivists, say the noncognitivists in ethics or aesthetics, regard their position as incompatible with this sort of agreement. But this is because they see themselves as belonging to an empiricist tradition going back to Hume according to which all motivations, attitudes, passions, feelings, sensations, and choices can, even in fully rational and informed agents, be no more than contingently related to their objects. This dogma, however, does not appear in other philosophical traditions. For example, both Plato and Aristotle can be interpreted to hold that there are motivations that every rational person must have; and in this respect at least they have been followed – although in quite different ways – by Kant and Sidgwick.[15] The relevance of this to the present issue lies in the fact that it seems possible to combine an acceptance of some such necessary connection between cognitive excellence and agreement in response (although not perhaps in a form acceptable to any of these authors) with the doubt that this connection entails that the responses are themselves cognitively assessible as true or false or even as justified or unjustified. It might be useful to consider the converse: whether one would, for example, think that *any* valid argument to the conclusion that all morally perfect agents agree in thinking logically about certain matters, e.g.

15 Some relevant passages: Plato, *Meno*, 77b–78b, *Gorgias*, 468c, *Protagoras*, 352a–355d; Aristotle, *Nicomachean Ethics* VII, iii, esp. 1147b; Kant, *Groundwork of the Metaphysics of Morals*, p. 460 (Royal Prussian Academy Edition), and *Critique of Practical Reason*, Ch. III; Sidgwick, *The Methods of Ethics*, p. 34.

consequences, would by itself establish that it is morally good to think logically about consequences. It would seem that whether an argument that establishes a necessary connection between some set of excellences and a certain pattern of response guarantees that such responses are assessible in terms of the excellences depends on the specific nature of its premises.

But if agreement cannot by itself be used against the mentalist, perhaps disagreement among the qualified responders can be used against some form of realism. A realist who holds that the C-response is some separable combination of pure cognitive state and noncognitive response may perhaps attribute some sorts of disagreement to the disturbing presence of the latter element. And even a realist who holds that the C-response is thoroughly cognitive may nevertheless regard it as a very specialized variety of cognition whose vagaries would not rule out an interpersonally consistent assignment of C-features via some other cognitive route. But it might seem plausible to suppose that disagreement among the qualified responders is incompatible with a realism according to which the C-response is not only cognitive through and through but is for us the basic epistemic state by which we recognize the C-feature. The idea is that the knowledge and other advantages included in our list ought to be sufficient to eliminate any possibility of uncorrectable error in identifying objects as having or lacking the C-feature. And this rests on the assumption that every instantiation of an intrinsic characteristic is entailed by or inductively implied by some fact that can be *independently known*.

But on reflection this assumption seems highly suspect. Such logical integration of knowledge may be an ideal of natural science, but natural science may not exhaust all knowledge. The idea of aesthetic facts that are not entailed or implied by any facts that could be known independently has been energetically defended.[16] At the very least, therefore, we need some additional reasoning to show that the assumption is compelling. Until it is brought forward the realist may be allowed simply to suppose, for example, that some qualified responders are better able to discriminate the C-feature than others, and to explain any disagreement arising among them in this way.

16 By F. Sibley, for example, in "Aesthetic Concepts," *The Philosophical Review*, LXVIII (1959), 421–450.

But the issue of the impact of disagreement on realism is not quite as simple as this. To see why, we must turn our attention from the qualified responders to the linguistic community at large. Unless we can find certain relevant patterns of linguistic agreement there, we will, given realism, find ourselves unable to justify the very supposition that the community possesses the concept of the C-feature. In order to be justified in supposing that a community possesses a concept we generally have to be in a position to pick out parts of its language – perhaps a term – as expressing the concept. But given a realistic view of the C-feature, we could justifiably suppose a term to play this role only if it were commonly applied to objects that we could understand either to have or to seem to have the C-feature. The possibility of a realist's ascribing the C-feature concept to a linguistic community therefore seems to presuppose the presence of certain patterns of prediction there, and these patterns seem tantamount to some form of interpersonal agreement – even if limited to some few paradigm cases.

But those mentalists who espouse a relativistic account of the C-feature in terms of the C-response may be able to do without such agreement. For they regard talk about the C-feature as reducible to talk about, or other kinds of expression of, the speaker's C-responses. And presumably we could identify that sort of talk, if it exists, if we were able to identify the concept of the C-response. But on some mentalist conceptions we should be able to do this simply by finding members of the community applying certain purely noncognitive behavioral or phenomenological criteria to themselves and others. A mentalist need not assert this, of course. He may conceive the C-response on the model of fear, i.e. as necessarily including certain specific judgments about its objects. Or he may simply hold that the C-response, while not tied to any specific thoughts about its object must be subject to certain orderly causal explanations which would imply certain regularities in the objects that provoke the response. If his conception of the C-response were of either of these types, then the mentalist would probably be just as dependent on some pattern of agreement in C-feature ascriptions as the realist. But a mentalist need not regard the C-response as thus restricted to certain objects. He may think that we can find it in a community just in case we can find a common recognition of certain noncognitive phenomenological or behavioral patterns. And once we have found the concept of the C-

9

response we need find no further patterns of classification in order to find the concept of the C-feature (should it be present). Thus it would appear that the absence of certain forms of agreement in the community at large would count against realism but be compatible with certain forms of mentalism.

This appearance is deceptive. It is perhaps true that if we *assume* that the speakers in a community in which no uniform pattern of C-feature predication emerges have the concept of the C-feature then this fact could only be explained by mentalism. But this does not show that the absence of the relevant forms of agreement is tolerable under mentalism but not realism. For there is the prior question whether the assumption is legitimate, i.e. whether the concept of the C-feature should be assigned to a linguistic community whose classifications of independent objects are in the relevant sort of disarray. The realist will insist that no reason has as yet been put forward to show that it could be assigned in such a case. And so far as I can see, that is correct. So we have still failed to produce a possible condition of disagreement that would settle the dispute in the mentalist's favor.

II

The mentalist has not yet had his full say about the question of agreement. Even if he admits the force of the preceding observations he may well suspect that we have been missing the point of what is really relevant in the matter of agreement and disagreement. Instead of dwelling on the implications of the possibility that we either agree or disagree in our ascriptions of the C-feature, we should consider just how contingent any possible pattern of our C-feature ascriptions would be.[17] It is not the disagreement present in a possible situation that argues against realism, it is rather the fact that whatever agreement is present might easily have taken some other form – that instead of finding *these* things funny we might have found *those* things funny instead, that instead of *these* things (apples and roses) looking red *those* things (grass and avocados, or for that matter, grass and bananas) might have, etc.

---

17 See Jonathan Bennett's defense of the distinction between primary and secondary qualities in *Locke, Berkeley, Hume: Central Themes* (Oxford: Clarendon Press, 1971), Ch. IV, esp. section 20.

We must be extremely careful in formulating any objection to realism based on such alleged contingencies. As we have seen, what makes a mentalist a mentalist is his opinion that there is enough in the nature of the C-response to enable us to identify it for what it is independently of first finding in it any *thought* about the C-feature. And we have also seen that this is exactly what the realist finds implausible. It is important to remember that it is precisely here that the dispute lies when trying to fashion a non-question begging argument against realism. It will not do for the mentalist simply to insist on the contingency of the connection between our C-responses and their objects if what underlies his claim is nothing more than the controversial assumption with which the realist disagrees. If he wants to merit our attention he must argue to the contingency from premises that the realist can grant.

The following is an attempt to fashion such an argument. To begin, suppose we grant the realist's assumption that a C-response is cognitive in the sense that it essentially contains some genuine thought of its object as having the C-feature. Now whatever else we think about C-features, it seems pretty clear that a C-feature is never an *identifying* feature of an object it characterizes – it is not one of these features one would *need* to know about in order to settle possible problems of distinguishing one object from another or problems of deciding what are or are not an object's proper parts.[18] Size, shape, and location serve to identify material bodies. Color, as ordinarily conceived, and not redefined by a physicist, is theoretically dispensable. Time and agent are among the identifying features of action, moral goodness is not. One story or joke may be distinguished from another by its content or by the precise words that make it up. Its funniness or unfunniness doesn't make it the story that it is. (There is strong reason to insist on these last two points, since we have to know exactly what an action or story is in order to know whether it is morally good or funny.)

The idea that C-features are supervenient, and therefore gratuitous from the point of view of strict identification, is not granted by some realists; for them the mentalist's argument is aborted

18 This is perhaps part of what Moore meant by his odd claim that intrinsic goodness is *not* an intrinsic property of a thing that possesses it. See "The Conception of Intrinsic Value" in *Philosophical Studies* (London: Routledge and Kegan Paul, 1922), esp. pp. 272–273.

here.[19] But some important realists would grant and even embrace the point, so we may continue the argument as addressed to them. Drawing the distinction between identifying and nonidentifying features leads to some important (if rather difficult to formulate) implications concerning the possibility of error. So long as we are not concerned to mark a thing off precisely, we may make some mistakes about its identifying features without jeopardizing our claim to be acquainted with it. But even so, the more frequent or substantial our mistakes about a thing's identifying features become, the more our claim to be experiencing that thing as an element of an independent reality is threatened. If I sincerely report to see an ordinary watermelon that I am holding in one hand as smaller than an ordinary grape that I am holding in the other, you may well suspect that I am undergoing some strange hallucination and reporting on the content of it rather than on the real objects in my hands. And you will be confirmed in this if my other alleged perceptions of their identifying features are equally eccentric.[20]

But the case is different with non–identifying features. Even if we grant the realist's assumption that these features are objective qualities or relations inhering in independent objects, experience *of* those objects does not by itself require a unique assignment of the features. This is shown by the fact that we may radically disagree about such assignments without even a suspicion arising that we are not disputing about the very same reality. We may be ever so color-blind, morally blind or perverse, and insensitive or even moronic in our sense of humor without losing hold of the world.[21] It follows from this that even if we agree in mapping C-features onto the world in such and such a way, we might *in experiencing the very same objective world* have mapped the features quite differently even though the objects mapped remain the same in all intrinsic aspects.

Radical, systematic error as to which things have a given C-feature is not incompatible with a correct identification of the things

19 I am thinking of realists who accept a *reduction* of C-features to the properties on which others would say they supervene – e.g., a deontologist who identifies moral rightness with the disjunctive property of falling under one or another of such and such rules or a color theorist who identifies the colors with various physical properties.
20 Cf. Bennett, *op. cit.*, p. 98.
21 The realist may point out here that a hold on reality is more than a hold on the objects of that reality. For if these eccentricities go far enough we will in fact regard a person as mad.

12

in question, whereas such error in the case of identifying features is. Identifying features are thus proof against radical misplacement in a way that C-features are not. This means that even if we suppose that the C-response essentially contains the thought of the object as having the C-feature, it could nevertheless have been evoked by objects quite other than those which in fact now evoke it. We do not have to deny the realist's basic claim in order to assert that had the laws of psychology been different, the things that now arouse a sense of moral approval or a feeling of amusement might not have and the things that do not now have even the slightest tendency to arouse these responses might. And all this might have occurred without supposing any alteration in the intrinsic natures of the objects themselves. Of course, if the realist assumes that here in the actual world we locate the C-features with a fair degree of accuracy, then he would have to say that in the possibility under consideration we would be systematically deluded. We would think things morally good, funny, or red that do not even come close to having these features. And what is more nightmarish, these illusions might be as internally and interpersonally consistent as our present patterns of response. We would and should have just as much reason to be confident in our judgments as we now have. So realism with respect to C-features not only entails the possibility of complete, undetectable illusion, but gives us no greater chance than that afforded by cosmic luck that we are not here and now in its grip. The old-fashioned skepticism cries out for the old-fashioned phenomenalist remedy. Rather than tolerate these dreadful notions of undetectable illusion and cosmic luck, we should adopt the mentalist interpretation of the C-responses with its more sensible and modest way of explaining their contingency.

The argument is, in its way, impressive and seems to present considerations with which the realist must come to terms. It depends on the assumption that where C-features are concerned, we can credit a thought (type) as being the thought of a thing that it has the C-feature without worrying about the character of the things at which the thought is typically aimed. The mentalist is not prepared to grant this with regard to identifying features for the simple reason that mistakes about them tend to draw a veil between the thinker and the alleged objects of his thought. A thought about a thing's identifying features has a certain double life: it enables us to be acquainted with the thing and at the same time to take in its character. Any flaw in the latter is at least a potential flaw in the former. The obstacle to the radical misplacement of identifying features is thus a *reference* problem – a problem of seeing a thought *as a thought about this or that thing*. And the mentalist has argued, persuasively, that there is no correspondingly serious reference problem raised by the radical misplacement of C-features.

But the reference problem is not the only problem with respect to the identification of thoughts. This can be seen by setting *de dicto* (or internally quantified) thoughts alongside the *de re* (or externally quantified) thoughts we have been hitherto exclusively examining. Since the reference problem is the problem of our right to credit someone with a *de re* thought about a particular object (e.g., the thought *of that object* that one perceives it to be square), it does not speak directly to the question of how we can credit someone with a *de dicto* thought (e.g., the thought that we perceive some object to be square). But surely there are limits to what we can accept here as well. A *de dicto* thought (type) could not plausibly be interpreted as the specific thought that *p* if that interpretation made all or most occurrences of the thought inexplicably false. We could not reasonably credit a thought (in a given community) as the thought that one is seeing something square if the thought never occurs in people when they are in fact seeing such a shape. And that we cannot credit this does not simply seem due to an inability to get into the heads of these people to see if the totally inappropriate thought really is there; for even if we could get into their heads (whatever that would be like) we would still have the problem of identifying what we found there. The mentalist's mistake lies in supposing that anything, whether a mental event or a bit of language, can be identified as being or expressing a specific thought – whether *de re* or *de dicto* – independently of determining its role in its subject's interactions with the public world.[22] Surely there is a truth problem, as well as a reference problem, in identifying thoughts of any type.

The implications of this for thoughts about C-features are immediate. The mentalist has argued that there can be no objection arising from the reference problem to one's identifying a type of

---

22 Cf. Wittgenstein's claim in *Philosophical Investigations* II, xi, p. 217, that even "if God had looked into our minds he would not have been able to see there whom we were speaking of" and the immediately preceding remarks. See also Part I, sections 452–453.

14

thought as the thought of a thing that it has the C-feature. But this is just to say that there is no problem in attributing these thoughts, *supposing that we can find them,* to the unlikeliest things. Well and good. But can we find them? It is one thing to ask whether a thought that we have interpreted in a certain way can, so interpreted, be understood as a thought about these objects, and quite another to ask whether it was reasonable of us to have interpreted it that way in the first place. The mentalist's argument was directed to the first question and not to the second. It is preposterous to think that *any* thought – even about nonidentifying features – could be interpreted without concern for the truth problem. A realist therefore is entitled to reject as senseless the hypothesis that in a given possible setting some thought (type) is functioning as the thought of a thing that it is morally good, funny, or red if that interpretation does not make the thought true or plausible often enough, and so he need not – given his insistence that the thought is essential to the C-response – be frightened by the possibility of our C-responses running riot. Thus it seems that the contingency has not been successfully argued from the realist's assumption that the C-response contains a thought about the C-feature.

III

From the discussion so far, it might seem that realism is merely a reactive (not to say reactionary) position. But realists have offensive strategies, one of the most important and interesting of which I should now like to consider. The argument I have in mind begins by granting provisionally the mentalist's claim that the C-response is noncognitive – some species of mere feeling, affect, sensation, etc. But which species? The feeling of moral approval is not just any pro-attitude; it is different presumably from something we might call aesthetic approval. Amusement is not just any form of affect; it differs from fear, excitement, delight, etc. And even if we grant that something's looking red to one involves some species of mere sensation not to be confused with genuine perception, that kind of sensation must be different from the kind involved in something's looking blue to one. But this need to *differentiate* the C-state leads the mentalist into a fatal trap. For he will find that he cannot differentiate the C-state except by referring in one way or another to the C-feature. This difficulty is most familiar in the case of mentalist accounts of the colors. It seems impossible to imagine how one could even begin to provide a conceptually necessary differentiating feature for a color sensation without mentioning the color of which it was the sensation. What makes the sensation of red different from the sensation of blue is that it is the sensation of *red*. Any other feature that would serve to demarcate the species of sensation, e.g., that it was correlated with a certain brain state, would seem to be a conceptually contingent feature of the state and thus would not provide the kind of differentia that explicates the concept of the color.

This type of argument has also been brought to bear on mentalist accounts of moral approval. The realist objects that some instances of approval cannot count as moral. But how can moral approval be distinguished from other types? The realist then goes on to argue in one way or another that we can do so only by reference to some judgment that is inextricably involved in the approval – some judgment ascribing moral features to things.[23] Moral approval can thus be differentiated only by reference to the feature or range of features that on the mentalist view it is supposed to explicate. From this the realist draws the inference that moral goodness (or some other moral feature) has the prior status.

The key premise in all such arguments is the assertion that in order to differentiate the C-response, reference must occur sooner or later, directly or indirectly, to the C-feature. The trick for the mentalist is to cast doubt on this premise without thereby denying its natural appeal. One way of doing this is the familiar maneuver which asserts the feature term to be ambiguous, meaning one thing when it names the C-feature (when it stands for a feature of independent objects) and meaning another when it occurs in the differentiating account of the C-response. In the former use it is to be given some complex, perhaps dispositional or emotivist, explication in terms of the latter use where it is to be understood phenomenologically or behaviorally.[24] The differentiation of the C-response does not therefore really involve reference to the C-feature

23 W. Alston provides an interesting example of this line of argument – as addressed to emotivists – in "Moral Attitudes and Moral Judgments," *Nous* 2 (Feb. 1968): 1–23.
24 Firth puts this forward as a live possibility for both color and moral terms in "Ethical Absolutism and the Ideal Observer," p. 324.

but only involves the use of the ambiguous C-feature term. Because the ambiguity (like ambiguities in general) may be masked, the key premise will seem to bear the realist's interpretation.

Since I am not strongly attracted to this reply, I mention it only to mark it off from another perhaps less familiar response to the realist's argument. This consists in the employment of two maneuvers. The first concerns the realist's challenge to differentiate the C-response from other responses in its genus. The maneuver is to reject the demand as illegitimate. It is not proper to argue from the fact that one thing is different from other coordinate items belonging to some common more general type to the conclusion that there is some concept which can be employed to differentiate the thing as a species of the type. A simple look at colors in the way that many realists conceive them should be enough to convince us of this. Red is certainly a color, and it is certainly different from other colors such as blue; but it is far from clear that it can be differentiated from these other colors in the way the realist demands a differentiation of the C-response. If conceptual analysis is formally analogous to definition of terms (and it is usually taken to be in at least the following respect) then some of our concepts will be incapable of analysis. And there is no reason why some of these unanalyzable concepts should not cluster together into families under some parental concept (which may itself be unanalyzable). (Note that in adopting this intuitionist strategy, the mentalist should not feel bound to adopt any of the typical intuitionist's other ideas. In particular he need not feel committed to the view that every unanalyzable concept is *simple,* if that insinuates not only that analysis cannot be completed but also that it cannot, as it were, get started. There is nothing in the fact that e.g., amusement is, in principle, not completely formulable that prevents us from listing any number of interesting conceptual truths about it – such as that it is a pleasant affective state disposed to express itself behaviorally and directed toward a perceived or contemplated object. What makes a concept unanalyzable is not the lack of formula but the conceptual space left beside it for a *distinct* concept that shares the formula.) The push to differentiate these family members from one another will be understandable, but unless resisted will inevitably lead to some form of circularity. That circularity in fact occurs, the mentalist will conclude, just at the point where we are forced to refer to the C-feature in trying to explicate the C-response. For the C-feature itself should be analyzed into the C-response and not vice versa.

Here the realist is likely to object that this reply could be accepted only on condition that it didn't seem as intuitively correct as it in fact does to differentiate the C-response by reference to the C-feature. One is not forced to make the differentiation, one is *drawn* to make it. The harder we focus on the C-response itself, the surer we become that it is a transparent phenomenon, one that appears to present some unique quality or relation to us. The more we reflect on the nature of amusement, for example, the more we are driven to see it as the *discernment* (or apparent discernment) of the funny. Amusement does not present itself to us as some opaque sensation like pain; nor can it even remotely be captured by any reference to behavior. There is more to amusement than laughter, which is also characteristically associated with various forms of hysteria. Amusement is marked off as what it is by the fact that it feels like the cognition of something about a thing. And the same, or something similar, can be said about the other C-responses.

Perhaps this line will not make sense to some mentalists – not strike them as answering to anything in their own reflective experience of the C-response. But I am certain that it will seem to do so for some, even if they regard my formulation as crude. Even these sympathetic mentalists, however, have a provocative and not contemptible reply (the second maneuver) reminiscent of moves originally designed to meet Moore's naturalistic fallacy. Let it be granted that the phenomenology of the C-response is as the realist says – that there is an important way in which moral approval, amusement, and something's looking red feel as if they fall on a different side of the cognitive divide from appetite, fear, and pain. But while far from irrelevant, this consideration does not settle the question of analysis. That the C-feature should or should not be analyzed into the C-response – indeed that any concept should or should not be construed as posterior to some other – need not be one of those transparently obvious truths that immediately recommends itself to any possessor of the conceptual scheme. Like all theoretical questions, it is a matter of finding a systematic organization of the scheme that satisfies various desiderata – only one of which is conformity to pretheoretical phenomenological intuition.[25] Whether the mentalist's construction of the scheme has other advantages that compensate, such as giving us a less cumbersome account of the apparent relativity of C-feature judgments and a less magical account of their internalist aspects, is a matter for painstaking evaluation about which men of theoretical good will may disagree. But what should be admitted by all is that introspective intuition does not settle the matter by itself, and thus that the way in which we were drawn to the differentiating account proposed by the realist does not really force our hand.

IV

The preceding discussion was obviously far too selective and incomplete to warrant sweeping conclusions. But it may be taken as illustrative, I think, of the vastness of the problem. The instincts that separate the mentalist from the realist involve or at least touch on the most basic matters of which philosophy treats: the nature of objectivity, conceptual analysis, essentialism, private languages, and so on. That is to say we should have been forced to face these and many other basic problems of epistemology, metaphysics, and philosophy of mind in pushing our discussions beyond the points at which I relaxed my efforts. In no case does this appear more forcefully than in the closing remarks of the last section. The realist we were considering there regarded what we might call the *phenomenological cognitivity* of the C-response as *the* salient aspect of the case, something that must either be explained away or yielded to. While the mentalist, paradoxically enough, was ready to treat these introspective mental data more casually, feeling that they may be made to yield to a theory defensible on other grounds. Here, quite obviously, we are confronted by unsettling questions of philosophical methodology – questions for which the special disciplines of ethics, aesthetics, and theory of perception may not adequately equip us.

25 The realist might try to appropriate S. Kripke's comments – intended for a quite different dispute – on the force of intuitive content. See "Naming and Necessity," G. Harman and D. Davidson eds., *Semantics of Natural Language* (Dordrecht, Holland, 1972), pp. 265–266.

2

Abortion: Identity and loss

Most philosophers who discuss abortion seem to presuppose that during any period of time in which a human fetus is not yet a human being abortion remains a matter of negligible moral consequence.[1] The extreme antiabortionist, of course, denies that there is any such period; but he too seems to accept the presupposition. For he argues as if everything depended on establishing conception as the point at which human life begins. The extreme proabortionist relies on the same presupposition. It enables him to move from the premise that no fetus ever fully qualifies as a human being to the conclusion that abortion at any fetal stage is permissible on demand.[2] Even moderates are generally so classified because they take some intermediate point in pregnancy (for example, viability) to be the beginning of human life, and hence to be the moral watershed at which abortion begins to be objectionable. Thus all parties to

From *Philosophy and Public Affairs* 13:1 (Winter 1984) 24–54. Copyright © 1984 by Princeton University Press. Reprinted by permission of Princeton University Press.

Many thanks to Philippa Foot, Miles Morgan, Christopher Morris, Gerald Smith, and other Los Angeles philosophers for their encouragement and criticisms. And thanks above all to Rogers Albritton for his patient advice.

1 The fact that the following discussion will be carried on in terms of "human being" rather than "person" requires some comment. This will, of course, make no difference to those who conceive of human beings as essentially persons. But to those who think that human beings *become* persons I would suggest the following defense of my procedure. Whatever new, and undoubtedly more serious, moral aspects come into play when persons are killed, the killing of a genuine human being, especially where this is not done wholly in the name of its own interests, raises serious enough moral issues just on the face of it to be worth considering. In the following I shall try to show that this appearance is correct.

2 To speak strictly, a fetus is the prenatal organism from about the eighth week on and is preceded by the zygote, conceptus, and embryo. In this paper I allow myself the common philosophical (and perhaps bad) habit of using "fetus" and "fetal" as general terms covering the entire series from single-cell zygote to full-term fetus.

the debate as traditionally conducted seem to regard the fetus itself as entering the moral drama in only one of two ways: either as a mere mass of cells which can be excised at the pregnant woman's discretion or as a human being with a full right to life of the very sort possessed by those who ponder its fate.[3]

But this presupposition may be false. At least it is at odds with two intuitions I have long found persuasive: (1) The first of these is that even a very early abortion stands in need of moral justification in a way that the surgical removal of a mere mass of tissue does not. Abortion is morally problematic not only because of its impact on the pregnant woman but also because of its impact on the organism that is killed and removed. The extreme antiabortionist will, of course, share this intuition, but it is deliberately weaker and vaguer than anything he could endorse as a final position. This is shown by its apparent compatibility with my second intuition: (2) That abortion occurring early enough in pregnancy, at least before all the organ systems of the fetus are complete, is not morally equivalent either to the killing of an adult or the killing of an infant. The early fetus not only fails to be morally protected by the same kind of right to life that mature persons possess, but its moral status also differs in some important way from that of the neonate.

The extreme proabortionist will, of course, endorse (2) but not the idea that it can be conjoined consistently to (1). But it is this conjunction that I find plausible. The early fetus is not, as the conservative thinks it is, under the full moral protections appropriate to a mature human being, but it is also not the morally negligible thing the liberal seems to think it is. To these two intuitions I shall add a third which sometimes strikes me as equally compelling: (3) As pregnancy progresses abortion becomes increasingly problematic from the moral point of view. More, and perhaps considerably more, is required to justify an abortion at six months than at one month. This intuition, which may well be widely shared, almost never finds a secure place in philosophical discussions of the abortion issue.

In this paper I shall discuss, in what will have to be a somewhat

---

3 Although some proabortionists think like Judith Thomson that even the possession of a full-fledged right to life would be rendered irrelevant by the fact that the fetus locates itself where it has no right to be and makes demands it has no right to make. See "A Defense of Abortion," *Philosophy & Public Affairs* 1 (1971): 47–66.

rough and schematic way, two alternative metaphysical theories of the status of the fetus and the nature of fetal development in which these moral intuitions could be seen to be satisfied. These theories attempt to articulate, each in its own way, the kind of individual identity that the fetus possesses, especially in relation to the identity of the future human being it will in some sense become. Each of them is offered as plausible quite apart from the question of abortion, for each does considerable justice to intuitions about fetal identity that arise from an attempt to take man seriously as a biological being. But their special relevance to this discussion lies in the way they satisfy certain requirements imposed by the first two moral intuitions. (1) will seem to have serious weight only if the fetal being affected by abortion is thought to be capable of receiving morally significant harms and benefits. If the fetus were viewed as a special kind of short-lived individual destined at birth to fade from existence as the human being replaces it, or as the early stage of a complex piece of biological machinery which a human being will only later come to possess, abortion would seem to pose no serious moral problem. It seems then that (1) demands a theory in which the future human being in some sense already exists in the fetus.[4] Intuition (2), on the other hand, with its denial that abortion is strictly comparable to standard cases of murder or even to infanticide, seems to require that there be a sense in which a human being does not yet exist *in utero*, or at least a way in which it does not yet fully exist there.

Any ontology of the fetus suitable for my purposes must thus satisfy both of these superficially conflicting demands. Each of the two theories to be presented in Sections II and III seems to me to do this and to satisfy other independent requirements more plausibly than other theories I have seen discussed or have been able to

---

4 That we can refer to a possible but as yet nonexistent human being who, if he comes to exist, will have some significant relation to that which the fetus will become is not, I think, enough to make abortion seriously problematic. For while it seems possible now to harm the interests of an as yet nonexistent human being who will in fact come to exist, I do not believe that one can in any way affect the interests of a merely possible human being who does not now and never will in fact exist—even by the very act that prevents it from ever existing. This is why birth control does not seem to raise a comparably serious moral issue. Richard Hare, it must be noted, does take the interests of merely possible people seriously in "Abortion and the Golden Rule," *Philosophy & Public Affairs* 4 (1975):201–222, esp. pp. 219–221.

construct. As indicated, the discussion will be programmatic rather than complete. In particular I shall set aside the obviously important question as to the precise time at which the human creature first exists as a full-fledged human being. My concern here is instead with the clearly identifiable but morally problematic period that comes first. In Section III I shall go on to argue that if either of the theories is true, then there is some way in which we shall be forced to see standard cases of abortion as inflicting on a fetus the loss of a future fully human life. In Section IV I shall reflect on the ethical implications of this result, trying to show that the initial moral intuitions are indeed secured.

I

The theory to be developed in this section starts with an examination of the extreme antiabortionist's premise that conception marks the beginning of human life. This premise includes at least two distinguishable claims: First, that conception marks the beginning of the individual, for example Socrates; and second, that it marks it as the beginning of a human being. The theory under consideration rejects the second claim, but finds something importantly suggestive in the first. For it does seem plausible to think that some individual entity begins to exist at conception to which the later human being will be intimately related, an individual biological organism of the species *Homo sapiens*. And this organism, while living within its parent, does not have the biological status of an organ. Its development is explained by reference to its own needs; and its emerging parts are assigned functions within *it* rather than within its parent. I shall call this entity, upon which our theory focuses, the *human organism*. This serves not only to give it a name but to distinguish it from the *human being* who will, as we shall see, only enter the picture later.

Now what is absolutely central to this theory is the claim that the human organism persists and continues to develop through fetal, infant, child, and adult forms, remaining numerically one and the same individual organism throughout the entire human life cycle. The theory regards this claim as conceptually unobjectionable and empirically verifiable. Despite its remarkable changes of form, there are no stretches in the life of the human organism, even in the amazing developments of the fetal stage, at which it is plausible

23

on biological grounds to suppose that a previously existing organism ceases to exist.[5] The smooth gradualism of fetal development is, of course, part of the reason.[6] But even more important to the case for organic continuity is the fact that this development proceeds according to a tendency and plan that we believe to have been fully present in even the earliest form of the zygote. (That "plan" is used in this context metaphorically is not, I think, a problem. The point is that the subsequent development is causally determined by special goal-directed factors present in even the earliest stages.) Throughout its life, the fetus has need of external objects and stimuli, whose absence will retard or even end its development. But we do not, according to the theory, interpret its interaction with them as altering its basic plan of development.

For this reason there is a clear difference between any event in the life of the fetus and the event of fertilization in the life of the ovum. The ovum has a developmental history of its own which is dependent on its own determinate nature and the internally encoded plan that this nature includes. But we do not suppose that this nature and plan by themselves account for the later development of the zygote and conceptus. We rather think of the latter as a new form of life to whose nature both the ovum and the spermatozoon have made significant contributions. Parthenogenesis, should it become possible, will be best conceived as a transformation rather than a development of the ovum – the parthenogenic agent being seen as having the power to change the ovum's essential nature, to make of it a new organism with a quite different teleology. The now purely imaginary possibilities of cloning and wholesale gene splicing should be viewed, according to the theory, in much the same way.

5 This may have to be qualified where monozygotic (identical) twins are concerned. If such twinning is genetically determined, then the pretwin zygote may have to be regarded as some special kind of proto-organism that ceases to exist in its own right as the twinning process takes place. If twinning is contingently produced by environmental factors, the pretwin zygote can be regarded as a human organism that might have gone on to develop through a normal human cycle but, as a matter of fact, ceases to exist in the twinning process. Since twinning is a striking discontinuity of normal development there may be nothing objectionably ad hoc in these qualifications. See Lawrence Becker's "Human Being: The Boundaries of the Concept," *Philosophy & Public Affairs* 4 (1975):334–359, esp. p. 340.
6 Continuity from conception onward is also emphasized by Richard Warner in "Abortion: The Ontological and Moral Status of the Unborn," *Social Theory and Practice* 3 (1974):201–222.

The second central thesis of the theory concerns the nature of the human (or, for that matter, animal) body, that is, the body of a human being. The theory rejects a certain, perhaps philosophically common, idea according to which the human body is a fully real organic *subentity* – one which, while logically incapable of intentional actions (that is, unable to read, converse, perceive), is the *primary agent* of a human being's metabolic and purely reflexive activities. So conceived, it is our body that digests, that converts nourishment to protoplasm, that sweats, that jerks when struck in certain ways, and *we* (human beings) are seen to metabolize, jerk, sweat, or even simply to occupy physical space only because our bodies do. According to this conception, we supervene upon, contain, or bear some other exotic relation to a distinguishable source of activities which then become attributable to us by a kind of logical courtesy. This idea can be seen most clearly in a certain perspective on extreme senility in which it is seen as the emerging or separating off of the body. The higher parts of the human person having, as it were, evaporated, the body is left behind unhappily bereft of its former companions.

The theory being considered rejects the idea of the body as real subentity. It instead takes the body, insofar as it is conceived as something incapable of higher activity, to be a product of *mere* abstraction. So taken, the body of a man is nothing other than the man himself, *just insofar* as he is a subject for physical, chemical, and biological inquiry.[7] This abstraction produces an object of thought which, in virtue of the relevant stipulations, is logically capable of movement and biological activity but not thought and volition.[8] But the abstraction of the body from the man, although no doubt culturally and psychologically profound, is seen by the theory as lacking the metaphysical significance often assigned it. Our living bodies are capable of behaving as they do only because

7 See Douglas Long's interesting discussion of an abstractionist account of the body as it fits into the issue of other minds in "The Philosophical Concept of a Human Body," *Philosophical Review* 73 (1964):321–337.
8 No doubt there is something appealing in the availability of such an object of thought, considerably more appealing than the availability of (say) the *nonmusical self*, an object of thought that includes everything in the human being other than his musical powers and capacities and is therefore logically incapable of composition and musical performance. Only people bizarrely obsessed with musical activity and ability would find it psychologically possible to think in such terms, while most of us find it convenient and satisfying to think in terms of the body.

we are, and senility is the deterioration of what was previously able *both* to metabolize and to think into what is now able only to metabolize.

The importance of the idea of the body to the abortion issue is clear. Given the availability of the conception of the body as subentity, the fetal organism could be dismissed as nothing more than that human subentity in its early stages.[9] On such a view, the fetus is the beginning of the body of an as yet nonexistent human being.[10] But, given the abstractive conception of body, things look very different. When man is seen as a single organism capable of a wide repertoire of behaviors ranging from the metabolic and automatic to the intentional and cerebral, a quite different picture of the relation of the primitive to the mature human organism becomes attractive: The primitive organism is seen as something which in the course of *its* normal development will take on new physical, psychological, and eventually rational powers. It will first acquire a form and capacity that will qualify it as animal; and it will subsequently take on mental, emotional, and volitional powers that will qualify it as a human being. But through all these changes it will remain one and the same biological organism. It must be admitted that only a perfectly amazing kind of organism could have this protean capacity, an organism which, even in its initial stages, would have to contain some kind of representation of all the structures of its maturity. But, according to the theory, that is exactly the kind of organism that modern biology has revealed the human fetus to be.

Is the zygote then nothing other than the human being in its earliest phase of development? Not, I believe, according to the conceptual intuitions of most people nor according to the present theory's interpretation of the grammar of "human being." Human organisms qualify as human beings only when they have reached a certain developmental completeness. "Human being" thus brings in reference to a certain (typically very long) noninitial phase in the development of the human organism, just as "adolescent" brings

9 Hugh McLaughlin identifies the fetus with part of the future person's body in "Must We Accept Either the Conservative or the Liberal View on Abortion?" *Analysis* 37 (1977):197–204.
10 This is of course not the position that the fetus is a mere mass of cells, and so it might be taken to generate a rather weak kind of antiabortion argument.

in reference to a certain developmental phase of the human being. But this reference does *not* establish a distinguishable individual. The adolescent is not distinct from the human being who is adolescent, and the human being is not distinct from the human organism which is a human being. The theory thus denies what in some philosophical circles has come to have the status of an axiom: that being a human being is an essential property.[11] Just as common sense discloses that the individual who is in fact an adolescent might never have been one (for example, might have died in childhood), so biological science shows us that the organism which is in fact a human being might never have been one (for example, might have been spontaneously aborted as a fetus).

It is not surprising that status as a human being should *seem* to be an essential property. The stage of the human organism in which it is a human being takes up, at least in familiar cases, the longest and most conspicuous part of its life. And there may be another, less respectable, reason. In determining whether the sortal "human being" individuates a substance per se or merely a stage of it, one must distinguish the question, Was there an earlier time at which the individual who is now a human being existed as a mere fetus? from, Did the human being already exist as a mere fetus? There is certainly a way of hearing the second question which requires that it be answered in the negative. But this fact by itself is metaphysically inconclusive, for it leaves us free to answer the first question affirmatively. In fact, something similar occurs for even the most uncontroversial stage sortals. Thus there is a way of hearing the assertion that the adolescent already existed as a mere child which makes it seem just as false. It seems that a certain, possibly deceptive ambiguity arises when such predicates as "already existed as" or "still exists as" are applied to subjects individuated by stage sortals such as "adolescent." But we can protect ourselves from metaphysical error here by simple linguistic measures. Thus we can see clearly that the child before us is the very same ongoing biological

11 I now find that W. R. Carter also advocates the stage-sortal conception of human being in "Do Zygotes Become People?" *Mind* 91 (January 1982):77–95. His basic argument is that there is no "natural breaking point" between conception and birth at which we could locate the beginning of a new substantial individual, and therefore that we may be forced to say that the fetus becomes, that is, takes on the attributes of, a human being.

individual as the future adolescent, and, according to the present theory, that the human fetus is the very same ongoing biological individual as the future human being.

"Human being" may seem to have two further peculiarities not shared by other terms that sort out the stages of human organisms. First, it may seem that we give proper names to human beings as such. And second, it may seem that we reserve, again for human beings as such, a special set of pronouns, including the philosophically fascinating "I." While both claims are arguable, I doubt that either is quite right. Even a convinced extreme proabortionist might be caught off-guard wondering exactly when he or she was conceived and whether he or she occupied a breach position in the womb. And it is difficult to suppose that because the Chinese regard themselves as already one-year-old at birth, their personal names and pronouns must be seen to have a different logic. But even if there were linguistic contexts in which it was off-limits to refer to fetuses by human names and personal pronouns, nothing devastating to the present theory would be entailed. For human names and personal pronouns might be restricted in this way simply because they carry in these contexts an implication that their referents are, at the time indicated by the reference, in the relevant developmental stage. Indeed, if "human being" were a stage sortal then any names given to human beings *as such* would have to carry some such restriction. The theory is thus inclined to treat the alleged fact of names and pronouns unextensible to the fetus as no more metaphysically telling than the fact that in certain cultures children's nicknames cannot be extended to adults. That we could not in such a culture properly refer to an adult as "Timmy" or "Freddie" (or that to do so would be either an insult or a joke) would not in the least entail that the individual before properly referred to as Timmy does not still exist. Without prejudice to the issue of the extensibility of human names, it will be convenient to introduce a convention yielding names that without question apply to biological organisms: Thus if "Smith" is the name of a human being we may refer to the human organism with whom he is identical as "Smith°."

Since the theory holds that the normal fetal human organism is going to become a human being it also asserts that the history of every human being is part of the history of some human organism. Thus whatever happens to Smith at t also happens to Smith° at t, whatever Smith does at t Smith° also does at t, and whatever state

28

Smith happens to be in at t is also a state that Smith° is in at t. So if Smith is bored at t, happy at t, engaged in philosophical reflection at t, so is Smith°. Of course, on the assumption of special reference conditions for human names, it will not follow from the fact that Smith is at t "just beginning to exist" (that is, is just entering the stage in which it can be referred to as "Smith") that Smith° is as well. But this is perfectly compatible with the theory. For this alleged fact about Smith does more than characterize the way Smith is at t; it also refers us to the Smithless pre-t world. Facts really confined to reporting the condition of Smith at t will transfer to Smith°.

So much for the outline of the theory as it bears on our present interests. As to the point in the normal life of the human organism when it becomes a human being, I offer only this observation: The biological perspective which we have been adopting tempts one to regard as especially significant the point at which the major organ systems, most especially the central nervous system, are completely formed.[12] This criterion is attractive even insofar as human mentality is concerned. For if we distinguish between the mental faculties that are developed as a normal human infant collects and sorts experiences of himself and the world, that is, the mental faculties that the infant or child comes to have in virtue of the learning he has done, from the underlying mental capacities that make this learning possible, it seems attractive to identify the latter as what is essential. (One also thereby avoids the somewhat awkward necessity of ascribing early learning to something other than a human being.) And it may well be that the underlying mental capacities that support the learning processes of the neonate are already contained within the fully developed nervous system of the very late fetus.

II

The first theory, as we have seen, connects status as a human being to the achievement of a certain advanced developmental *stage* in the

12 Although the overall morphology is sketched in quite early in pregnancy, the distinctively human convolutions of the brain may still be developing in the eighth month. See Jean Blumenfeld's excellent discussion of fetal brain development in "Abortion and the Human Brain," *Philosophical Studies* 32(1977):251–268. Also see Becker, "Human Being," pp 341–345.

life of an underlying organism. (We may therefore call it the "stage theory.") The theory to be developed in this section, however, returns to the more familiar idea of "human being" as a substance sortal which applies to an individual throughout its entire career. The central idea is that fetal development is a *process* in which an individual human being gradually comes to exist.[13] (So we may call it the "process theory.") This conception presupposes a general metaphysics in which it is possible for individual substances to come into (and go out of) existence *gradually*. And because of the problematic nature of this general metaphysics, the strategy of this discussion will have to be somewhat different. With the stage theory, what most needed discussing was not the perfectly familiar and apparently noncontroversial general metaphysics of underlying substance and developmental stage but rather the somewhat surprising application of that schema to the case of human organism and human being. In the present case, however, the problems are reversed. If one thought that genuine processes in which substantial individuals gradually came to exist were really possible, it would seem immediately plausible to identify fetal development as just such a process. The trouble is that one is likely to think either that there is no plausible general argument in favor of the existence of such processes or that there is some logical incoherency in the very idea of them. I shall therefore have to make some brief remarks in response to both these doubts before applying the general theory to interpret the identity of the fetus.

The central feature of the process theory is that the coming to be of substantial individuals may be a genuine *process* in time in the course of which the prospective individual comes into existence gradually, entering the world by degrees. The ontology in question thus involves the idea of the extent to which an individual has at a given time become fully actual or real – or, as I shall sometimes say, the degree to which it already fully exists. It will be helpful in understanding this conception of coming to be, which we may call

13 Lawrence Becker, ibid., p. 335, also adopts the view that "entry into the class of human beings is a process." But, unlike me, he seems to think the partial human reality of what he calls the "human becoming" to be in itself of no moral interest. For him the whole problem is when the process is finished. Joel Feinberg also discusses a "gradualist potentiality criterion" which may be compatible with my idea of the becoming process. See "Abortion," in *Matters of Life and Death— New Introductory Essays in Moral Philosophy,* ed. Thomas Regan (New York: Random House, 1980), pp. 183–216.

gradualist, to contrast it with the rival *antigradualist* idea. The anti-gradualist finds only two kinds of processes involved in the typical way in which artifacts such as houses and biological individuals such as human beings are introduced to the world. First there are preparatory processes: Boards and bricks are assembled together in preparation for the coming to be of the house, and cells are organized in various complex configurations in preparation for the arrival of the biological animal. Second, there are the finishing processes in which the newly formed individual is perfected by various changes and additions which take place in *it.* During the preparatory processes the individual does not yet exist, and during the finishing processes the individual already fully exists.

The antigradualist, in other words, seems to be committed to the totally instantaneous and catastrophic (in the mathematical sense) introduction into the world of the new individual. Let's call this sudden existential leap the "pop." The gradualist finds the idea that artifacts and human beings pop into existence extremely artificial and implausible. On his view, gradual and continuous phenomena have been radically misrepresented in the interest of logical neatness and simplicity. Of course, the antigradualist has a reply. The pop, he will insist, while indeed implausible, is not implied by his theory. For the *vagueness* of the substance sortal under which the new individual is individuated (for example, "house" or "human being") makes it impossible to identify any precise temporal point as the first moment of its existence. The beginning of all individuals, biological or artificial, is shrouded in vagueness, and that, according to the antigradualist, is why we are intuitively set against the idea of the pop.

The letter of the objection has been attended to, the gradualist will respond, but not its spirit. The pop is implausible not because of vagueness but because of our clear intuition that the coming to be of a new individual is the passive equivalent of the making process. If a builder's making a house or mother nature's making a human being are genuine processes taking time then so too are the coming to be of a house or human being. The vagueness that protects the antigradualist's account has nothing whatever to do with the fact that a thing is coming to be. Vagueness surrounds our concepts in all directions. It arises from a natural desire that our standard vocabulary be learnable and applicable in ordinary epistemic contexts and not from an attempt to accommodate our

31

metaphysical intuitions. To see this, consider the sometimes heard logicist proposal to reconstruct a version of our language more free from ambiguity and vagueness than what we now have, so as to be able to think about the world with greater precision. Suppose we were to succeed in doing so for at least that range of discourse describing fetal development and the beginnings of human existence. Our revised language might then have the resources to represent the pop that was formerly hidden by the vagueness of our unrevised language.[14] But would having the existential pop really be one of the gains in this reconstruction of our ordinary notions? The gradualist finds it implausible to think so. He will say that the "improved" concepts are in this respect really no improvement, not because they give definite answers where our old, familiar concepts could give none at all, but because they give the wrong answer where the old ones gave the right answer. Where the status of a shack or a hut is concerned our concept of "house" may simply fail to provide for a definite decision. But where a house under construction is concerned our concept provides us with a definite characterization. The thing in question is very definitely a *house under construction*, and is definitely neither a completed house nor a mere assemblage of materials for the building of a house. And as the construction progresses the object's right to be called a house increases accordingly. The gradualist supposes that our ordinary concepts recognize and make room for processes in which things come into existence and that the motivation behind this is to be distinguished from the very general linguistic considerations that produce vagueness.[15]

The thought that the process theory is *logically* incoherent comes from two sources. First, it is undeniable that its adoption will involve nontrivial logical complications of various sorts. We will need a predicate admitting of degrees for existence or reality; we may,

14 Perhaps our concept of "human being" would have been lost in the process of reducing vagueness. But this would only mean that our old concepts had been doing us the disservice of misrepresenting the true character of the newly emerging individual. When put into sharp focus the situation presents us with the instantaneous coming to be of an individual K where "K" replaces our previous vague concept of a human being.

15 Vagueness will, of course, confront the gradualist if he should try to pinpoint precise moments when the process of coming into existence begins and ends. But it will also face the antigradualist with respect to the precise beginnings and endings of what he regards as the preparatory and finishing processes.

depending on how the logic is worked out, also need a graduated notion of identity; and, as I shall suggest below, our conception of the extension of a predicate will certainly have to be revised. One may well complain of such complications, but from a certain philosophical perspective such complaints do not themselves constitute objections. Logic may well have to be complicated to accommodate the unruly character of our actual thought rather than our thought rendered simpler to fit an elegant logic.

The second source of worry seems even less creditable. The process theory posits a special kind of noninstantaneous change. Ordinary change over time is nothing more than the gradual acquisition by an already fully existing individual of new attributes. If this were the only variety, it would of course follow that any individual undergoing noninstantaneous change would have to be as fully real at the beginning as at the end of it. But the process theory explicitly denies that all noninstantaneous change is like this, insisting that there is a fundamentally different kind of constitutive change in which an individual gains or loses attributes as part of the process of gradually coming to be. And given that this is its distinctive claim, its defenders should not be daunted by objections that arise from attempts to model coming to be on some other kind of change. For example, if one tries to picture something coming into being as like someone coming into a room, the former idea will immediately lose its distinctive character and collapse into a species of mere change of attributes.[16] But it is all too evident that such picturing begs the question against the claim that coming to be is a unique kind of change.

Although it is no part of the present project to devise a complete conceptual scheme for the gradualist ontology of becoming, a few remarks in that direction may make clear what is at issue. A more or less Aristotelian version of the process theory would assume that any individual object or being is basically individuated as the individual thing it is by one of the sortal predicates that hold of it. For Smith, this individuating *substance sortal* is (*pace* the first theory) "human being" while for his house it is the sortal "house." The

---

16 The example is borrowed from Roderick M. Chisholm whose objections to the idea of gradual coming to be seem to me to involve this kind of modeling. See "Coming Into Being and Passing Away," in *Philosophical Medical Ethics: Its Nature and Significance,* Stuart Spicker and H. Tristram Engelhardt, eds. (Dordrecht: D. Reidel, 1977), pp. 169–182.

idea that some human beings or houses are incompletely real at a given time is tantamount to the idea that individuals of these kinds may fall under their substance sortals in two different ways. This means that the extensions of these substance sortals must divide into two distinct classes – one containing the fully realized individuals and the other containing the only partly realized individuals of the kind in question. We may call sortals with this kind of two-part extensional structure *complex* to mark the contrast with *simple* sortals having a one-part extension.

Several other kinds of related sortals should be mentioned. First there are those complex sortals each of whose extension classes includes the corresponding extension class of the substance sortal. These are the *generic sortals* of the substantial kind in question. "Mammal" and "animal" are, in this sense, generic sortals of human beings, while "building" and "dwelling" seem to be generic sortals for houses. Generic sortals preserve the distinction between partial and full reality found within the substance sortal. Thus a partly actual house is only a partly actual building while a fully actual house must be a fully actual building.

True generic sortals, which are complex, must be distinguished from those simple sortals which apply to all the individuals, whether fully or partially real, falling under the substance sortal. Let's call such simple sortals *mock-generic*. "Construction," in one recognizable sense, is a mock-generic sortal for houses. Every house *and* every house under construction is equally, in this sense, a construction. "Construction" thus clearly differs from the true generic "building." For while every partly actual house is no more than a partly actual building, every such house is already a full-fledged construction.[17] Another type of important simple sortal comprises the stage sortals that apply exclusively to *partly* real individuals of a given kind. We may call these *proto-stage sortals*. "House under construction" is clearly a proto-stage sortal of houses, for an incipient house can be a full-fledged house under construction without being a fully real individual house. Unlike substance sortals and true generics, both mock-generic and proto-stage sortals fail to provide within their own extensions for the distinction between full and partial reality. Partly real individuals can fully and un-

17 When "S" is a simple sortal, the claim that "x is a full-fledged S" means that S clearly and unambiguously includes x in its extension.

ambiguously satisfy the criteria associated with such sortals. The simplicity of these sortals can therefore be misleading. We must be on guard not to infer from the fact that we have found a full-fledged S that we have found a fully real individual. For "S" may turn out to be a mock-generic or a proto-stage sortal for a substantial kind that admits of gradual coming and ceasing to be.

We must now consider how all of this is to be applied to the fetus. There seem to be three choices. The fetus could be identified with the collection of biological materials in the process of being transformed into a human being; it could be identified with the human being that is coming into existence; or it could be seen as yet some third kind of object that either gradually ceases to exist as the human being becomes increasingly realized or that continues to exist throughout the human being's life as a constituent entity. Both versions of the third possibility seem implausible for reasons that have been discussed in connection with the stage theory. The developmental succession of fetal stages does not strike us, as the transformation of the caterpillar into the butterfly strikes some, as involving the gradual ceasing to be of an independent biological organism. Nor, if we reject the view of body as component sub-entity, are we left with any constituent part of the later human being with which the fetus could plausibly be identified. The first possibility seems even less plausible. A fetus does not seem to *be* a collection of anything, even biological materials, although it is of course in some sense composed of such a collection.

But it may also seem unacceptable to identify the fetus with the human being who is coming into existence. The fetus is perfectly definite – it can be seen, touched, probed, and measured. It has a fully determinate, although constantly changing, morphology and histology. All this makes it seem fully and not just partially realized. Nevertheless, there is something wrong with this objection. There is nothing in the way I have defined gradualism that commits it to the absurd view that objects in the process of coming into being should be empirically indeterminate. A house under construction can, at a given moment, be characterized with every bit as much precision as a fully built house. Its incompleteness lies only in its relation to the special sortal that best indicates the kind of thing it is, namely, "house." Thus there is no reason in the kind of full empirical reality that the fetus possesses to reject the claim that it is the human being in the making. And this is indeed the position that the gradualist who applies his process theory to human becoming ought, I think, to take.

The resulting picture is this: The fetus is a human being in the making, a partly but not fully real individual human being. However, the fetus is also a full-fledged fetus, fully satisfying the appropriate criteria. There is no contradiction in this because "human being" is the substance sortal for the individual in question while "fetus" is what I have called a protostage sortal. As the stage theory insisted, the fetus changes and acquires new attributes. But the process theory has the resources to enable it to deny the stage theory's claim that such change is merely a change of attributes. According to it, the fetus is most tellingly described as a partly existent individual human being, and its acquisition of new forms is best seen as part of the process of coming to be. A similar reinterpretation of the status of the human organism is also possible. While it is correct to see a full-fledged biological organism from conception on, it is wrong to interpret "biological organism," in this sense, as a substance sortal. It is more naturally seen, the process theory will insist, as a mock-generic sortal that stands to "human being" in the way that "construction" stands to "house." A fetus is indeed a full-fledged organism, but this is quite consistent with the claim that such a full-fledged organism is not a fully real individual. One must not be misled by the fact that the incipient human being gets a secure status as a coherent continuing object of biological interest before it is a fully real individual.

Of course, this identification of the fetus as a partly real human being will help sustain my initial moral intuitions only if it can be made immediately or very soon after conception. But conception seems an eminently plausible candidate for the role of starting point of the becoming process. Given that human beings are biological beings and given that the first theory was correct in rejecting the conception of the body as brutish subentity, the beginning of the formation of our bodies would seem to be the beginning of our own formation. And the embryological evidence is clear that the processes of cell differentiation and migration in which the various parts of the body come to be differentiated begin almost immediately after conception.[18] As to the question when the becoming process is over and the human being fully realized, the tentative

18 The earlier qualifications about twinning will have to be made here as well.

remarks made earlier about the counterpart question of the first theory seem equally appropriate. It is natural to think that the becoming process is over when the higher nervous system is developed enough for the organism to start learning, in the fashion of the normal neonate, the ways of the world.

III

We can now see that both the stage theory and the process theory secure the existential ambiguity we were seeking and that they do so in quite different ways. On the stage theory, the normal fetus will some day be a human being even though it cannot now be correctly described as one. On the process theory, the normal fetus is already to some extent but not fully a human being. Either of these theories does better justice, I would argue, to our biologically informed, extramoral intuitions than either the extreme antiabortionist's view that a fetus is, even in its earliest stages, a fully existent human being or the extreme proabortionist's view that in early pregnancy the human being is in no way already in the picture. But I would like now to consider what the positive aspects of these theories, the way that each sees the human being as already present, imply about the fetus's capacities to be touched by good and evil. Both theories regard the fetus as something that will, under favorable circumstances, come or continue to exist as a human being. Whether we see it as a human organism or as an incipient human being, the normal fetus that is not going to be aborted may have great *human* goods and evils, indeed a whole human life, in *its* future. And a fetus that is going to be aborted might well have had that life were it not for the abortion. So to the extent that having a human life is a good, abortion can be, it would seem, a bad thing or *loss* for the fetus.[19] It should not, however, be seen as an intrin-

19 In "The Evil of Death," *Journal of Philosophy* 77 (1980):401–424, Harry Silverstein argues that "loss" in the literal sense implies subsequent existence in a deprived condition. It is clear, on the other hand, that those who with me speak of "loss" of life through, for example, accident or illness mean to call attention to the difference for the worse from the point of view of the subject that the accident or illness makes by causing it to be true that he will not have the life he would otherwise have had, and do not mean to imply that the subject will subsist in some existentially deprived state. Since it seems perfectly intelligible, it is perhaps not important to establish whether this usage constitutes a metaphor or an ordinary sense.

sically bad thing. If it is bad, it must be so extrinsically, bad in the difference it makes to the being's future. Events are extrinsically bad, in this sense, when they affect one's prospects for the worse. Some extrinsic evils make things worse by causing the future to contain positive intrinsic evils, for example, pain and suffering. But this is by no means necessary. Losing one's inheritance, for example, may not cause impoverishment; indeed it may leave one with a perfectly agreeable life. But it may still be seen as a very bad thing when one reflects on the really splendid life one might have had.

What we thus need to know when we assess an event as extrinsically good or bad is the way the future *would have been* but for the event. The metaphysical status of such conditional states of affairs is, of course, philosophically problematic, and to the extent that my conditional future really is indeterminate at a given time, events that occur then lack this kind of positive or negative extrinsic value for me. But we ordinarily assume that the future is not, relative to different things that might occur, completely indeterminate. Winning the lottery, getting married, being cured of cancer, are thus seen as good things, while failing the bar exam, being jilted, and losing one's wallet are seen as evils. Of course we may be wrong. Value judgments of the type in question, because they presuppose some knowledge of the counterfactual future, may go wildly astray. The apparent misfortune may turn out to be a blessing in disguise and the seeming stroke of luck the very stuff of tragedy. This risk of error, however, does not and should not stop us from making judgments of extrinsic value as best we can and from shaping our prudential and moral choices in light of them.

Abortion is an event in the history of a human organism (on the first theory) or incipient human being (on the second theory) that has tremendous impact. In most cases the creature thereby loses the whole human life it would otherwise have come to have. For this reason abortion can be, from the point of view of the fetus, a far from inconsiderable extrinsic evil.[20] Or can it? At this point a number of objections will come to mind.[21] And the best way to

20 My defense of this proposition against certain objections will recall points made by Thomas Nagel in "Death," *Nous* 4 (1970):73–80.
21 Silverstein, in "The Evil of Death," discusses the Epicurean objection to the idea of death as an evil, namely that as long as we exist death is not with us and when it comes we no longer exist. He thinks the root of the objection is the

proceed is to consider them one by one. Perhaps it will seem to some that a loss cannot constitute a real evil unless what is lost is already wanted – or, if this is too strong, something the creature would have wanted were it to have considered the matter. Whichever condition of actual or potential desire is selected, it is clear that a totally unconscious fetus cannot qualify. It neither wants nor envisions a future; nor, in any relevant sense, is it able to. But one must say in response to this objection that it is extremely implausible to insist on desire or foreknowledge as a requirement for the possibility of extrinsic evil. Suppose some fiendish experimenter surgically deprives a fetus of the possibility of future sexual activity.[22] Should the fetus survive to maturity as a fully existent human being, he can rightly regard that long past experimental surgery as having been a very bad thing for him indeed. And in so doing he need not suppose that, as a fetus, he had any conception

idea that one's future death does not now timelessly exist and is therefore not now available as an object of those negative attitudes that would constitute it as an evil. My guess, however, is that Epicurus could admit the timeless presence of one's future death, but would still hold that it is irrational to think that it could be evaluated from the point of view of one's welfare. Nagel's discussion in "Death" (pp. 76–78) suggests to me a relevant distinction between temporally indexed and temporally vague conceptions of human good. Some datable conditions (for example, pain) affect one's welfare at a precise time (often at the very time they occur) while other perhaps equally datable conditions (for example, being unable to live up to one's early promise) seem to affect one's good in a much less datable and more general way. Epicurus's assumption, I suspect, is that future nonexistence, if it were to be an evil at all, would have to be an evil of the first sort, affecting our welfare at the very time it occurs. But since all such evils presuppose the subject's existence, the idea that nonexistence is such an evil is absurd. If this is the Epicurean assumption, it is by no means easily discredited. The basic difference between such a skeptic about death and his critics is that he is unimpressed by the fact that most of us seem to find it quite possible to consider the alternatives of staying alive and being dead and to form a decided preference for the former. He finds this preference irrational, not because nonexistence isn't available as an object to consider, but because it cannot be assigned any value that could make sense of the preference. His critics, however (and I am clearly among them), find the apparent fact of the preference sufficient reason to believe that death can be assigned a value (presumably a nonpositive value) that makes sense of the strong preference for life. And, it must be added, when we reflect on whether death is preferable to life, we cannot be supposing that our preference itself will constitute the evaluative difference. Otherwise we would have nothing to reflect on. That attitudes, and even the possibility of attitudes, are not the whole story about the evil of death is something I shall be arguing for in what follows.

22 This is like an example of Michael Tooley's in "A Defense of Abortion and Infanticide," in *The Problem of Abortion,* ed. Joel Feinberg (Belmont: Wadsworth, 1973), p. 64.

or attitude toward his future. Of course, in this case, the evil event would bring suffering. And this may lead someone to suggest that, where fetuses are concerned, an event can be extrinsically evil only by bringing *positive* future evils, for example pain and suffering. But this is equally implausible. For suppose the researcher had deprived the fetus not only of its sexual potential but also of the emotional and intellectual potential it would need to understand and regret its condition. Far from having set things right, this would only have made the harm done by the experimentation greater.

Of course, the case of abortion is quite different, for what is lost there is not some particular kind of future good but future life itself. So perhaps what failed to be true in general will be true here, and death will be a loss only when it frustrates future directed desires and plans. On this view, it is an adult's interest in his future that gives him something to lose in death.[23] And a child or infant, having little perspective on its future, will have correspondingly little to lose. One is bound to admit that there is an important element of truth in this modification of the first objection; what we have planned and hoped for may constitute an especially important kind of loss. But it must also be said that this is certainly not the whole story even for adults. The future that one now dead had planned and hoped for might, after all, have turned out to be very unsatisfying to him, and good might have come to him from changes in his life that he never imagined. And even if the hoped for future would have proved to be as good as expected, it seems odd to explain the badness of its loss by reference to the hope rather than to the good things the future would have contained. Consider a person who finds himself with all his ambitions fulfilled and interests secured. Or, even better, someone who, *much* more than most of us, lives for the present, taking little interest either in what his future will be like or whether it will exist at all. Do we regard death as less of a loss for him than for the rest of us? In some ways, perhaps, yes. But in some important ways, no. And I would not find it absurd for someone to suggest that in dying such a one loses more than we do. In any case, if the good lost in death may bear little relation to what the deceased envisioned and desired for his

23 See John Perry's "The Importance of Being Identical," in *The Identities of Persons,* ed. Amélie Rorty (Berkeley: University of California Press, 1976), pp. 67–90.

future, the fetus's present incapacity to envision a future at all is no objection to its possible vulnerability to that same kind of loss.

It should be noted here that it is possible to speak of a human being as having come into possession of a new life. This may be, as when a student graduates, no more than a pleasant metaphor. But it is possible to take the idea with a certain philosophical seriousness, not unlike the seriousness some philosophers have attached to the idea that a prisoner may emerge from prison as a new person.[24] The common philosophical idea is to split the concept of a person or, in this case, of a person's life into two subconcepts. In one broad sense we each have one and only one life. In the other narrow sense we may have many. And this idea of lives within a life might be thought to have relevance to the present issue. For someone might suggest that death can deprive us only of the life (in the narrow sense) that we now have. One might think of life in this sense as a kind of artifact, something we, in part, make for ourselves out of the circumstances luck has thrown our way. This "artifact" consists partly in a network of ongoing associations and activities and partly in the current personality, character, interests, and abilities that shape our experience of them. It consists in what we do and can do, what we know and love, where we go and why. And it is this and only this present network of possibilities that we stand to lose in death.

This objection is relevantly different from the last one. It is not our anticipations and projects that make us vulnerable. Rather it is our current possession of the as yet unexhausted good of our present life, a good that the fetus cannot possess and therefore cannot lose. But despite its attractiveness, this idea seems to me to express at best an incomplete picture of what one loses in death. It likens loss of life to the loss involved in extreme dislocation or exile, as when a child, having lost its parents, suddenly finds itself in an orphanage with no one and nothing the same. In such cases one loses almost

---

24 In "Later Selves and Moral Principles," in *Philosophy and Personal Relations*, ed. Alan Montefiore (Montreal: McGill-Queen's University Press, 1973), pp. 137–169, Derek Parfit describes *alternative* "Simple" and "Complex" views of personal identity with different moral implications attaching to each. It seems to me possible, however, to regard the two views not as competing explications of the same concept but as marking off two different relations each of which may have its own moral relevance.

all of the life one has had, and this indeed can be tragic. But surely part of the special evil of death lies in its final foreclosure of all possibilities of change and growth – not the least important of which is the possibility of coming into possession of new lives. It is, of course, true that the only life we now know that we can lose in death is the life we already have. But in the death of anyone, and particularly of an infant, one central mystery lies in our sense that we mourn a loss of which we can know very little.[25]

Still, the child and even the infant loses at most *part* of its life, while the fetus is alleged to lose *all* of it. For although the fetus is alive it has not yet come into possession of the human life we are here speaking of, nor can it until it is already a full human being. And this fact may itself be thought to show that any talk of the fetus losing its human life is incoherent. For it may be said that when a person's life is cut short the evil is done in the first instance *to his life* and only derivatively to him. To die in childhood or infancy is to be deprived of a natural life span; such a death makes one's life a stunted and unshapely affair. And even death in middle age denies one the chance to find the right finish, the right way of tying things up and rounding things off for the best. But the fetus, as we have seen, has no human life already under way that can be spoiled or even made slightly worse by death. So on this view, abortion cannot be regarded as an evil for it.

In reply it must be said that the generalized version of this claim, the idea that a lost future good must be one that would have added to the intrinsic value of a person's life as already in progress, seems false. At times, life offers us a prospect that is in some clear sense intrinsically good (like the prospect of an extramarital affair with someone deeply loved) but that cannot, because of what it is in itself, add to the intrinsic value of our life as already established.[26]

25 Consider the death of Mozart and the musical mystery it poses. Supposing that he would have lived as long as Michelangelo but for the attack of rheumatic fever that claimed him at thirty-five, he would have worked into the period of Schumann and Chopin. What the masterpieces we would now have would be like is something we can know almost nothing about, save that they would have been incalculably great and that the whole course of nineteenth-century music would have been very different.

26 The problem in the case of the affair may well be more than just a matter of consequences. Certain intrinsically good states of affairs may fail to fit the value system of a given life and may tend therefore, simply by their occurrence, to spoil or make nonsense of it. The determinate character of our actual history may make it impossible to intrinsically enhance our lives by the addition of

42

Consider, for example, the case of an old man about to die. He has had a normal life, has no outstanding plans and projects, and is not terrified or troubled by the thoughts of death. Suppose a doctor can give this man an additional six months of life by administering some new drug still in the experimental stage. And suppose further that although the old man is now understandably indifferent to the prospect of the reprieve, he would in the end be glad of it if it arrived despite the fact (let us also suppose) that it would not contain any achievements, personal discoveries, reconciliations, or insights and would unfortunately contain more discomfort and less pleasure than he is used to. Far from having the character of final *coda*, the added six months would, if he got them, be anticlimactic, detracting a bit from the beauty of his life as a whole. And for these reasons, it may well be that the extension cannot be seen as one which would add to his life's overall intrinsic goodness. But even so, since the man would be glad to have had the additional six months, there seems to be a very good reason to give him the drug. For in so doing, the doctor would be doing the *man* a real service, although not the special service of enhancing the long-term project we call his *life*. The moral of this for the case of abortion seems clear. If the old man can sustain a real loss (should the doctor decide not to give the drug) that is not to be explained as a blow to his life, then the fetus may be able to lose its whole future in just this way.

The objector may reply that I have underestimated the significance of the fact that the human life of the fetus has not yet begun, for it consists not in the fact that all injuries are injuries to lives but in the bedrock fact that the limits of a life (in what I before called the broad sense) are the limits of a creature's capacity to lose its future. To convince us, he may ask us to imagine a possible world in which the biological facts of human life are quite different. Instead of dying in old age, the human being lapses into a coma and gradually shrinks to the size and condition of a fetus. At this point some womb, artificial or natural, must be provided until it is born again. In its second life it remembers nothing of its first and may even have, within the limits of its continuing genetic makeup, a some-

certain indisputable intrinsic goods. G. E. Moore provides for this point in his notion of "organic wholes." See *Principia Ethica* (Cambridge: The University Press, 1903), esp. pp. 27–31.

what different appearance and personality. Lives are repeated several times until the organism finally wears out and really dies. Now let us suppose that Jones is a being in such a world currently in his first life. Let us further suppose that Jones cares only for his present life and is unwilling to take the necessary steps to ensure his survival to the next. He holds in effect that, whatever the underlying metaphysics, the boundaries of the life he is now living in some sense individuate a unique subject of goods and evils with which he psychologically identifies and in which he takes an exclusive prudential interest. That he is a human organism or human being that will be able to lead other lives seems to him to have no relevance to his present interests. And, the objector will conclude, Jones's attitude is intuitively correct, for it is just the attitude we should have were we suddenly to find ourselves in such a world.

But surely extreme caution is required in thinking about such bizarre possibilities. For our immediate intuitive reactions, having been formed in a world in which the real possibilities are very different, may prove inadequate. We must try to imagine what such a creature's intuitions would be, all other intuitions being suspect as parochially irrelevant. Of course, we must first be sure that the imaginary biological facts really do the intended job, that is, that we really have before us a case in which one and the same individual survives through various human lives. Let us suppose therefore that something like a genetic blueprint for the entire series is present in the original fetus and that the tendency to develop through the entire series is part of its nature. But whatever fact it is about these creatures that inclines us to think them capable of multiple lives, their own recognition of this fact and their own thought of themselves as having this capacity would surely have a special evaluative significance for them. Since it would be natural for them to see each of their successive lives as something like a reincarnation, they would be bound to feel, and would be encouraged to take, an interest in their past and future lives that would be, even more than our interest in the lives of our parents and siblings, quasi-prudential in character. They would be consoled by learning that their past lives had been happy, and they would be disturbed by the thought that their future lives might be unhappy. In short, in at least one strand of their evaluative thinking, they would surely be inclined to think in terms of a common subject of all their lives, a subject to which all the various goods and evils in

44

them could be attributed. The Jones the objector has pictured in such a world would thus be something of a skeptic, and it is doubtful that his skepticism would have more power to threaten the natural intuitions of his own kind than the analogous skepticisms of our world have to threaten ours.[27]

It is now possible to see that the objections we have been canvassing make a common charge. They claim and argue that it is only when the fetus's present and the future it would have had but for our choice to destroy it are connected by relations stronger (more specific) than that of being different parts of a possible history of one being that its death can be seen as an extrinsically regrettable loss. In each case, I have in effect accepted the idea that the stronger connection proposed is relevant – that it does create the possibility of a special kind of loss. But I have tried to show that there is a type of loss that remains even when all of these special connections are absent. This is the loss whose possibility is provided by the fact of individual continuity itself, by the fact that the very same human organism or incipient human being here present would later have enjoyed a human life but for the abortive procedure that destroys it. It is nothing other than the fact of this loss, I think, that makes abortion a moral problem.

IV

In this final section I want to try to sort out some of the moral implications of the kind of metaphysical status the two theories have assigned to the fetus with particular attention to the kind of moral constraints that arise from the fact that the fetus has something important to lose in being aborted. Specifically, I will try to state how it is that the second negative intuition, the idea that early abortion cannot be regarded either as a violation of a mature right to life like our own or even as comparable in moral gravity to infanticide, is satisfied. And I will also, of course, try to sustain the first intuition by motivating the idea that the fetus's susceptibility to loss brings it under some important moral protections.

To do this, I will need to invoke some version of the common division of morality into what are often called the spheres of "justice" and "benevolence" (although, as will become apparent, I think

---

27 Which is not to say that it would have none.

these particular headings can be misleading). I follow a Kantian tradition here in thinking that one important part of morality is made up of constraints on our behavior toward others that spring from our recognition of others as mature agents on an equal moral footing with ourselves.[28] The fundamental attitude underlying virtuous action of this type seems to be respect for what can be thought of as the moral authority of others. Defining the scope of this authority amounts to specifying the rights that mature moral agents have over each other. But what is characteristic, interesting, and important about these rights for our purposes is that they exert their force on others only in virtue of actual (or in some situations, counterfactual) exercises of will. Take, for example, the well-known rights of life, liberty, and the pursuit of happiness. Among the several moral reasons you may have not to kill me, take me captive, or subject me to your idea of the good life, perhaps the most important lies in the simple fact that I *choose*, or would choose were I to consider the matter, that you do not. Viewed in this way these rights are nothing other than equally distributed moral powers to forbid and require behavior of others, and violations of them are nothing other than refusals to respect the exercise of these powers.

The picture of morality as a nexus of independent spheres of authority to permit, forbid, and require is, in one special use of the term, a picture of "justice." But while justice in the more ordinary and contemporary sense enters into the definition of these spheres, especially with regard to property, most violations of these rights are not altogether naturally described as injustices. I propose therefore to call this first part of morality the *morality of respect* and the rights that it includes *rights of respect*. These rights are marked by an often mentioned common grammatical feature whose presence is easily explained. Since what is constrained by someone's choice is in a perfectly obvious sense constrained by *him*, the constraints

---

28 I am also clearly drawing here on H. L. A. Hart's conception of natural rights. See "Are There Any Natural Rights?" *The Philosophical Review* 64 (1955):175–191. In some respects Hart's "Bentham on Legal Rights," *Oxford Essays in Jurisprudence (second series)*, ed. A. W. B. Simpson (Oxford: The Clarendon Press, 1973) and reprinted *Rights,* ed. David Byons (Belmont: Wadsworth, 1979), gives a clearer picture of the type of right in question, although here in a legal rather than a moral setting.

generated by rights of respect are obligations owed *to* individuals and not merely obligations to act in various ways with respect to individuals.

The other relevant area of morality is quite different and, in one way, much easier to understand. The constraints that arise in it are not grounded in the will of others but in consideration of the good and evil that our actions may do to them. Since the basic motivation of virtuous action here is concern for the well-being of others, I shall call this the *morality of humanity*. This part of morality, unlike the morality of respect, extends its protections to immature human beings and other creatures presently or permanently incapable of joining the community of moral agents. In fact, it seems tempting to think that it especially serves to protect them and not us. As a young person becomes an adult and more responsible for his own successes and misfortunes he tends, I suspect, to exchange some protection under the morality of humanity for protection of his developing authority under the morality of respect. This may be why our humane obligation to look after the abandoned child seems so much more obvious and pressing than any similar obligation to look after the derelict even though each be in equal danger without our aid. However, the name "humanity," like "benevolence," must not be allowed to obscure the fact that the obligations of humanity are sensitive to special natural and institutional relations that exist between moral agents and those toward whom they act. For example, parents have a much weightier obligation under what I am calling humanity to avoid harming the interests of their own infants than they have to avoid harming the interests of those of their neighbor.

It is interesting to ask whether there are rights in this part of morality and if so what the propriety of speaking in this way can consist in. People are sometimes tempted to think that the obligations that remain once we have subtracted those of respect are in some unique way grounded in the purely self-referential necessity of promoting virtue and avoiding vice. This conception is fundamentally unsound, I think, and speaking of rights here is one way of expressing one's objection to the error. Any part of morality can be practiced with an eye to one's own virtue, justice as well as benevolence. The humane part of morality, no less than the other parts, gives rise to obligations and prohibitions in large part grounded in relevant facts about others. And it is for this reason that the discharge of one's obligations under humanity is a matter in which the community or even the law may take an interest.

The rights of animals provide a good illustration of this. When animal lovers speak of animal rights (say a right against wanton abuse or torture) they mean to be reminding us of three things: (a) that prima facie we *must not* subject animals to certain forms of suffering and pain, (b) that the law ought to take an interest in enforcing these prohibitions, and (c) most important, that the ground of the moral constraint that is here active is the welfare of the animal itself (and not the moral virtue of the human agent). In these ways the morality of respect and humanity are alike. In both we look to something about the creatures our action affects and to our connections with them to find the ground of the requirement or prohibition. The difference, as we have seen, is that in the one the obligation, grounded in the will of the other creature, is therefore owed to it whereas in the other the obligation is not grounded in the other creature itself, that is, in its will, but in its well-being.[29] For this reason an obligation under benevolence may sometimes require us to do what is neither willed nor wanted by the affected party, as parents educating their children well know.[30]

But what are the implications of all this for the abortion issue? One thing is evident. Neither fetuses nor infants are yet in posession of rights of respect. And this explains my original intuition that abortion cannot be seen as a violation of the kind of full-fledged right to life that we possess. Fetuses, like animals, do not *require* us to do anything; nor do they have any wills to contravene. They are incapable of the authority that is the ground of the respect owed to others. Here it must be stressed that one does not constrain others in the relevant way simply by disliking or reacting negatively

29 With rights of respect, x's obligation *to* y matches y's right *against* x. But while rights under humanity do not give rise to obligations *to* the right-holder, I am inclined to think that such rights can properly be said to be *against* those specific individuals whom morality requires to take a special interest in the right-holder's welfare. Thus a child may have special rights under humanity against its parents.

30 In this kind of case it would not be natural to speak of the child's right to the unwanted benefit as what constrains the parent. Still the child does have a right to the benefit and there would be no impropriety in speaking of that right constraining the parent in cases where the benefit is not unwanted. The constraints of humanity are brought under the idea of "rights" only insofar as the benefits are not unwanted or disliked. Here we perhaps hear an echo of the connection between rights and will found in the morality of respect.

to what they do. Such a reaction may well create strong reasons of humanity to desist. But one is not showing respect for a creature in expressing humane concern over its discomfort. (This distunction can also be seen when one reflects that a person may explicitly refuse to activate rights at his disposal while continuing to show extreme displeasure at the very action he has the authority to prevent, as when a lender makes it clear both that he is very distressed by the nonpayment of a debt and that he nevertheless does not yet demand payment.)

Nor should we let the absurdity of crediting the fetus or infant with rights of respect be obscured by the fact that the prohibitions created by these rights are typically in force unless the right-holder has explicitly indicated otherwise. It is true that one cannot defend removing life-sustaining equipment from an unconscious adult on the ground that he never explicitly said (supposing him never to have considered the matter) that one must not. But this is because one must presume that the injured man's will is in a general way set against actions that would lead to his death and that he would not make an exception in this case. But we cannot make sense of the idea, and therefore cannot be obliged to presume, that the fetus's will is set in a general way against anything; and we cannot therefore respect any such will in refusing to abort it.[31]

If this is right and fetuses do not fall under the morality of respect, they must therefore lack an important right to life which we possess. And, although I will argue shortly that they do fall under the morality of humanity, it is possible to see why even their protectedness there should seem to fall short of the infant's. The obligations of humanity are, as noted above, sensitive to various natural and institutional relations that exist between the agent and the being toward which he acts. It is one thing to foreclose on the mortgage

---

31 Here someone might suggest that we are able to respect the future retrospective will the fetal being would come to have were the abortion not to occur. Although I am doubtful that such a strategy could plausibly bring abortion under the morality of respect, a similar strategy does have some attractiveness in the case of the fetus who is not killed but who is deprived, for example, by an experiment, of normal future human intelligence and volition. That the future will of the creature would have been retrospectively set against such interference can seem not irrelevant to the character of the offense. For a discussion of these kinds of moral situations see Joel Feinberg's "Is There a Right to be Born?" in his *Rights, Justice, and the Bounds of Liberty: Essays in Social Philosophy* (Princeton: Princeton University Press, 1980), pp. 183–216, esp. p. 214.

of a brother or a friend, another to foreclose on a colleague or a neighbor, and yet another to foreclose on a stranger (supposing, of course, that none of them had any right of respect against the action). That we think such relations make a difference is one of the more important ways in which most of us are not utilitarians. Of course, relations of friendship and kinship matter very little where, for example, the killing of infants is concerned; we are simply not to kill any infant whether our own or a stranger's. But while it is true that these kinds of particular relationships seem irrelevant to the inhumanity of killing fully actual human beings it does not follow that the very special relationship of acting toward such a fellow human being is irrelevant to the inhumanity of killing. Most people would think it matters very much whether we kill a retarded member of our own species or an equally intelligent chimpanzee. And so it is not surprising that it should also seem to matter whether a fetus is unequivocally a human being, as the extreme antiabortionist insists or something less, as on our two theories. For if our most psychologically salient conception of the human community is as a community of fully actual human beings, it will naturally make a difference whether the fetus is one of us in this full sense.

But if the fetus has no rights of respect and it is not yet a full-fledged member of the human community, why should we have to take it into account at all, morally speaking? Here I would answer that the question of whether a creature's good or ill needs to be taken seriously cannot be wholly separated from the question of what that good or ill consists in. This, I think, is one of the most important truths in classical utilitarianism. According to both our theories, the fetus is a being to some extent capable of losing a fully human future life, the very kind of life we now enjoy. And it is hard for me to see how the loss of an object of this significance, the loss of the very thing that for ourselves we hold most important in the world, could have no moral weight. In any case, there is surely no precedent for thinking that it could be ignored, for there are simply no other situations in which such losses are at issue where a morally sensitive agent ignores them. The fetus, I feel, must have a right that its future welfare count for something and thus that there be a sufficiently strong moral case for sacrificing its good. And to the extent that the ties of biological kinship themselves add special weight, it will have an especially strong version of this right against its parents.

In this regard, the process theory gives a somewhat different result from the stage theory. To the extent that the human being already exists it is susceptible to the loss of future life and its rights under humanity come into play. But to the extent that it does not yet fully exist it cannot, it would seem, suffer this or any other loss and is to that extent removed from moral consideration. But what in this regard the process theory loses in moral impact, it seems to gain back in its implication that abortion directly concerns a creature with some claim already to *be* a human being. Abortion on this view therefore falls under the part of humane morality that looks after the welfare of human beings, or at least that special part of it that treats of the transitions in the course of which human beings move into and out of existence. For if, as I have already indicated, the morally binding force of humane considerations varies according to various dimensions in which the object affected is nearer to or further from us, the fact that the fetus is to some extent already a human being, already to some extent one of us, can only make its loss, however qualified, count for more. And as the fetus becomes more fully human the seriousness of aborting it will approach that of infanticide. In this way the process theory, unlike the stage theory, validates the third moral intuition that later abortions are more objectionable than earlier ones.

It is clear then that the two ontologies point to a limited, if important, moral consequence. Even the early fetus is a creature whose status arguably brings it at least within the fringes of the morality of humanity. How powerful its rights are against other competing moral forces is the very important problem of casuistry that I have gladly left aside. Women have rights of respect over their own bodies and rights of humanity concerning their own happiness, rights which cannot be ignored. How the complex web of moral forces vectors out in particular situations is, as Aristotle would say, what the wise man knows.

51

3

The right to threaten and the right to punish

Most of us feel certain that punishment is, in many cases, fully justified. But as to the nature of the justification we are perplexed and uncertain. I do not refer here to punishment within the family. Parents are natural educators morally charged with the task of turning their young dependents into civilized adults, and they need, common sense insists, the possibility of punishing to succeed. But civic punishment, in which one adult is made to suffer for his past wrongdoing by other adults who officially represent the community, raises different problems.[1] It is not, of course, that we doubt its utility. Common sense urges, no less here than in the case of family discipline, that some form of civic punishment is necessary for a decent social order. The difficulty lies rather in the question of authority or right. For on the modern liberal view, adult criminals are not dependents of the community, and the community is not assigned the moral task of forming or improving their characters. How then does its right to punish them arise?

The major source of theoretical difficulty here is the fact that the restrictions, confinements, and deprivations of property and life that make up standard civic punishments would, if imposed in nonpenal contexts, be opposed by various important moral rights

From *Philosophy and Public Affairs* 14:4 (Fall 1985) 327–373. Copyright © 1985 by Princeton University Press. Reprinted by permission of Princeton University Press.

I would like to thank Philippa Foot, Miles Morgan, Stephen Munzer, David Sachs, the Editors of *Philosophy & Public Affairs*, and, especially, Rogers Albritton for helpful comments on earlier drafts.

1 I would simply call this kind of punishment "legal" if I were certain that having a code of punishable behavior and designated authorities to punish always, even in very simple societies, adds up to having a legal system. In any case, I shall help myself to the word "crime" for the kind of thing that is properly punished by this type of punishment.

of liberty, life, and property. If these evils did not come by way of just punishment, a person subjected to them could object to his treatment in ways that would have serious moral weight.[2] To understand how civic punishment can be morally justified, therefore, we must first understand why these familiar rights do not stand in its way. There is, it is important to note, a parallel theoretical issue in the case of self-defense. In defending oneself against an unjust attack, one may put the attacker at some risk of being harmed or even killed, a risk that one could not create in most other contexts without violating some of his rights. Here, however, we feel that we can explain why an attacker's objections to such a defense do not count. How could morality first declare that certain aggressions would be serious violations of our rights and then extend to these aggressions an immunity from interference comparable to that which it assigns to innocent actions? But no parallel explanation seems available in the case of punishment. We cannot punish a crime until it is beyond influence.

If criminals fully retained their ordinary rights to liberty, life, and property, these rights would either raise a morally decisive barrier against punishment, in which case it would *violate* them, or they would create an obstacle that a case for punishment could override, in which case it could *justifiably infringe* them. Justified punishment could not, of course, violate rights. But perhaps it could be thought to infringe them. This idea invites us to include proper punishment in the class of actions, such as the expropriation of private property in time of national emergency, in which we regretfully but justifiably encroach upon someone's rights in order to prevent some evil. But, upon reflection, this assimilation appears doubtful.[3] For justified infringement of rights is a special moral circumstance creating special moral demands not present in the case of punishment. When one has harmed someone in the course of justifiably infringing his moral rights, it is always appropriate and sometimes required that one express regret and offer compensation.

---

2 Having a moral right, in the sense I intend throughout this article, is having a moral status in virtue of which one's objecting (or objecting that could be done on one's behalf) to what others might (or might not) do creates at least a prima facie obligation that they refrain from doing (or not doing) it.
3 Herbert Morris expresses such a doubt in "The Status of Rights," *Ethics* 92 (Oct. 1983):45, and also offers some plausible objections to received conceptions of infringement.

But when punishment is fully justified, expressing regret seems, at most, morally optional, and making compensation seems definitely out of place. We do not feel that a properly punished criminal is entitled to either.

It thus appears that a morally justifiable practice of punishment can neither violate *nor* infringe a criminal's rights. And therefore the central problem for any moral theory that takes both punishment and rights seriously is to show how this can be so despite the fact that in punishing we subject people to treatment that in other contexts would violate or at least infringe their rights. This is not, of course, the only interesting moral question that can be raised about punishment. A particular punishment might be unwise or unkind without violating any rights. But, as a natural working hypothesis, I shall assume that when punishment is *unjustified* because of the evil imposed on the punished person, it is unjustified as a violation of one or another of his rights. In discussing the question of rights, therefore, I shall often speak as if I am discussing the general question of justification. If this assumption should prove false, my argument will bear only on the specific question of the right to punish, that is, the question how punishment can be shown not to violate a punished person's moral rights.

The way I shall set about answering this question differs from the way state-of-nature theorists often proceed. They typically begin by assuming a nonproblematic right of private punishment (or, as I shall say, retaliation) in a state of nature. And from this they infer that the central philosophical problem for the theory of civic punishment is to show how such a right can be preempted by the state.[4] Now, accepting their idea that the right to civic punishment must somehow arise out of a more fundamental right to private retaliation, I agree that this is an important problem. But even in the case of retaliation, there is a more basic question. To give an adequate account of justified retaliation in a state of nature we must be able to explain why an offender's moral rights do not stand in opposition to the evil inflicted upon him. Justified retaliation raises, therefore, the same fundamental question raised by civic punishment. And since it is this question that I wish to answer, I shall avoid altogether the less basic question how a

4 The problem that occupies Robert Nozick in Part 1 of *Anarchy, State and Utopia* (New York: Basic Books, 1974).

community can rightfully forbid private retaliation and force its members to accept instead the protections of civic punishment. I shall do this by restricting the discussion to communities whose members prefer the protections afforded by their practices of civic punishment to those they could hope to gain by threatening retaliation.[5]

Before presenting my own account, it may be well to consider briefly how some familiar theories would address the problem of the right to punish. If any of these theories had a fully satisfying account of this right, there would be no need to continue looking. We may begin with consequentialist theories. Act consequentialism justifies an individual act of punishment by direct reference to its results. Among the most useful of these results is strengthening the deterrent effect on others of the ongoing threat. Since this consequence is a conspicuous social benefit, a plausible consequentialism cannot set it aside as irrelevant to the question of justification. Indeed, it is by reference to this kind of benefit that, under this theory, most justified acts of punishment receive the major part of their justification.

In rule consequentialism this kind of benefit enters into the justification of the practice of punishment as a whole and therefore also into the justification of acts of punishment. For a practice, insofar as it can be consequentially justified, includes those events that help constitute its existence, and these constituents must, in the present case, include the particular acts of punishment that would not otherwise occur. These acts are therefore a large part of what is justified when the practice as a whole is justified. And their deterrent effects on others are a large part of what does the justifying. It thus appears that both kinds of consequentialists are ready to justify punishments, at least in part, by reference to their deterrent effects on others. And even in rule consequentialism, the deterrent effects on others of a *particular* act of punishment may, in theory, tip the balance so as to justify the practice that contains it and, therefore, serve to justify the act itself.

To apply consequentialist theory of justification to the question of rights, we seem driven to the following result: Punished persons

---

5 To further lighten my burden, I shall also limit the discussion to punishment for acts that clearly violate people's public moral rights, acts such as murder, theft, assault, and fraud.

have no rights that stand against their punishment because, in part, punishing them is so often useful in helping to deter others from committing crimes. But I, for one, find this answer deeply disturbing. There may indeed be situations in which utility decides the presence or absence of moral rights. But to justify punishment in this way is to say that properly punished people lack the relevant rights because, in large part, they make such useful object lessons for others. In no other case, however, do we suppose that ordinary rights to liberty and life fail to apply *because* their application would stand in the way of some socially profitable use of people.[6] Our rights, by their very nature, are kinds of moral properties that resist such attempts to justify incursions upon them. The most that can follow from an appeal to the general utility of using people is that any rights that stand in its way may be justifiably infringed. But it is implausible, as we have seen, to regard punishment as justified infringement.

A deterrent theorist might escape this kind of objection by restricting his appeal to the deterrent effects of punishment on the person who is punished. Punishing in an attempt to make a criminal's future behavior morally acceptable could not naturally be construed as making use of him. And in aiming at the social utility that would result from this improvement rather than at the punished person's edification, punishers would not be liable to the charge of paternalism. The trouble is that such an account restricts the class of cases in which punishment can be justified and thus unreasonably restricts the kinds of liabilities to punishment that can be created. Suppose, for example, that we discover that a certain type of person is psychologically capable of committing only one murder. Such a person need never murder at all, but if he does murder once he will never murder again. If such people could be identified, we could not on this view rightly punish them for murder since we could not justify this punishment as a way of keeping them from committing future murders. And this seems to imply that we could

6 The military draft in wartime may seem an exception to this claim. But even here it would be odd to argue directly from social need to the conclusion that people have no right not to be forced into military service. Claims about what is *owed* the community in return for alleged benefits received from it are at least implicit in all common-sense justifications of conscription. Moreover, it may be possible to view conscription as a justifiable infringement of liberty rights and to interpret the various forms of preferential treatment accorded to veterans as forms of compensation.

not, except as a bluff, have the threat of punishment for murder stand against them in our penal code. But this implication seems absurd. Surely we might rightly make them liable to punishment in hope of deterring the single murder that each is capable of committing.[7]

We must also consider the family of retributivist theories of punishment. Often, caught up in establishing a supposed duty to punish, retributivists do not directly address the question of right. But when they do, some retributivists invoke the idea of *forfeiture*. The rights that would otherwise have barred us from doing the sorts of things we do in punishing, for instance, depriving the criminal of liberty or life, have been forfeited by his own behavior. These rights are seen as conditional and, therefore, liable to deteriorate or disappear unless preserved by a certain moral prudence. This conditionality can be seen as a basic feature of the operation of natural moral law that provides an independently intelligible "clearing of the way" for retribution.

The appeal to forfeiture as an independently intelligible moral mechanism is, however, problematic. The proper authorities are entitled to punish Jones, a generally decent young man who has foolishly stolen Smith's car, by depriving him of up to the amount of liberty forfeited in the theft. But suppose that before any such punishment takes place, Smith, for reasons having nothing whatever to do with the theft, kidnaps Jones and deprives him of exactly that amount of liberty. In this situation it is natural to suppose that Smith not only wrongs Jones but specifically violates his right to liberty. Perhaps this is because Jones forfeits his right to the community as a whole and not to Smith in particular. But suppose that the community in which Jones lives has the unjust practice of seizing and confining political dissenters. And suppose that shortly after his crime Jones, who also happens to be a dissenter, is officially seized and, for a time, quarantined to prevent the spread of his political views (views having nothing to do with his theft). Again, we would naturally suppose that Jones's right to liberty had been violated by his community, even if he were confined only for a period that would constitute an acceptable punishment for his theft and were never punished thereafter. But surely all this strongly

---

7 This objection, suitably modified, can also be used against other educative and reformist conceptions of punishment.

suggests that the conditionality of Jones's right to liberty (the conditionality invoked by the doctrine of forfeiture) makes essential reference to punishment.[8] Jones has not forfeited his right without qualification, he has forfeited it in that he may be subjected to a certain penalty (presumably the proper penalty for the crime) by certain people (presumably those with the right to punish him). It seems, therefore, that the idea of forfeiture in this kind of case comes to no more than the idea that the criminal's rights do not in fact stand in the way of his being punished. The appeal to forfeiture does not, as it first seemed, provide an explanation of why this is so.[9]

It is sometimes thought that the force of an appeal to forfeiture lies in the moral necessity of reciprocating respect for rights. But

8 To deny this would be to adopt a theory of forfeiture according to which Jones's crime has to some extent made him an *outlaw*, someone whose basic moral rights do not stand in the way of a certain amount of ill-treatment whether or not it comes by way of punishment. Someone who held this idea of forefeiture might try to show that it could be restricted in various ways by moral and legal conventions. He might in this way hope to account for the fact that, in our own moral and legal systems, Jones forfeits his conventionally specified liberty right only in that he may be punished. On such a view, forefeiture would be restricted only in some systems of social morality; in other morally acceptable systems outlawry in some degree would be the regular consequence of crime. It is this last suggestion that I find disturbing.

9 Forfeiture of the kind we are discussing might be distinguished from forfeiture whose very possibility is created by a contract that both creates a right and specifies the precise ways in which it may be lost. Some philosophers might appeal to forfeiture of the latter kind by construing the right to punish as deriving from a hypothetical social contract that both creates and limits various social rights. On such a picture, our natural disapproval of, for example, murder and assault, would lead us to design our rights in a way that stipulated forfeiture for such acts. And certain other natural desiderata would lead us to specify that this forfeiture be to the community for the specific purpose of punishment. While tempting, this kind of account raises some difficult questions. First, there is the familiar problem of the actual moral force of a hypothetical agreement. Second, it would have to be shown that such a view can make sense of the morally intuitive upper limits on punishment. And this would be difficult, I think, even if the hypothetical contractors were trying to minimize the likelihood of the worst things that can happen to them. For in the design of their future practice they will focus not so much on individual crimes, and how best to deal with them, as on the bearing of alternative possible practices on their lifetime prospects. And since one very bad, but empirically possible, lifetime prospect is to be a *repeated* victim of a certain kind of crime, it may be reasonable to design the practice so as to tolerate, under certain empirically possible situations, Draconian penalties. Finally, this picture of the right to punish seems to give no account of the right of retaliation in a state of nature – a right which, to my mind, not only exists but raises the same basic theoretical problem as does the right to punish.

it is not clear how this necessity can help explain why the loss of rights arising from nonreciprocation focuses so precisely on punishment. Moreover, such an account is hard pressed in other ways. If respect is treated as an *attitude*, then many people who never steal may have as little respect for property as Jones, who may have uncharacteristically succumbed to an unusually strong temptation.[10] Yet these others do not, in virtue of their attitude, forfeit any rights. If, on the other hand, respect is taken to refer only to actions, then it is not clear what role the idea of reciprocation is to be assigned. Suppose Smith wrongly takes Jones's car at the very same time that Jones takes his. They apparently reciprocate the same degree of respect for each other's rights. But surely this does not mean that neither may be punished. Crimes may be punishable even though everyone commits about the same number of them.

A retributivist may, however, omit any appeal to forfeiture in his account of the right to punish. He may argue that the special moral character of retribution, its status under justice as something *deserved*, demands that morality make room for it.[11] Morality would, on such a view, be internally inconsistent if it fully extended ordinary rights into penal contexts. Since it is not inconsistent, a person who gets what he deserves cannot object by appealing to any moral right. When retributivism is thus conceived, evaluation of its account of the right to punish must focus on the moral cre-

---

10 There is also the difficulty of explaining why Jones doesn't lose his rights only for the period in which he remains disrespectful of others' rights. Without such an explanation it will not be clear with what right we punish people who have reformed in the interval between crime and punishment.

11 Some quasi-retributivist conceptions that bring punishment under the heading of rectification also do without forfeiture. Versions of these views can be found in Herbert Morris's "Persons and Punishment," *The Monist* 52, no. 4 (October 1968): 475–501, and in Jeffrie Murphy's *Retribution, Justice and Therapy* (Boston: Reidel, 1979), pp. 73–115 and 223–49. Such accounts, while attractive in many ways, face a number of problems. If punishment is modeled on the payment of a debt or the cancellation of an illicit liberty, it must be explained why the matter cannot be set right, voluntarily, in other ways. Moreover, in clear cases of rectification, there is the possibility of transferring the misappropriated property or power either to its rightful owner or to someone with a better claim to it than the wrongful possessor has. In punishment, however, there is a "taking away" from the criminal without any obvious transfer of what is taken away to anyone else. For some other criticisms of these views see Richard Burgh's "Do the Guilty Deserve Punishment?," *Journal of Philosophy* 79, no. 4 (April 1982): 193–210.

dentials of retribution itself. Since a critical examination of these credentials would take me beyond my present purpose, I shall make only two brief observations. First, it seems clear that retributivism is burdened by a prima facie mystery. The idea that it is just (and, therefore, in some sense morally good) to harm someone's interests simply because he has wrongly harmed someone else's interests is, when considered in the cold light of reason, hard to understand. Second, one may doubt that an appeal to particular moral intuitions can help to dispel the mystery. For while we would often be inclined to assent to the claim that a particular person deserves to suffer for what he has done, the thought behind our inclination may not be adequately expressed in the precise words we accept. Our underlying thought may simply be that the criminal ought to be punished for his crime and that his punishment will be justified not by its effects but by the fact of the crime itself. But this intuition can be valid in the nonretributivist account of punishment that I shall now present.

This conception, unlike those we have considered, gives equal attention to two temporally distinct components of the practice of punishment. The first is establishing the real risk of punishment, creating serious *threats* of punishment designed to deter crime. The second is, of course, the actual *punishing* of those who have ignored the threats. According to this conception, the standard theories err in assuming that the right to threaten punishment derives from the anticipation of an independently intelligible right to punish. The central idea of this conception is, in contrast, that the right to make people liable to punishment is the *ground* of our right to punish.[12] Another way to put this claim is to say that according to conventional theories one cannot object to being subject to the threat of punishment because one will not, if one commits the offense, be able to object to being punished, whereas on the present view, it is because one could not object to the threat in the first place that one cannot, later, object to being punished.

12 Thomas Hurka advances this idea in "Rights and Capital Punishment," *Dialogue* 21, no. 4 (December 1982): 649. (But he seems to take it back or at least to modify it on p. 659, where he asserts that punishment, by which I take him to mean punishing, is impermissible unless *it* promotes the social good.) Hurka suggests a view of punishment in many respects like the one I am advancing, but he defends it on p. 650 with what seems to me a very dubious libertarian argument.

To create (or establish) a threat against x, in the quasi-technical sense that I intend in this discussion, is *first, deliberately to create a real risk that x will suffer a certain evil if he does or omits a certain specified action and second, to warn x of the existence of this risk, where by these means x may possibly be deterred from the act or omission.*[13] I mean this quasi-technical use to include the making of ordinary sincere threats.[14] In this most simple case the conditional danger lies in the intention of the threatener to carry out the threat. But in typical practices of punishment the conditional danger derives from an already existing "machinery" of the law. This "machinery" is, in large part, made up of the dispositions of various functionaries to make their assigned contributions to the process by which guilty persons come to be punished. But I shall also be considering a kind of general threat in which the danger is created by activating artificial devices. To speak of a threat in such a case will further extend the ordinary notion, which normally includes the idea that the threatened evil will come by way of some intentional human action.

When we create threats of punishment we are, according to the theory I wish to develop, justified by our rights of *self-protection*.[15] It is morally legitimate to create these threats because it is morally legitimate to try to protect ourselves in this way against violations of our moral rights. Viewed the other way round, we cannot object to certain deterrent threats of punishment that stand against us because others have a right to try to protect themselves from us by these means. The theory asserts that a practice of punishment is at its moral core a practice of self-protective threats.

I shall try to make this two-stage conception of punishment clearer and more plausible in the course of the discussion. But even from the present sketch one can see that it is in some ways like both standard deterrent and standard retributive theories. Like

---

13 As I mean it, the warning condition is satisfied where a general risk that applies to x is publicized but x does not, through his own fault, become aware of it and in cases where x knows of the risk independently of any explicit warning that might be given.

14 But mere bluffs and threats in which the threatener hasn't really decided whether he would carry out the threat are excluded.

15 In "The Doomsday Machine: Proportionality, Punishment and Prevention," *The Monist* 63, no. 2 (April 1980), Lawrence Alexander distinguishes two different practices within what we call punishment, one of which rests on what I call rights of self-protection.

the former, it refers the justification of punishment to the goal of prevention. But unlike them, it does not try to justify *acts* of punishment as means to that end.[16] Only the prior threats are justified in this way. Like familiar retributive theories, it is backward-looking in its account of the right to punish, but unlike them it invokes no primitive notion of desert. Instead it explains the right to punish by reference to the right to establish the original threat.

This conception raises two different questions. First, whether the right to create the threat of punishment is, as I claim, grounded in a right of self-protection. Second, whether the right to punish is, as I claim, derivative from the right to establish the threat. The first question is not totally independent of the second, and we therefore need a strategy for resolving all of its independently resolvable parts. The strategy I have chosen is to construct an imaginary practice of threatening in which all threatened evils are to be delivered by fully automatic devices. This twist allows us to examine the moral basis for making threats in abstraction from the question of the specific right to carry them out. The kind of automated practice I will construct is, of course, meant to be *purely self-protective* in its function and moral ground. I shall examine such a practice in Section I, where I shall not presuppose that it is, apart from its automatic character, the moral equivalent of punishment. I shall compare the two practices in Section II, where I shall argue that they are indistinguishable in the distribution of acceptable penalties. I will try to show that, apart from the question of the right to carry out actual punishment, there is nothing in the workings of a justified practice of punishment that prevents us from seeing it as a practice of self-protective threats. I shall confront the final difficulty in Section III, where I shall try to show how the right to punish can derive from the right to create the earlier threat.

16 In this respect it may seem to be like the well-known mixed views of punishment put forward by John Rawls in "Two Concepts of Rules," *Philosophical Review* 44 (1955): 3–32, and H. L. A. Hart in "Prolegomenon to the Principles of Punishment" in Hart, *Punishment and Responsibility* (New York: Oxford University Press, 1968). In their rule-consequentialist aspects, however, both these views (if my previous argument was correct) justify acts of punishment, taken collectively, by reference to their collective preventive effects. The crucial distinction in these theories is between whole (practice) and part (act) while in the present theory it is between the earlier threat and the later punishment.

Let us imagine ourselves existing at some time in the future when, our social structures having been destroyed by earlier upheavals, we come together to form a new community. Being scientifically very advanced, although no more moral or prudent than we were, we are together capable of making fantastically complex devices that can (at least as well as we can) detect wrongdoing in our new community, identify and apprehend those who are responsible, establish their guilt, and subject them to incarcerations (and perhaps other evils) that I shall call mechanical-punishments, or m-punishments for short.[17] Let us further imagine that we have lost whatever taste we once had for retribution and are interested only in protection. The devices attract us, therefore, in their deterrent rather than in their retributive capacities. Furthermore, we are not particularly concerned with the theoretical question whether using the devices for protection would constitute a new form of civic punishment. We are prepared, however, to acknowledge that there may be limits within the morality of self-protection that resemble limits on justifiable punishment. And we are therefore glad of the sophistication of the devices, which may not only be programmed to mete out different m-punishments for different crimes, but may also be set, in virtue of their remarkable (but not infallible) ability to determine the state of mind in which someone committed a crime, to withhold m-punishments in kinds of cases that we do not wish to bring under the threats. We are also glad that the devices can be so conservatively programmed that they will never be "fooled" into m-punishing the innocent. For, as it happens, we prefer this form of safety even though it means that the devices may sometimes fail to identify the guilty, a possibility made even more likely by our further wish that they be programmed to "pay" scrupulous attention to civil liberties in their criminal "investigations."[18]

17 The antecedents of these devices in the current literature are Lawrence Alexander's Doomsday Machines which differ from our devices in offering only one drastic penalty for any crime, and James Buchanan's automatic enforcing agents in *The Limits of Liberty* (Chicago: University of Chicago Press, 1975), p. 95.
18 Throughout this article I shall simply ignore the difficulty of justifying a practice that, like all actual practices, sometimes punishes the innocent. And by imagining devices that are programmed to operate under all the principled constraints that

It is not surprising that we are drawn to the prospect of deterring crime by means of the general threats posed by these devices. We are attracted, to be sure, by their efficiency and powers of discrimination (which I am supposing to be at least as great as ours), but we are even more pleased to leave the unpleasant business of enforcement to nonhuman enforcers. For it must be remembered that these automatic devices, while marvelously sophisticated, are not persons responsible for authentic moral choices. Should we choose to use them, their operation would involve only that choice and the choices that determined their design and program. To insure the completeness of this desirable isolation from human control let us also suppose that once the devices have been activated for a certain predetermined period, they cannot then be interfered with. For the choice whether or not to stop or alter them could, at some point, be tantamount to the choice whether or not someone will be m-punished.

The fact that our only choices are initial ones seems to throw new light on the question of our right to protect ourselves by way of threats. Without the devices, an effective system of deterrent threats can exist only if some of us are prepared to make independent choices to carry them out. And these independent acts must, it naturally appears, be justified in one of the familiar but unsatisfying ways already considered.[19] With the devices, however, there are no such independent choices. There is instead an initial choice to establish an ongoing deterrent threat, where it is foreseen that this will, in all probability, cause m-punishments to occur. In this situation, our choice to bring about future m-punishments is *derivative*, an unavoidable consequence of our more basic choice to set up the threat. That this is so is shown by the fact that we would not choose to create the threat if we foresaw that m-punishments would occur without protecting us, but that we would choose to create the threat if we foresaw that it would be so effective that m-punishments would never occur. And it is morally significant that our choice to bring about m-punishments is, in this sense, derivative. For derivative choices may sometimes be justified by that

would govern the best human punishers, I hope to avoid any objection to their automatic and artificial character.

19 I shall argue in Section III that this appearance is deceptive, and that the justificatory structure of an actual punishment system is really like that of a system of m-punishment.

which can be said for the basic choices to which they attach. In our new situation, therefore, we may be able to see how to justify bringing about m-punishments even if we cannot see how to justify independent choices to carry out threats that have failed.

This restructuring of the problem would not be available if we were retributivists using the devices as surrogate retributors. For then each m-punishment would be a kind of end for us. But our actual end is nothing other than protection from crime. And it is the threat of m-punishment rather than m-punishment itself that we call upon this end to justify. It is important, however, to see that our choice is to create a *real* and not a deceptive, threat. A deceptive threat may have the advantage of not leading to any m-punishments, but it will not protect us as well as a real threat. For some people will have to know of the deception. And, in the scientifically advanced community we are imagining, others will surely suspect it. More important, such deception would be morally insupportable. It is one thing for a private individual to protect himself by bluffing. But it is an altogether different thing for civic authorities, acting in their official capacities, to practice wholesale deception in a matter as vital as this to each citizen's interest. We therefore have both practical and moral reasons to create a real threat if we create any.

It does not, however, follow from the fact that our threat is real and will, therefore, almost certainly lead to m-punishments that our initial justification must appeal to the anticipated deterrent effects of those m-punishments. If such an appeal were necessary, then the future m-punishments themselves, along with the threat of them, would enter our scheme of justification as means of protection. But the justification we seek makes no such appeal. We see that each m-punishment will occur as the result of the previous existence of a real threat, and we insist that each such prior threat be completely justified by reference to the protection that *it* can be expected to create.

To see how this justification works, we may begin by considering the initial period from the moment of activation up through the occurrence of the first crime that the devices will subsequently m-punish. We do not know exactly how long or short this period will be. But we have good empirical grounds for believing that, given human nature, it cannot be very long. The activators must therefore ask themselves whether they would be justified in establishing the threat (with its risk of giving rise to m-punishments) for any stretch of time that might realistically constitute this initial period even if the deterrent force of the threat were not to be reinforced by the publicized occurrence of any m-punishment. This is to insist on a justification for activating the devices for any such stretch that appeals only to protection that would result from the publicized fact of activation itself (from the general belief that the devices will work) and from possible artificial demonstrations of their effectiveness.

If the protection created by these factors alone would justify establishing the threat for any such duration, then the first m-punishment would clearly be justified, not as a means to later protection, but as an unavoidable empirical consequence of our having enjoyed an earlier protection.[20] And each subsequent m-punishment would presumably be justified in the same manner, by reference to the period of threatening that preceded it. Of course, there may come a time when the deterrent effects of publicized m-punishments become essential to the continued justifiability of the ongoing threat. If, fantastically, all m-punishments were kept secret, some would-be criminals might eventually cease to believe in the reality of m-punishment. But given that each actual nonsecret m-punishment is justified by reference to the threat that preceded it, each may be allowed to contribute its deterrent effects to the case for the continuing threat. For it does so as something already justified quite independently of those effects.

The key to this scheme is the fact that activation for a shorter term never depends for its justification on activation for a longer term. The first, second, third, etc. m-punishments are therefore each justified as empirically unavoidable costs of and not as producers of protection. Each m-punishment is seen as the byproduct of a period to which it does not contribute any deterrence. And it is nothing other than the fact that there is no separate choice to bring about the m-punishments, that our choices are tied together in a single initial choice to activate and create the standing threat, that makes this pattern of justification stand out.

20 Speaking of the justification of m-punishments is, of course, shorthand for speaking of the justification of the original activation insofar as it was foreseeable that they would result. As already noted, m-punishments are not real actions, and the devices are not real agents. So, strictly speaking, m-punishments are not the sorts of things that can be morally justified or unjustified.

On this conception, everything depends on our initial right to protect ourselves by placing would-be criminals under real threats. This right is akin to, but in some ways different from, the right of self-defense and the right to construct protective barriers. It allows us to make offenses less tempting by attaching to them the real prospect of costs, in this case costs that may, as a matter of the operation of automatic devices, follow crimes. If each member of our imaginary community possessed such a right and exercised it by authorizing that all others in the community be placed under the discipline of the devices not to commit offenses against him, then the activation could, on the present view, be completely justified.

The claim that there is such a right is made plausible by considering other, more familiar, self-protective rights that permit us to create serious risks for wrongdoers. First, we may mount appropriately limited, violent self-defense against attacks on our persons and property. Second, we may erect barriers, such as difficult-to-scale fences, to prevent such attacks. Third, we may arrange that an automatic cost *precede* or *accompany* the violation of some right, a cost that is not designed to frustrate the violation but rather to provide a strong reason not to attempt it. The one-way tire spikes placed at the exits of private parking areas provide a commonplace example. And fourth, we may confine those who have shown in the crimes they have committed that they cannot be controlled by other strategies of self-protection.

The first, second, and fourth of these familiar rights are, most fundamentally, rights to render or try to render someone incapable of committing or consummating some crime or crimes. In defending ourselves, we try to frustrate an offense by disabling the offender.[21] The harm we thereby create may be justified as a means of incapacitating the criminal *or* as an unavoidable side effect of an attempt to block the crime. In erecting very high fences or in confining the incorrigible we attempt to render would-be offenders unable to undertake various offenses. The third right (like the right to which we appeal in activating the devices) has, however, a different strategic character. In attaching costs to crimes, we attempt to prevent an offense by giving the would-be offender reason not

---

21 Philippa Foot points out to me that one might do this by psychological rather than physical means, by falsely saying, for example, "Your son has been killed."

to undertake it.[22] But both the basic strategies of incapacitation and threat are designed to protect, and both involve, as we have seen, a connection between the commission of a crime and the possibility of a resulting evil.

Each of these familiar four rights of self-protection has the same wide scope, holding not only within civil society but also in a state of nature. Individuals in a state of nature may defend themselves, set up obstructive barriers, establish automatic costs to accompany violations of their rights, and confine those who are incorrigibly dangerous. I also claim that they have the right to which the activators appeal, the right to use devices that promise costs to follow violations of rights. I cannot, of course, prove this. But reflection on certain features of the other rights of self-protection makes this claim plausible. Consider, for example, the form of self-defense in which the evil that results for the attacker is a side effect rather than a means of defense. The moral acceptability of this form of self-defense shows clearly that the evils created by a legitimate strategy of self-protection need not be justified by reference to *their* effects.

The comparison with the right to create threats of evils to precede or accompany an offense provides even more support. Suppose the best fence that someone in a state of nature can erect to block an attack on his life cannot stop some vigorous and agile enemies. He would then, under this right, be permitted to place dangerous spikes at the top of the fence in order to discourage those who could otherwise scale it. These spikes, like the more familiar ones in parking lots, would not stop a would-be offender who is willing to accept any cost, but they would provide most would-be offenders with excellent reasons to hold back. But suppose, to take the story one step further, our defender cannot arrange the spikes so that they offer a threat of injury to someone entering his territory but can arrange them so that they clearly offer a threat of injury to an enemy leaving his territory after an attack. And suppose that the latter arrangement would discourage attacks just as effectively as the former. It would, I submit, be very odd to think that he could

---

22 The prospect of a vigorous self-defense may also, of course, give a would-be offender such a reason. But the justification for risking injury to an attacker in defending ourselves does not, I am supposing, arise out of our prior right to create the threat of this injury. If one thinks otherwise, then the justificatory structure I allege to be present in the case of punishment is already present in self-defense.

have the right to build the first kind of fence but not the second.[23] What morally relevant difference could it make to a would-be wrongdoer that the injury whose prospect is designed to discourage him will come earlier or later? In either case, the injury is not there to stop him if he tries to attack but rather to motivate him not to attack. But building the second kind of fence is nothing more than creating an automatic cost to *follow* an offense. It is, in fact, a very primitive kind of m-retaliating device.

If we do indeed have the self-protective right to create the prospect of such costs, then each of us would, prior to the establishment of a public system of protection, have the right to protect himself by activating a suitably programmed personal m-retaliation device like the public devices that, thanks to our combined resources, we now possess. Of course, even in our imaginary situation we do not have such personal devices, but the fact that we would have the moral right to use them bears directly on our present problem. For each of us may now contribute that private self-protective right to the general authorization to activate the public devices we actually possess. But here a new problem arises. For even if everyone, as I am supposing, prefers protection by the devices to protection by other available means, not everyone is likely to prefer protection by the devices *and* the risk of suffering m-punishments to protection by other means *and* the risk of suffering from the use of those means by others. Some people, whom we may call *rejectors*, will surely fear the increased risk of suffering for their own future crimes more than they welcome the increased protection against the crimes of others. But we may safely assume that most people, whom we may call *acceptors*, will prefer the practice of m-punishment, all things considered, and would therefore agree to its full implementation.

It is the acceptors who will, in the situation I am imagining, bring about full activation of the devices in a series of partial activations. Their first step will be to activate the devices with a program that

23 It would not, in every case, follow from the fact that he could build the second kind of fence instead of the first that he could build a fence that combined the two threats. My view here is that there is a single self-protective right to attach deterrent costs to offenses whether these costs are to precede, accompany, or follow the offense. If this is correct, then it is plausible to think that there must be a common limit to the total costs that can be attached to a given offense. The fence that poses a two-way threat might exceed this limit.

places everyone under threat not to violate the rights of any acceptor. In doing this each acceptor will draw on his own right to make private self-protective threats. The acceptors will then proceed to ask each rejector, in turn, to permit them to extend the operation of the devices so that all are placed under threat not to violate *his* rights. Since even the rejectors welcome the increased protection against crime provided by threats of civic m-punishments, each will be willing. For in accepting this offer of protection a (former) rejector incurs no new risk for himself. His risk of being m-punished comes not from his own acceptance but from that by others. Each person's right of self-protection will thus be exercised and everyone will be brought under the discipline of the devices.[24]

It is important to see that this justification for placing rejectors under the threat of m-punishment is not an argument from fairness. It is not that a rejector may be made subject to the threats because he himself wishes to be protected by those same threats as they fall on others. If that were the argument, the rejector could escape the liabilities of the practice by simply withdrawing from its protections. Instead, the situation in a civil society is the same as in a state of nature, where it is clear that one person may make reasonably limited threats of m-retaliation against others quite independently of whether any of them returns the threats. The source of the first person's right to threaten lies in his legitimate interest in safeguarding himself from the possible misconduct of the others rather than in what the others must, in fairness, accept in return for their threats against him. It is for this reason that one cannot gain moral exemption from these threats by renouncing the use of them. (The same thing also holds of self-defense. One does not lose the right to defend onself against a wrongdoer if, strangely, he has renounced the right to defend himself.) So once a rejector sees that, whatever he decides, others may justifiably subject him to the discipline of the devices, he will see that he has every reason to authorize his own protection.[25]

24 While the acceptors would have agreed to the full practice, and so to their own liability to m-punishment, the full practice does not come about by way of any such agreement. As it happens, no one actually agrees to his own full liability to m-punishment. For that liability always arises by way of other people exercising their right of self-protection.
25 Of course the rejectors might agree among themselves to refuse the protection

70

Our justification for activating the devices is now complete. Because of its special character, it escapes the earlier objections to the familiar deterrent and retributive theories of punishment. It is clear, for instance, that in placing someone under a threat in hope of keeping him from crime, we are not using him. This does not mean, of course, that threatening in the interest of self-protection is never morally objectionable. To threaten someone is to bring a certain kind of force to bear on him (a force that we identify as intimidation when it is not justified), and such force in human affairs is often wrong. But threatening a person so that he will act in certain ways and using him so that others shall act in certain ways involve quite different moral relations to his will. That a threat is

of the devices and to form instead a partial state of nature within the community, in which their relations with each other would be reciprocally disciplined by threats of retaliation and their relations with acceptors would be governed by their own threats of retaliation and the acceptors' threats of m-punishment. But there are reasons to doubt that any agreement to execute such a limited escape from the devices would be clearly enough in their interest to be stable. One gain from such an agreement would be the reduced risk involved in violating the rights of other rejectors (since retaliation is less sure than m-punishment). One loss would be an increased risk of misplaced retaliation by other rejectors. (Acceptors are less vulnerable to this risk since rejectors know that the devices will punish all improper retaliations.) But the gain is of doubtful importance. For to the extent that the rejectors' choice to forgo protection by the devices indicates that they have little to protect, they may be unattractive as targets of criminal opportunity. (While disadvantaged criminal rejectors may, for reasons of convenience, prey largely on other disadvantaged rejectors, they may stand to gain relatively little real advantage from this.) And the loss is significant. For to the extent that the rejectors' choice indicates that they are indifferent to the moral order, the risk of misplaced retaliation by them is indeed frightening. Thus even if the rejectors would prefer no practice of m-punishment at all, they will have reasons to prefer a total practice to a partial practice of the type in question. Moreover, whenever any party to such an agreement broke faith and went over to the acceptors there would probably be, if the above is correct, even more reason for others to follow. (And such defection could not rationally be prevented by threatening reprisal or even by threatening specially dreadful retaliations for any crimes that defectors might commit against the remaining rejectors. For reprisals or improperly severe retaliations against acceptors by rejectors are themselves crimes that the devices will m-punish.) Of course, if the original acceptors could rightly, as I think they might, make it impossible for the rejectors to communicate, for instance, by surprising each of them with a sudden, irrevocable, and required choice, then the rejectors, assuming that an agreement to reject the practice would be in their collective interest, would be in a prisoner's dilemma. For each would see that no matter what the others did, he would be best off choosing more rather than less protection. Assuming that a fully general practice of m-punishment would be socially beneficial overall, this is a case in which a prisoner's dilemma would work for rather than against the community as a whole!

71

designed to make the threatened party behave as he morally should is a fact that gives it, if not full justification, at least some moral support. However, the fact that an injury to someone helps keep others in line is almost nothing in its moral favor. This means that while a right to punish a criminal in order to deter others cannot be basic (but must, when it exists, derive from some more fundamental right), a right to compel potential criminals to respect one's rights could be basic.[26]

Nor is it the case that we must appeal to forfeiture in order to explain our rights of self-protection. In fact, such an appeal would be subject to the earlier objections. We get a better explanation of these rights if we focus on *actions* and the protections that morality may assign to or withhold from them rather than on *agents* and the general rights they may keep or forfeit. Innocent actions that do not menace others are *morally protected*. This protection consists in the fact that we may not in general attempt to prevent them coercively or frustrate them violently. Violations of important moral rights are, on the other hand, *morally exposed*. That is, we may try to prevent or frustrate them by means that would, in other contexts, violate their agents' rights. That morality should withhold some protection from some seriously wrong actions is easily understood. For these are the very acts that, morally speaking, should not take place. And, to draw a final contrast with retributivism, the explanation of why rights must be contoured so as to permit threats, namely, the appeal to the need to protect ourselves from crime, has an obviousness and compelling clarity missing in retributivists' accounts of the right to punish. That morality should expose wouldbe wrongdoers to threats in order to prevent wrongdoing is easier to understand than that morality should expose actual wrongdoers to retribution.

Before concluding this examination of m-punishment, we must briefly consider the upper limits on the severity of the m-punishment that may justifiably be threatened for a given type of crime.[27] That there are such limits and that they are a proper part

---

26 It will become clear in Section III that I think it *can* be morally permissible to punish someone with the intention of deterring others, so long as the right to punish is independently secured.

27 In "The Doomsday Machine" Alexander claims that we may threaten those who are competent and free with *any* penalty for any violation of our rights. He argues from an alleged lack of constraints on the self-protective right to construct

of the morality of self-protection can be seen by looking at other self-protective rights. The moral right to defend our property does not permit us to kill a burglar whom we know intends us no physical harm. Nor may we erect an extremely dangerous barrier to prevent harmless trespassing. These examples show that the morality of self-protection contains its own rough standard of proportionality. While we may attempt to prevent more serious crimes by creating risks of greater evils, some evils are too great for some crimes. This idea of proportionality is *not* tied to the ideas of retribution and desert. No retributivist claims that the right of self-defense is a right of retribution, but no retributivist can plausibly deny that the right of self-defense is governed by some requirement of proportionality.

The theory of these limits is complex and difficult, and I can here make only some general and tentative suggestions. Using self-defense as a guide, it seems that we do not have to justify particular self-protective threats by any hard and fast criterion of expected general utility. Someone defending himself against an attacker is not burdened by the need to justify the degree of danger that his defense creates by reference to its chance of success. He is entitled to defend himself in ways that put his attacker at risk of evils that are intuitively proportionate to the intended offense even if there is very little chance that the defense will succeed. The same is surely true of self-protective threatening. A penalty cannot be ruled out

dangerous barriers such as moats and electric fences. But I think there are substantial constraints even here, constraints that may easily be obscured by the fact that these barriers are generally created to prevent a variety of crimes ranging from relatively minor intrusions to very serious assaults. With such a wide range of protection in mind we tend to allow the barrier to create dangers that might be unacceptable if it were used to prevent only the less serious crimes. Thus it would be more defensible to put a very dangerous electric fence around one's house than around a vacant piece of land from which one wished to discourage poaching. And in the latter case, I think it would be seriously wrong to erect such a fence. One should not be confused here by the fact that we may not be obligated to *remove* a barrier that is no more than appropriately dangerous for typical wrongdoers when we realize that some particular wrongdoer may have a special liability to be hurt by it. That is, after all, a special case. Alexander is scandalized by the thought that we might be able to frustrate or deter a crime but not morally permitted to do so. One can understand this reaction but nevertheless feel certain that such cases are frequent. It must be remembered, however, that if a wrongdoer has proved himself ready to brave all obstacles that we may properly place in the path of his crimes, we may call upon the right of preventive confinement. But we should not confuse this right with the right to carry out threats.

simply because the threat of it creates more danger for potential wrongdoers than protection for potential victims of crime.

It also seems clear that self-protective threats are not subject to the retributivist's standard of equivalence – that the degree of the threatened evil must equal, or at least not exceed, the degree of the evil created by (or intended in) the offense. For if, in a single self-protective response to a possible crime, we may not create an evil for the would-be wrongdoer exceeding that present or intended in the offense, it is hard to see why the *sum* of our self-protective responses to that crime should not be governed by the same limit. But, intuitively, there is no such overall limit, and its adoption would not seem advisable. Self-protective threats of m-punishments will be our defenses of first resort, serving to keep contemplated offenses from ever eventuating. Their capacity to play this role would be considerably diminished if potential criminals knew that any injury they might receive from a victim's self-defense would reduce their m-punishment. Indeed, such an arrangement would sometimes encourage criminals to persevere when they might otherwise be stopped by fear of a vigorous defense. And in some instances it would mean that criminals could not be penalized at all. Consider, for example, a case in which one breaks the arm of an assailant in an unsuccessful attempt to prevent his breaking one's own arm. It seems absurd to think that we must program the devices to withhold m-punishment in such a case.

It also seems absurd to suppose that strict equivalence sets the limit for any individual self-protective response. We may certainly risk breaking both arms of an assailant to keep him from breaking one of ours. And we may threaten m-punishments that are, by ordinary preference rankings, worse than the evils typically inflicted by the crimes they address.[28] There is, however, one consideration that suggests that the limits on what may be threatened must often be set somewhat lower than the limits on what may be done in self-defense. When a threat is made we cannot be sure that this is our last chance of self-protection. But when we are forced to defend ourselves, it is almost always because our other options have run out.

28 This is true for serious crimes that because of standard insurance typically result in negligible net loss to the victim and crimes, such as some violations of privacy, that typically result in no harm at all.

The aim of self-protection does not, however, provide a carte blanche. Self-defense does not, as I have noted, justify any degree of violence against any attack. And some form of proportionality must surely also be observed in making threats of m-punishment. But it is an important and interesting question just why this should be so. Assuming that a potential criminal does not have to violate our rights, why must we take care not to threaten him with too much in order to deter him?

Morality, I have claimed, exposes wrongs so that they may be prevented or frustrated. It therefore designs variances in some of our rights so that these rights will not interfere with a range of defensive strategies. The question before us is why our rights do not give way so completely that any defense or any threat may be directed against any offense. The answer, I think, is that they retain some force in order to protect those aspects of ourselves and our lives that go beyond any situation in which we choose to commit a crime. Someone who disregards a serious penal threat jeopardizes not only himself and his interests as they are then, but also himself and his interests as they have been and will be. In imposing limits on the dangers that may be placed in his path, morality refuses, in effect, to regard him at the time of a criminal choice as a fully competent disposer of the whole of himself and his life.[29] We may wonder whether morality would extend this protection to beings who were fully rational and totally consistent over time. But it is surely appropriate for us. For human criminals, like the rest of us, have interests and psychological identities that vastly exceed what they can see and defend in a single part of their lives. Morality requires some respect and protection for these larger components of a criminal's identity and good even while it permits us to protect ourselves against him. The result of these conflicting moral pressures is, as one would expect, a compromise.

This compromise naturally results in an upper bound to what may be threatened for a given crime, a limit that wisely allows more serious m-punishments to be threatened for more serious

29 This is, in one sense, paternalistic. But not in the way in which paternalism is usually thought to be objectionable. Objectionable paternalism prohibits people from doing what they may wish to do on the ground that it may be bad for them, and so causes complaints from those who are protected. The present constraints, however, raise objections not from those whom they protect but from those whose protection they limit.

crimes. Such a constraint sets a limit to the worst thing that may happen to a wrongdoer as a direct effect of the threat against him.[30] A limit of this form can also be defended from the point of view of the comparative importance of the various rights involved.[31] If one is trying to protect oneself from having one's pocket picked one should simply not have the life of the potential pickpocket at one's disposal as material from which to fashion threats. A credible threat of death for such a crime would be a grave moral indignity which even the certainty of deterrence would not diminish.

The ceilings on what may be threatened for different categories of crime must also vary to some extent with several factors other than the seriousness of the offense. First, it is plausible to think that the ceiling may be raised for persons who are especially dangerous, people who have shown themselves ready to commit serious crimes.[32] Second, the ceiling may be raised for crimes that are especially prevalent or are threatening to become so. Here the limit on the threatened evil may be raised generally and not only for people who have demonstrated their particular dangerousness. But this factor should be allowed much less influence than the first. For it is natural to suppose that circumstances largely beyond one's control should not significantly increase one's penal liabilities.[33] Third, the ceiling may be raised for crimes whose detection rates are especially low, at least if this promises a noticeable gain in prevention. But this too would have a limited impact for the reason just mentioned. (This third factor, it should be noted, creates a special theoretical problem that will be important later. In effect, the more severe m-punishments introduced by this consideration

30 By a direct effect I mean one that falls within the direct intention expressed in the threat. If the threat is a threat of death, then death can be a direct effect. If, however, the threat is of a certain term of imprisonment, and such imprisonment quite accidentally happens to cause death, the death is not a direct effect of the threat.

31 See Hurka's "Rights and Capital Punishment," p. 652.

32 Of course, at the moment someone commits a serious crime he is undeniably dangerous. Dangerousness must therefore refer to the general disposition of a person toward the type of crime in question during some fairly long period of time. Taken in this sense, a person may commit a crime without having been dangerous.

33 But to allow this factor to have some influence is not to use the additional jeopardy to a particular potential criminal as a means of deterring others. The additional strength of the threat against him simply addresses the fact that he is a member of the community and that members of the community have, in general, shown an alarming tendency toward the crime in question.

are justified only because the guilty are less likely to suffer them. And I believe this means that what is justified in such a case is not the straightforward threat of an m-punishment but the threat of a certain [no doubt vaguely specified] *probability* of receiving an m-punishment. In real practices of punishment the analogous threats are, I shall claim, justified only as threats to *try* to punish.)

II

In imagining our new community and its amazing devices we have, in effect, examined a particular type of protective social practice, the practice of m-punishment. One of its features, the fact that no persons have to carry out the threats, clearly distinguishes it from punishment. And the fact that it is fully grounded in rights of self-protection might appear to mark another difference. My task in the rest of this article is to show that neither of these features is incompatible with the thesis that acceptable practices of m-punishment and acceptable practices of punishment have, *au fond*, the same moral nature. In this section I shall address the second feature, arguing that the penalties of any intuitively justified practice of punishment would be what we should expect if the moral point of the practice were self-protection. Some terminology will be helpful here. Let's say that a possible practice of punishment and a possible practice of m-punishment are *counterparts* if both threaten penalties of just the same severity for just the same crimes.[34] The thesis that I now wish to defend is this: Every intuitively justified practice of punishment has as its counterpart a practice of m-punishment justified by rights of self-protection, and vice versa. I shall call this the thesis of the functional moral equivalence of counterpart practices (or, for short, the thesis of functional equivalence). This thesis is composed of two claims: first, that exactly the same offenses are properly penalizable in each practice and, second, that all offenses properly penalizable in both practices are penalizable to exactly the same degree in each.

We may take up the somewhat less difficult question of degree of penalization first. It is hard to see how punishments or m-punishments could ever, in being too mild, violate the rights of

---

34 I shall also speak of similarly positioned threats and penalties in counterpart practices as counterpart threats and counterpart penalties.

those who come under threat of them. Our question therefore becomes whether some properly penalizable crime might be subject to a justified threat of a certain punishment even though the counterpart threat of an equally severe m-punishment would be too harsh, or vice versa. Now it seems hard to imagine that a punishment for a given type of crime might be acceptable but the counterpart m-punishment too severe. If a crime is serious enough to be punishable with a severe penalty it must be a very unwelcome violation of rights and therefore subject, under the right of self-protection, to the threat of a severe m-punishment.

However, it might seem that justified m-punishments could be *more* severe than justified punishments for the same crime. For we have seen that the right of self-protective threatening is not subject to retributory equivalence as a limit on what may be threatened. But, so far as I can see, our ordinary intuitions about particular punishments reject this limit just as decisively. At least this is true if retributory equivalence is determined by anything like usual preference rankings. Consider, for example, our typical legal penalties for crimes against property. Surely the average person, even the average thief, would prefer to have his car stolen than to be confined for a month or two. And the same disregard for retributory equivalence is present in many common punishments for assault and molestation. Not very many people would prefer spending six months in a typical American jail to receiving a serious beating that left no long-term disability. Yet this sentence would not seem overly harsh as punishment for such a crime.[35]

Alan Goldman, who remarks on these disparities, finds our intuitions in these cases are paradoxical because he holds that a theory of forfeiture is the most plausible account of the right to punish.[36] In rejecting that account, however, the present theory of punishment rejects the paradox. When considered in light of retributive principles, these widely accepted punishments can, it is true, seem absurdly high. But if our intuitions are to provide any kind of useful touchstone we must not ignore them when they operate

---

35 A disproportion between harm done in the commission of a crime and harm received in punishment can hardly be avoided in punishments for attempted but unsuccessful crimes. Here retributory equivalence must refer, I suppose, to the harm intended by the criminal.

36 "The Paradox of Punishment," *Philosophy & Public Affairs* 9, no. 1 (Fall 1979): 42–58.

most independently of theoretical preconception. And I can see nothing in our actual working intuitions about the upper limits on degrees of punishment that is hostile to the idea that punishments may be set as high as m-punishments. Moreover, each of the special factors that can properly influence the severity of self-protective threats seems equally capable of influencing our feelings about punishment. Consider, for example, the higher penalties we often assign to repeat offenses. Past conviction operates here as a criterion of dangerousness with respect to the type of crime in question. It is also true that we sometimes feel justified in threatening somewhat greater punishments for crimes that are especially prevalent in the community as well as for crimes that pose especially difficult problems of detection and conviction.

Having looked briefly at the question of degree, we must turn to the more difficult question whether counterpart practices would justifiably threaten penalties for just the same offenses. At first, it seems clear that wherever we properly threaten punishment the counterpart threat of an m-punishment would be equally justified on purely self-protective grounds. This is true even for threats against attempted crimes. If we did not bring substantial attempts under threat of m-punishment, would-be criminals would know that they could, without risk, always place themselves in an advantageous position from which to decide whether or not to risk committing penalizable crimes. They could start the project and then decide to abort it if the risk of proceeding seemed too great, or to complete the project (under the favorable terms secured by their preparation) if the risk seemed low. Not to place some attempted crimes under threat of penalty would be very dangerous.[37]

37 The punishment of unsuccessful attempts to commit crimes presents theoretical difficulties for more than one conception of punishment. The class of attempted burglaries (whether completed or not) is wider than the class of burglaries (since all burglaries have been attempted but not all attempted burglaries succeed), and therefore we have more to fear from a burglary than from an attempted one. This suggests that the ceiling on the self-protective threat against attempted burglary should be set somewhat lower than the ceiling on the threat against completed burglary. On the way of looking at the matter most congenial to my theory, we do not make any threat specifically directed against attempted *but unsuccessful* burglary, since that class of action is not particularly dangerous. Rather we make a threat against attempted burglary (whether successful or not) but stipulate that, in cases where an attempt succeeds, the force of the threat is preempted by the force of the threat against actual burglary. As Bentham pointed out, it would be a serious defensive error to make the penalties for attempted

A more serious challenge to functional equivalence is presented by people who give evidence that they are incited by the prospect of penalties to commit the very crimes to which the penalties attach. It might seem that such people would, if not compulsive or incompetent, be punishable even though it would not be sensible to place them under self-protective threats of m-punishment. In one kind of case (certainly the most familiar), we may know that a person is *sometimes* led toward crime by the prospect of a penalty that usually deters him. It is plausible to think that we may let ordinary general threats of m-punishment stand against such people, even against those particular crimes that they may commit because of the threats. For were we to exempt such crimes, knowledge of the exemption might encourage these people to indulge their more ordinary criminal motives in the hope of seeming to have acted from the special motive. There seems nothing unjust in increasing our overall protection against someone who is free and able to avoid committing crimes by allowing threats to stand against him on the rare occasions when they do more harm than good. In another (and certainly rarer) kind of case, we may know that a person is so frequently and strongly incited by the prospect of penalties that he would be less dangerous overall were he exempted from the usual threats.[38] We might, of course, be inclined to keep him under them for fear of the effects on others of exempting him. For if we did exempt him, some people who do not suffer from his condition might commit crimes in the hope of appearing to suffer from it. But to refuse for this reason to exempt the known victims of this kind of irrationality would be morally questionable.

crimes as severe as those for completed crimes, since that would eliminate an important incentive to abort crimes under way.
38 Note that it might be sensible to place such a person under threat of m-punishment for any criminal act that he can be determined to have committed from more ordinary criminal motives. And if he were sufficiently alert and had enough self-control, these special threats might give us all the protection we could get in the normal case. For the moment that he became aware that he might be about to commit a crime in some perverse reaction to being threatened, he would remember that the special threats do not, then and there, apply to him. The reaction would therefore subside, and he would be brought into a more rational relation to the special threats that stand against him. Substituting these special threats would not make sense, however, if he could not remember their special character or if he could not control his emotional reactions once they had begun. But in that case, he is under such serious psychological handicaps that we may surely doubt that he is fit for punishment.

80

It would seem to be a matter of using them to gain protection against others.

I am, therefore, inclined to think that such people may not be brought under self-protective threats of m-punishment. And this means that there is, in theory if not in practice, a class of free, but extremely irrational, wrongful acts that may not be m-punished. But how do such offenses stand with regard to punishment? It is not, I think, counterintuitive to judge that the people who commit them are irrational and abnormal in a way that throws doubt on their fitness for inclusion in a genuine practice of punishment. To present them with the prospect of punishment would, in effect, be to *invite* them to commit crimes. A certain kind of retributivist will, of course, disagree with this exemption, finding in this kind of perversely undeterrable crime need for the most stringent, and therefore the most criminally exciting, punishments. But here, I cannot help thinking, retributivism shows itself in a disadvantageous light.

We must now turn to the question whether every m-punishable crime is also punishable. Here different problems arise. The cases that most call for examination are those in which real punishment seems illegitimate despite the fact that an objective violation of rights has occurred. The question we must ask is whether these cases would also be excluded from a just self-protective practice of m-punishment. To begin, we may consider punishment of innocent third parties, for example, punishing parents for crimes committed by their children. Such a form of punishment is certainly ruled out by ordinary moral intuition. But threatening third parties might be a very effective means of self-protection. Nevertheless, I think we can see why these threats would be morally illegitimate considered strictly under rights of self-protection. For whether or not they succeed in deterring a given crime is not ultimately in the hands of the party who is in risk of receiving the penalty. And, no matter what the gain in protection, it is manifestly unjust to threaten to inflict an evil on someone when it is not up to him to do that which will prevent it.[39]

39 That this third-party constraint holds properly of the morality of self-protection (and not just of the morality of retribution) can be seen in the case of self-defense. We can construct imaginary examples in which a wrongful attack by one person could be physically frustrated by means of violent reactions directed against another person who is no party to the attack. Imagine a pair of Siamese twins,

It is also important to consider cases in which punishing would not be justified because of the criminal's special mental condition at the time of the crime. We may first consider the already mentioned case of compulsion.[40] It might seem that there could be no self-protective point to placing compulsives under threat. But this is incorrect. If genuine compulsives were excluded, some people who are not true compulsives would be encouraged to commit crimes in the hope of seeming to have been compelled. And since neither we nor the devices can ever be absolutely certain that someone acted wholly by compulsion in committing a crime, even those who give every indication of having been compelled may actually be faking. We therefore have deterrent reasons for refusing to exempt genuine compulsives from our threats. And the thought that we might properly do this is encouraged by a possible analogy with self-defense. We are not obligated to worry about the chance that a defense may be unable to frustrate a crime. Indeed, we are entitled to defend ourselves in ways that can harm an attacker even if we are virtually certain that we cannot succeed because of, say, the attacker's strength. Why then should we worry about the fact that our threats in some cases probably cannot succeed because of someone's compulsion?

The difference is this: Self-defense against an actual criminal is justified as a way of disabling him, while threats are justified as a

A and B, joined so that both will be seriously injured or die if B is shot but so that B will not die or be seriously injured if only A is shot (if A is killed B may be surgically separated and saved). Suppose that A assaults you with the intention to do you grievous bodily harm (dragging the reluctant and vainly struggling B along). You have a gun, but are physically prevented from aiming it at A. You can, however, injure or kill A by shooting B. But surely, even though you would be within your rights to shoot A, the attacker, you cannot shoot the innocent B even to protect your life. This is not because injury or death is something that B does not deserve. If you were able to shoot and injure A his injuries would not, I think, be counted by the theory of retribution as part of his just deserts. These would come only later in his proper punishment. You may not shoot the innocent B because you are not defending yourself against *him*. This very fundamental constraint on activities of self-protection is primarily a matter of what may be in itself intended or done as a means. We must not let it be obscured by overattention to cases in which self-defense puts nonattackers at risk incidentally. Third-party threats would, of course, make direct rather than incidental use of a danger that is not in one's power to prevent.

40 Perhaps compulsion is a matter of degree. If so, then when there is at least some freedom there may also be room for limited threats and hence for limited penalties. Note also that threatening certain people might actually enable them to break the grip of what would otherwise have been their compulsions.

way of giving a potential criminal reasons. Defending oneself is therefore an activity in which the attacker is simply acted upon. In threatening, however, one assigns a morally essential active role to the threatened party. He is to consider the reasons he is given by the threat and is, if all goes according to plan, to refrain from certain criminal choices at least partly for those reasons. It is one thing to cast someone in this role who (we are certain) will ignore the reasons. But it is quite another to assign the role to someone who cannot be influenced by them. That would be unjust. Nothing like this injustice is present, however, in the case of self-defense that cannot succeed.

The same argument applies, of course, to any mental state in which a person is unable to take account of his reasons for action, for example, hysteria, extreme depression, and a variety of mental illnesses. A related but somewhat different reason applies to people who do harm unwittingly without thereby violating any duty of precaution. Someone who acts in this way is simply not in a position to bring a threat of m-punishment into his deliberation about what he sees himself as doing. Placing such choices under threat of m-punishment would, again, be unjust. It would assign a role to the threatened person that he will be unable to play given what he knows.[41]

---

41 Acceptable threats to hold someone strictly liable for a type of proscribed action are, I think, best conceived as threats that warn people to take extreme precaution not to do the action, even unintentionally. If someone has taken every extreme precaution that can reasonably be required, he may not, on my view, be penalized. The strictness of strict liability cannot properly be strictness in principle. Holding someone subject to threats for forms of behavior that he, through his own fault, does not know to be proscribed is, I think, a special form of strict liability. (Any adult would, of course, have to be mentally defective not to know that the kinds of actions we have been discussing are crimes.) Each of us is, in effect, under threat to take care to learn what is proscribed by the penal code before we act in a manner to which the code may address itself, and the penalty for a failure to take this care, when this leads to the commission of a crime, is the very penalty set for that crime. On this view, when someone is properly penalized for a law of which he was ignorant, the threat with reference to which he is penalized must involve the general (and generally understood) warning to take care to inform oneself about the contents of the penal code. And the evil referred to in this threat is not a penalty, in the usual sense, but rather the prospect of receiving one of a number of different penalties in case the failure to inform oneself leads one to commit one of a number of different crimes. Such threats are special in lacking a full description of the threatened danger. But, since one can always find out the precise character of the danger before one runs afoul of it, they can be fair.

Suppose, however, the problem that raises the question of punishability is not lack of freedom or relevant factual knowledge. Suppose someone knowingly commits a crime who is free in the sense of being able to engage in and act on his practical deliberations but is unable to understand or appreciate the moral order behind the penal code. Suppose, for example, that we were to discover the existence of a genetic amoralism, a condition that deprives its victim of any moral sensibility or internal moral motivation but does not affect any other cognitive or deliberative faculty. Some genetically amoral people are, we discover, good citizens in whom any antisocial motives are held in check by the nonmoral civilizing motives that affect us all: desire for the esteem of others, fear of disgrace, and especially fear of civic sanctions. Others, perhaps a significant proportion, are criminals. Now, surely we could threaten those genetically amoral people who are free, clearheaded, and concerned for their own well-being with m-punishment in an attempt to deter them from crime. But since they are not, in some sense, morally responsible for what they do, could we punish them? Here again I think it is important to consult our moral intuitions in practice rather than when they have passed through the filter of retributive theory. If we do, I think we shall conclude that whether someone is to blame for his own amorality or immorality is, by itself, irrelevant to our actual decisions when and when not to punish him. We routinely punish and, I think, rightly punish sociopathic criminals whom we have absolutely no empirically respectable reason to blame for their conditions. What matters to us is whether they clearly understood the threats against them and were capable of being deterred by them.[42]

But what about the more extreme case of people who are free in the way we have been considering but whose moral *and* nonmoral sense of reality is not as it should be? Take someone who believes that God tells him to kill as many people as possible. Of course, we sometimes suppose that people who suffer from such massive delusions are in the grip of these delusions in a way that undermines

42 Our own legal systems make knowing right from wrong a condition of punishability in at least certain kinds of cases. But in practice I think that this condition cannot require more than that one be well aware of the contents of the moral code of one's community and the character of its major moral distinctions. And this is a kind of knowledge that genetically amoral and other disturbed persons could fully possess.

their freedom. But perhaps this is not always true. We must therefore consider possible cases in which people who are disturbed in their thinking but are nevertheless free and able to deliberate, commit crimes. Now we certainly feel that punishment ought to be ruled out in many such cases. And the question is whether the practice of m-punishment would treat these cases in the same way. There is, I think, one reason to think it would. For even if a madman can deliberate, he may not be able to grasp the danger posed by threats of m-punishment; or while he may in some sense grasp the danger, he may be unable to give it proper weight in his deliberation. The rationale for not including such people under threats is therefore the same as that for excluding compulsives. It would be unjust to create dangers for them that they cannot escape or cannot have a reasonable chance of escaping.

But perhaps not all mad criminals are unable to give threats of m-punishment enough weight in their deliberations. Perhaps there are some who retain enough hold on reality to appreciate the full force of the threats. Indeed I suspect that we are confronted with just such crazy but deterrable people in increasing numbers – terrorists and fanatics who act in the name of insane causes but who seem, since they take considerable trouble not to be caught, capable of being influenced by threats. Such people could certainly be placed under threat of m-punishment. But it is equally true, I think, that they may be threatened with punishment properly so called. And I am sure that the thought that they are punishable accords with the ordinary judgments of most of us. It is undeniably true that there is a sense in which such people are often not to be blamed for what they do. They are not like those of us who commit crimes from familiar and contemptible motives of greed or lust, and they may be no more responsible for their disturbed outlook than genetically amoral persons are responsible for their lack of genuine moral motivation. But there is a sense in which they may be held responsible for the real crimes they commit. For they commit them freely and deliberately in full knowledge that they are under threat designed to deter them. This sense of responsibility is usually enough to satisfy our everyday sense that punishment is in order, and, if I am right, it also ought to be enough for us in theory.

Two observations may help make the thesis of functional moral equivalence more plausible in these cases of mentally disturbed criminals. First, the fact that a disturbed person is at various times deterred by threat of m-punishment does not entail that he is, in the relevant sense, deterrable at the time he commits a particular crime. Justice requires that a threat apply to a criminal choice only if *in making that choice* (or the choices that lead to it) the criminal is able to understand the threat that applies to him, is able to appreciate the threatened penalty as something unwelcome, and is able to avoid the crime. Second, we have imagined that the devices are programmed to mete out m-punishments for any crime that was properly subject to our self-protective threats. But there can be genuinely humane (and therefore moral) reasons not to punish a crime, especially when the offender is mentally disturbed, that do not call into question our right to punish. If we wish to get a fair comparison of the two practices, we must either imagine ourselves as punishing whenever we see ourselves as having a strict moral right to do so or, preferably, we must imagine the devices to be programmed with principles of humanity as further constraints on their operation.

III

The thesis of functional moral equivalence should, to the extent that I have succeeded in making it out, incline us to take seriously the idea that the moral essence of a just practice of punishment and that of its counterpart practice of m-punishment are the same, that both are systems of deterrent threats fully justified by rights of self-protection. But a difficulty remains. For real punishment involves not only creating threats but also carrying them out and therefore raises questions that do not arise in the case of m-punishment. While the dangers to potential wrongdoers may be no greater under a practice of punishment, their realization will require real persons to perform various real actions all of which will clearly stand in need of some kind of moral justification. And it may seem that no appeal to our right to protect ourselves from possible crimes could serve to establish a right to do anything about those crimes once they had become actual. But the problem is, in a way, even worse. For the right to which we appealed when activating the m-punishment devices was the right to attach *automatic* costs to crimes. But in the case of punishment we need to appeal to a right to attach costs that will have to be imposed by human agents. Thus we seem forced back upon a particularly acute version of the difficulty with which we began.

But while it is true that the move from threats of m-punishment to those of punishment generates these new and difficult philosophical problems, it is, in my view, a mistake to assume that only an *independent* account of the right to punish can solve them. For this is to assume that the right to establish the threat of punishment is posterior in the order of explanation to the right to punish. But while very natural, this assumption is, I think, mistaken. In my view, the right to establish the real threat of punishment is the moral *ground* of the right to punish. I shall presently try to defend this hypothesis. But first we should briefly consider how the hypothesis would, when added to our previous results, enable us to reach the conclusion that practices of punishment and m-punishment rest on the same moral foundation.

To say that the right to establish a genuine threat is prior to the right to punish (or that the former right grounds the latter) is to make two claims: first, that the right to set up the threat can be established without first raising the question of the right to punish and, second, that the right to the threat implies the right to punish. According to the first claim, a case that prescinds from any consideration of how one will later be justified in punishing and concentrates exclusively on what is to be said for and against the creation of the real prospect of punishment for crime (that is, the real likelihood that a criminal will be punished) can be sufficient to establish the right to the threat of punishment. If this claim is true, then in our moral deliberations about setting up a practice of punishment we may regard the creation of the threat *as if* it amounted to causally determining our wills so that we would in fact try to punish crimes and would do so without raising any further question of right.[43] But this is to claim that the right to set up the threat of punishment may be treated as if it were the right to threaten that which will come about automatically, that is, as a causal consequence not subject to a certain kind of further moral scrutiny.

The first claim therefore implies that the right to establish threats of m-punishment and the right to establish counterpart threats of punishment are on the same moral footing, that the right to attach

---

43 That is, not raising any further moral questions about our right to punish kinds of crimes that are properly placed under the threats.

automatic costs must generalize into a right to attach costs that are either automatically or personally imposed. For apart from the fact that the threat of punishment is the threat to *do* something (the fact that we are to set aside), the morally relevant structure of the situations in which we establish the counterpart practices is the same. In both there are holders of rights who wish to protect themselves from potential violators of these rights, and in both there is the possibility of creating conditional dangers that will tend to deter crime. And according to the second claim (that the right to the threat implies the right to punish), considerations that suffice to establish our right to the threat of punishment will also suffice to establish the right to punish when the time comes. Since we are now justified in creating the real prospect of punishment we will later be justified in punishing. The thesis of the explanatory priority of the right to create the threat of punishment thus means that a practice of real punishment, both at the time it is established and later, has the same basis in moral rights as its counterpart practice of m-punishment.

But why should we believe that the right to establish the threat is prior? The ultimate plausibility of the hypothesis lies in the fact that it gives a more satisfying account of the right to punish than any alternative. The best defense here, as in the case of other highly theoretical moral claims, is an argument to the best explanation. I shall not, therefore, attempt any kind of proof. There are, however, certain reflections that can make my hypothesis seem dubious (or even incoherent), and it is to some of these that I now turn. One line of thought begins with the way in which establishing real threats of punishment must involve the formation of conditional intentions. In the simplest case an individual threatener must himself form an intention to punish crimes, and in more complex cases various members of a penal establishment must form various intentions that together could be thought of as a collective intention to punish crimes. Once one sees the role of intention in the creation of a threat of punishment, one will be reminded that, in standard cases, the moral justification for forming an intention is dependent on the justification one anticipates having later for doing the thing intended. And, generalizing on these standard cases, it will seem that the justification for establishing a threat could not be prior to the justification for punishing.

That the justification for forming intentions is usually parasitic on the anticipated justification for the thing intended is not surprising. In the vast majority of cases there is nothing of moral interest to assess in the formation of an intention other than the independent moral character of its object. The typical intention has no morally interesting life of its own. What will bear on people's good or ill, respect or violate their rights, is the action intended and not the coming to intend it. In this respect, however, conditional intentions whose expression is designed to deter or induce future action in others form a very special class. This is all the more true when the insincere expression of these intentions is, as in the case of promises and official public threats, morally questionable. In such cases, morality takes an interest not only in what we ultimately do but also in whether or not we form the intention to do it. Moreover, these intentions are embedded in actions, promises, and threats, that clearly have an impact on the good or ill of ourselves and others and therefore have a striking moral character of their own. The conditional intentions to punish or to contribute to a joint undertaking of punishing contained in the setting up of a practice of punishment are not, therefore, typical. It is not plausible to say of them that they have no moral interest apart from that of their objects.

That this is so can be seen by reflecting on the case of sincere promises to pay for future services. On the view that the justifiability of forming an intention always derives from the independent justifiability of its object, we could be justified in sincerely promising to do something only if we could justifiably do that thing independently of having been justified in making the promise. But this is not always the case. We may be morally permitted to do some things only because we *were* morally permitted to promise to do them. For example, the guardian of a ward and his estate would not, typically, have the moral right to disburse the ward's funds to *give* someone something for services rendered the ward in the absence of any prior agreement, but he surely would have the moral right to *pay* someone for services rendered under an earlier contract justifiably entered into in behalf of the ward's interests. Appeal to the ward's interests here plays a crucial role in accounting for the right to expend the ward's funds. This can be seen by noticing that a promise to pay made by the guardian in the foreknowledge that the services would be rendered *whether or not* there was a prospect of payment might create no moral claim on the ward's funds. If this were so, a plausible explanation of why the guardian may honor a promise made in order to secure the welfare of the ward but may not (with the ward's funds) honor a promise made in indifference or hostility to the interests of the ward is that in the former case, but not in the latter, making the promise was justified in the first place. In such cases the question of primary moral moment arises at the time the promise is made: Can it be justified by the way in which it may be hoped to benefit the ward? And it is important to keep in mind that we are not speaking here of insincere promises. The question is whether the guardian would be justified in making a promise with the full intention to honor it.

The same moral structure is present, I would argue, in the case of threats. What one may sincerely threaten to do in order to avoid certain things is not always determined by what one could do independently of the fact that one had the right to threaten. But suppose it is granted that certain promises and agreements involving the formation of conditional intentions can be independently evaluated in the way indicated. It might, nevertheless, be argued that it is a mistake to think that this can be generalized to the case of threats. For the relevant kind of case arises only when there is a way for the justification of an earlier act to carry forward to a later one. What enables the justification for the guardian's rightful promising to ground the later justification for making payment seems to be the fact that once he has promised, he is *obligated* to pay. Obligation contains permission, and therefore provides a moral medium that can carry an earlier justification forward.

This, in effect, threatens to reduce my view about punishment to absurdity. For, the objection continues, it is absurd to suppose that one could have the right to establish a real threat of punishment but not, *ceteris paribus*, the right to punish. In the case of the guardian's promise the analogous absurdity (that he might have the right to make the promise but not, *ceteris paribus*, the right to honor it) is avoided by the convenient fact that promises create obligations that carry permission forward. But there is no comparable forward-reaching moral mechanism in the case of the threat. For there is no general obligation on the part of penal authorities to punish every crime they have the right to punish. It must be, the objection concludes, that the moral alignment between threat and punishment is due to the priority of the right to punish rather than the priority

90

of the right to threaten. This is, perhaps, the most serious line of objection to my conception. To escape its force, I must be able to explain how a prior right to establish the threat of a given punishment *could* transfer forward to the right to mete it out. *And I must be able to explain this in a way that never presupposes that the right to punish has been secured first.*

I shall now try to construct just such an explanation. It consists in a series of steps that lead from threatening to punishing such that each step not only implies the next but, if I am right, implies it without presupposing it. The steps are these:

(1) *At t_1,* x cannot object to the fact that we then create a real threat that, if he commits a crime of type C at t_2, we will thereafter try to see to it that he receives a punishment of type P.

(2) *At t_1,* x cannot object to the fact that, if he commits a crime of type C at t_2, we will thereafter try to see to it that he receives a punishment of type P.

(3) *After t_2,* x cannot object to the fact that, if he has committed a crime of type C at t_2, we are trying to see to it that he receives a punishment of type P.

(4) *After t_2,* x cannot object to the fact that, if he has committed a crime of type C at t_2, we are actually seeing to it that he receives a punishment of type P.

(5) *At and for some time after t_3,* x cannot object to the fact that, if he has committed a crime of type C at t_2, we are subjecting him to a punishment of type P.

(6) If x has committed a crime of type C at t_2, then *at and for some time after t_3,* x cannot object to the fact that we are subjecting him to a punishment of type P.

The steps are to be interpreted as follows: "We" refers to all citizens who authorize members of the penal establishment to fulfill their various functions in the case of x's crime. "Seeing to it that x receives a punishment" refers to the complete performance of all these functions, that is, investigating the crime and apprehending, convicting, and fully punishing x for having done it, all carried out in the name of all the authorizing citizens. And "trying to see to it that x receives a punishment" refers to this collective activity insofar as it is begun but is uncertain of completion despite the best efforts of all concerned. (We can, in the intended sense, be trying to see to it that x receives a punishment in the detective work done before x is identified as the criminal.) T_1 is the time at which the threat is created, t_2 the time at which the crime in question is committed, and t_3 the time at which the punishment begins. And

at each step, the kind of objection that x lacks is one whose force would show the presence of some moral right and could, therefore, obligate us to see to it that the objectionable state of affairs did not obtain. I shall speak of a state of affairs to which x cannot, in this sense, object as one that is morally acceptable to him.

(1) is, of course, our starting place. It asserts that at t_1 we have a moral right, so far as x is concerned, to create the threat that we will try to see to his punishment if he commits a certain crime. To make the assertion as plausible as possible, we may suppose that x's mental condition makes him a clear candidate for placement under penal threats and that the threatened punishment is appropriate to the crime. To create this particular threat is to shape the present order of things so as to make the conditional (that we will try to punish x if he commits the relevant crime) probable, and to warn x that this has been done. Often, in creating such a threat, we actually succeed in making the conditional *true*. That is, we succeed in affecting the present order of things so that if the threatened party does commit a future crime, we will, in accordance with our present intentions and plans and only because of those intentions and plans, try to see to his punishment.[44] Suppose that in creating the present threat against x at t_1 we actually succeed in making the relevant conditional true in this sense. Assuming that our sincere threat is a morally appropriate self-protective measure, x cannot at t_1 object to our making this conditional as likely as possible. But then he cannot object that in making it as likely as possible we actually make it true. And if he cannot object to this, he cannot object to the truth of the conditional itself. Moreover, none of these inferences seems to depend on some hidden way in which the implying proposition presupposes the implied proposition. The best explanation of why x cannot at t_1 object to the fact that we will try to see to his later punishment should he commit the crime seems to consist in the fact that he cannot at t_1 object to our creating the self-protective threat that we will do so. (1) therefore implies (2) without presupposing it.

(3) brings the acceptability (unobjectionableness) expressed in (2) forward to a time after the crime has occurred. In both steps the

---

44 "Because" here indicates that the attempt to punish would not follow the crime if we had not formed the earlier intentions and plans. It does not, however, express a sense of causality incompatible with human choice. Often we would not in fact make a choice had we not made some earlier one.

same conditional state of affairs (if x commits the crime at t_2, then after t_2 we try to see to it that he is punished) is said to be morally acceptable to x. In (2), that state of affairs is seen by x from an earlier perspective, and in (3) it is seen by him from a later perspective contemporary with our attempt to punish him.[45] Either step *could*, for all we yet know, be prior in the order of explanation to the other. The earlier acceptability could be derived from the anticipated acceptability of trying to see to x's punishment. Or, as I claim, the latter could be based on the former. In any case, it is certainly tempting to think that one of these steps must explain the other.

But whichever we take to be prior, we have strong reason to reject any suggestion that the two judgments may *differ* in truth value. For if they do come apart in this way, it must be that they express incompatible moral conceptions. Relative to a single morality, a given state of affairs will be morally acceptable to x at all times if it is acceptable to him at any. This is because the notion of having a morally relevant objection that I intend here is *objective*, not a matter of whether x *knows* a good objection but whether there *is*, in principle, one that could be put forward in his behalf. And an objection that could be put forward for x at one time could, in principle, be put forward for him in some form at any other time. If, for example, x can rightly object at t_2 that trying to punish him harms his interests without furthering ours, he could have rightly objected at t_1 that the punishment we then threatened might turn out to be like this. But both we and x then knew that although this unhappy result was a real possibility, it did not provide x with a legitimate objection.[46]

Moreover, we should not be misled by the possibility that new

---

45 (2), therefore, uses the future tense while (3) uses the present tense. But these uses of tense are unessential. Each step could be expressed in a tenseless idiom.

46 The moral structure of our situation here must be distinguished from that of nuclear deterrence. There, in the hope of reducing our chances of being attacked, we threaten to do that which will, among other things, destroy innocent third parties. If such threats could, as some believe, be morally justified, they would be justified despite the good objections of these innocent third parties. Their objections would be overriden by the expectation that the threat will help us avert disaster. Should such a threat fail to deter an attack, our expectation will be proved false and the innocent third parties' objections will remain unopposed by any cogent moral counterargument. The present derivation, resting as it does on the claim that there is *no* good objection to creating the threats, could not even begin in such a case.

information may arise between t_1 and t_2 that would make the attempt to punish morally objectionable. Even if such a development could not have been predicted in a particular case, provision for it could and, in principle, should have been made. The threat should have been conditionalized so that it would not apply in case the unexpected information did arise. For example, even if we could not have predicted that x would become a kleptomaniac we could and should have restricted our threats against him so that they would not apply in this eventuality. This technique for bringing threats and attempts to punish into moral alignment in no way presupposes the explanatory priority of the one over the other.[47] It is nothing other than an expression of the requirement that (2) and (3) be equivalent. And it is just this required equivalence that explains the possibility of deriving (3) from (2). The important point is that the equivalence holds because the relevant notion of acceptability is governed by a constraint of temporal neutrality and not because an objection to the threat must derive from some prior objection to punishing. This explanation can be understood quite independently of resolving the question which step comes first in the order of explanation.

Let us now consider the inference from (3) to (4). The reference to "trying" in (2) and (3) is, I think, essential if threats of higher penalties can be justified, as I think they can, by reference to unusually low detection rates. In these cases the original threat is acceptable only because we may fail to bring off what we threaten. What x cannot object to at t_1 in these cases is not, in the first instance, the prospect of our actually seeing to it that he receives the specified penalty in full, but rather the prospect of our trying to see to it.[48] This means that we must find a way of bridging the gap between the attempt and the thing attempted. My strategy for this rests on two premises. First, that trying to see to it that x is fully punished is, once the attempt begins to be successful, the very same activity as seeing to it that he is fully punished.[49] And second, that the

---

47 I have already argued that the morality of self-protective threatening can account for all, or most, intuitively plausible limitations on punishing.

48 I assume here that it would be unintelligible to suppose that a morally unacceptable prospect could be rendered acceptable by lowering the probability of its realization, but that it is fully intelligible that a prospect of someone's attempting something might be acceptable, not because of the low probability that the attempt will occur, but because of the low probability that it will succeed.

49 This is relevant because (1) through (6) can be understood to refer directly to

acceptability of an action or activity under one description entails its acceptability under any other true description. This second premise results directly from the fact that the notion of acceptability contained in my argument is to be understood in an "all things considered" or "*überhaupt*" sense. One has or lacks an objection in this sense to an action (or to a state of affairs containing an action) no matter how the action is described. Seeing to x's punishment will therefore be acceptable to x, all things considered, just in case it is the same activity as trying to see to x's punishment.

My identification of these activities rests on a general claim that trying to do something and actually doing it can be the very same action or activity differently described. I do not claim, of course, that in a protracted but eventually successful attempt to open a door one is from the very start actually opening the door. For such simple actions as this, only the last moment of a successful attempt belongs to the action attempted.[50] But for most activities that include a variety of different actions as parts, actual performance is to be identified with attempted performance from the moment that the attempt begins to succeed. For example, a doctor's attempt to heal someone completely (once it begins to succeed) and his healing that person completely are the same activity. And the same is true, I claim, for a successful attempt to bring someone to full justice and the actual bringing of him to full justice. If our attempt to see to it that x is punished for his crime is, all things considered, acceptable to x, our actually seeing to it must also be acceptable to him.

This account of the inference from (3) to (4) is, like that of the inference from (2) to (3), neutral with regard to priorities. Some description of what we are doing in regard to x must, one thinks, be the morally *relevant* one, the one that explains why he cannot object. But when our action is both a trying and a doing, the inference from its acceptability under one description to its acceptability under the other holds whichever description has explanatory priority. That there is no basis for insisting that the

---

our activities. For example, (3) can be rewritten: "Our *trying* to see to it that x receives a punishment of type P for having committed a crime of type C at t_2 is (after t_2) something to which x cannot object," and (4) can be rewritten: "Our actually *seeing* to it that x receives a punishment of type P . . . . "

50 Even in such a simple case I would deny that a trying can be successful only in virtue of being succeeded by a doing that is no longer a trying. Otherwise there could be no such thing as a trying that succeeds from the very start.

acceptability of the doing (the succeeding) must ground the acceptability of the trying can perhaps be seen by drawing an analogy with the logic of permission.[51] You may grant me permission to try to A without granting me explicit permission to A. Indeed, when it is highly unlikely that I can A, permission to try may be all that you are in a logical position to grant. More to the present point, it may be that you are willing and able to grant me permission to try to A if you believe that my chance of succeeding is low, but you would not otherwise be willing or, perhaps, able to grant me permission to A. But if in such a situation you do grant me permission to try to A, there can be no further question about my A-ing having been done with your permission should I succeed. This suggests that it is intelligible to begin with the thought that in certain cases morality grants us a permission to try to see to it that someone receives punishment from which we can *infer* that, should we succeed, we will have acted permissibly.

Thus, both the inferences from (2) to (3) and from (3) to (4) depend on what might be called the logic of the relevant notion of moral acceptability to x and on the fact that the states of affairs judged to be acceptable to x in each pair of statements are, in one way or another, identical. The inference from (4) to (5) is based on the principle that it cannot be acceptable to x that we do a number of things unless, in so acting, it is acceptable to him that we do each of them. The action referred to in (5), punishing x, is a proper part of the activity referred to in (4), seeing to it that x is punished. There is no way in which x could lack an objection to the whole of that activity if he had an objection to this part of it. The acceptability to x of our punishing him is not, however, prior to the acceptability to him of our seeing to it that he is punished. For the latter involves bringing x to trial and convicting him, and x may rightly object to any punishment not embedded within such an acceptable whole.

Only the inference from (5) to (6) remains to be considered. Suppose we ascribe to (5) an underlying form in which what x cannot object to is the conditional proposition as a whole. Then the inference to (6) will call upon a modal principle similar to one found in the logic of possibility. That acceptability should be governed by such a principle does not seem odd. For it is very like a

---

51 Suggested by Rogers Albritton.

form of permissibility, permissibility as seen from the point of view of a person acted upon, and permissibility can be understood as possibility in a normative system. On the other hand, if we ascribe to (5) an underlying form in which under a specified condition (x's committing a crime) x lacks an objection to a nonconditional proposition (that we subject him to a punishment), then the inference to (6) requires nothing but *modus ponens.*

If this account of the relation between these steps is correct, it follows that if a threat of punishment could be fully justified by the rights of self-protection that justify a threat of m-punishment, the force of these rights would carry forward to the act of punishing. If the urgency of self-protection makes moral room for threats it also makes moral room for punishment. But this means that a justified practice of punishment *can* be intelligibly conceived to have the same moral essence as its counterpart practice of m-punishment. It is possible to hold that punishing a criminal for a crime does not violate his rights *because* subjecting him to the threat of punishment for such a crime did not violate his rights in the first place.

I now wish to consider a possible criticism, the reply to which will help bring out an important feature of this conception. The objection is directed against the very idea that the later acceptability of an action can derive from the earlier acceptability of its prospect. It starts with the initially plausible looking assumption that if the explanatory structure I invoke to explain punishment is valid, it should also apply in purely prudential situations. Consider the following fascinating case invented by Gregory Kavka.[52] An eccentric millionaire offers N a fortune to form the intention to drink a toxin that will make him feel rather ill. N would, quite sensibly, be glad to accept such a temporary unpleasantness in order to get the fortune, but that is not what he has been asked to do. He is offered the fortune as a return not for the action itself but for forming the *present* intention to perform it at a later time. And worse, the eccentric millionaire can tell whether N has succeeded in forming the desired intention by interpreting his brain states, and insists on paying N well before the toxin is to be drunk. Kavka thinks that it is at least very doubtful that in such a bizarre situation the unhappy N *can* rationally form the intention to drink the toxin. For as N thinks ahead to the time of the action, he can see that he will then

52 "The Toxin Puzzle," *Analysis* 43, no. 1 (January 1983): 33–36.

have a serious reason not to drink the toxin and no reason what-soever to drink it.[53] And foreseeing that he will be in such a state, he cannot with justification form the intention to drink it.

Kavka's doubt is very plausible. Indeed, I feel convinced that under the terms of the case N cannot rationally form the intention to drink the toxin. But if the case of punishment contains a viable justificatory structure, why isn't it also present here? Why couldn't N simply regard forming the intention to drink the toxin as an item of prior justification that will lend its justification to the later act? Our sense that drinking the toxin would not be rational seems to show that it is at least very doubtful that things can be conceived in this way; and this may suggest that there is something amiss in the very idea of actions being derivatively justified by reference to earlier actions or conditions that refer to them. But this suggestion rests on a false assimilation. The sphere of purely prudential rationality unconstrained by morality has features that rule out the special structure present in punishment. When prudential rationality is at issue, one is not, I think, able to separate the question of an action's justification from the question of the reasons one has for doing it. If one's reasons are good enough the action is prudentially justified; otherwise, it is not. In the toxin case the benefits that attach to forming the intention can provide no reason to do the intended action and thus cannot make it acceptable even in prospect.[54]

This difficulty need *not* arise, however, when the question of justification is moral. For a moral justification need not be a function of one's reasons for acting. I am morally justified in reading your book because I have obtained your permission to do so; but my

---

53 N is not allowed to induce false belief in himself or to provide himself with independent moral motivation by, e.g., promising someone to drink the toxin.
54 David Gauthier in his recent paper "Deterrence, Maximization and Rationality," *Ethics* 94, no. 3 (April 1984), presents a view in which, so far as I can see, it would be rational for N to drink the toxin given the benefits that attach to forming the sincere intention to do so. For Gauthier advocates assessing the rationality of individual actions by first assessing the rationality of the largest temporal stretches of activity in which they occur (see p. 488). What he fails to make clear, at least to me, is how an agent who follows this policy is to think of his reasons. Is N at the later time to think that he has a good reason to drink the toxin despite the fact that no good will come of it? And if so, what does this good reason amount to? Or is N to think that this kind of choice can be rational in the absence of any reasons to make it? Neither option seems to me inviting.

reason for reading the book is certainly not that I obtained this permission but that I hope thereby to amuse or instruct myself. The moral justification for an act of punishment does not have to lie in the punisher's reasons for punishing. Nor does his justification have to provide him with reasons to punish. Motives that do not in themselves morally justify an action can nevertheless constitute one's real reasons for doing it, and be perfectly acceptable in this role. In the case of punishment, such motives are not hard to find. Among them are those in which the two standard theories try to find its justification, righteous anger, and a desire to maintain the deterrent credibility of the penal institution.[55] Even more conspicuous, at least in complex practices like our own, are those mundane motives that arise from the fact that those who punish are expressly charged and employed to do so. Given that the punisher is in some sense aware of the justification provided by the right to make the earlier threats, he cannot be blamed for acting on reasons provided by any of these motives. And because we, as threateners, can foresee that we, as punishers, will have such reasons for punishing, it can be fully rational of us to form the collective conditional intention to punish.

Other objections could be made to this conception of the moral relation between threatening and punishing. But here, as in earlier

55 The present theory can therefore accommodate some of the claims of retributivism as an account, not of the right to punish, but of a morally legitimate rationale for exercising part or all of that right. Nothing I have said so far implies that the natural desire to make wrongdoers suffer, given that one had the right to do so, is contrary to moral virtue. And its moral acceptability is suggested by the fact that benevolence does not seem to condemn us in taking some satisfaction in evils that wrongdoers suffer as, e.g., accidental results of their crimes. These natural attitudes must, of course, be held within certain bounds; otherwise they become cruel and vindictive. And perhaps the appropriate limit for *this* part of morality is some version of retributory equivalence. Note that the motive for punishing provided by our righteous anger, like that provided by our prudent desire to preserve the credibility of our penal institution, would not seem to generate the obligation to punish in any particular case. But that obligation might sometimes arise from other considerations. I see no reason, for example, why a penal code might not rightly mandate punishment for certain crimes or why authorities might not rightly promise the general public to punish in certain kinds of cases. Moreover, I find myself strongly attracted to the idea that punishment of a crime can express the value society attaches to its victim and to his violated rights, and that not punishing or punishing too little may, in some cases, do the victim or his memory a moral injury. (For a discussion of other things that punishment might express see Joel Feinberg's "The Expressive Function of Punishment," *The Monist* 49, no. 3 [July 1965]: 397–408.)

parts of the discussion, limitations of space have forced me to set aside some interesting problems and complications for other occasions. I have tried only to present a forceful sketch of an overall line of defense for what I consider a plausible but largely ignored theory of punishment. The heart of the theory is, as we have seen, the special justificatory structure described in this section. This structure may be, and I think is, present in moral and quasi-moral phenomena other than punishment. But in no other part of morality is its presence more plausible or, given that it is valid, its recognition of greater practical importance. I say this because I not only believe, as my objections to the standard theories have indicated, that punishment has been misconceived philosophically, but also that it has suffered from these misconceptions in practice. Our major mistake, I have argued, is to have focused too much on the punishing and too little on the creation of the threat of it. My hope is that with the correction of this faulty focus, we may be able to see that punishment requires of us neither an act of faith in the justice of retribution nor any neglect of rights for the sake of effects.

4

Reply to Brook

Richard Brook raises three objections to my account of the right to punish.[1] He first presents a supposed counterexample, the case of the special nuclear threat. He then argues that, despite my rejection of forfeiture, I actually presuppose that some people have and others have not forfeited a right not to be threatened. And finally he suggests that, while I reject any justification appealing to the use we can make of someone in punishing him, my own justification covertly appeals to the use we can make of someone in threatening him. Of these, the first is the most important. So let me start with it.

I claim that if someone has no good moral objection to our sincere threat to do something bad to him if some event occurs, then, *ceteris paribus*, he will have no good moral objection to our actually doing it if the event does occur. Conversely, if someone has a good moral objection to our carrying out a conditional threat against him, then he had, *ceteris paribus*, a good moral objection to the original threat. But I qualify or restrict these claims in three important ways. First, I use "threat" in a special sense that excludes bluffs. We threaten someone in this sense only if we create a real risk that we (or our agents) will carry out the threat.[2] Second, by having a good objection to something, I mean having a moral right to be free from it.[3] Someone may, in this sense, have a good objection to something

From *Philosophy and Public Affairs* 17:3 (Summer 1988) 240–247. Copyright © 1988 by Princeton University Press. Reprinted by permission of Princeton University Press.

1 Richard Brook, "Threats and Promises," *Philosophy & Public Affairs* 17. No. 3 (Summer 1988): pp. 235–239.
2 See Warren Quinn, "The Right to Threaten and the Right to Punish," (reprinted as essay 3 in this volume) p.61, including n.14. (This and all subsequent page references are to the reprinted version.)
3 Ibid., p. 92.

without actually objecting to it or without wishing that it not happen. It might even be irrational or wrong to object. For some things that infringe a right can nevertheless be expected to benefit the holder of the right or others, and in some of these cases it might be imprudent or even indecent of him not to waive the right if he can. A right to be free from something, in the intended sense, is a prima facie moral immunity. It is the basis for a morally active *demand* that something not be done. And such a right is infringed when the thing is done even though the right has not been waived, that is, even though morally effective permission has not been given. Third, I did not argue in my article that if it is permissible to make a threat it must therefore be permissible to carry it out. As Brook notes, I left it open whether, as some think true in the case of nuclear deterrence, a good objection to a threat might be overridden by factors that could not later support its being carried out.[4] In such a case the objection would create a prima facie but overridden obligation not to make the threat and a conclusive obligation not to carry it out. I mention these three points only because I think they indicate how difficult it will be to find convincing counterexamples of the kind Brook needs. These will have to be cases in which someone has *no right whatsoever* not to be placed under a sincere threat even though it is clear that he will have every right not to have the threat carried out.

In Brook's example, he threatens some innocent persons with nuclear retaliation and thereby reduces their chances of being killed in a war. Since it is hard to imagine a professor (except perhaps at MIT) making such a threat credible, I shall change the case to one in which the threats come from governments. For the sake of realism let us suppose that innocent American civilians (henceforth, "we") and our Soviet counterparts both benefit from the fact that there is a real Russian deterrent threat against us. This is because the threat tends to prevent a first strike by our government (thus protecting the Russians) and so reduces the likelihood of Soviet retaliation (thus protecting us). The presence of both these protections deprives us, Brook would say, of a good moral objection to the threat against us.

I strongly disagree. Presumably the imagined situation does not differ from the real one in this respect: the Soviet government would

4 Ibid., pp. 93–94, n. 46.

threaten us with nuclear annihilation in order to protect itself and its citizens and *not* in order to protect *us*. But if we civilians are, as I am supposing, innocent, then surely we have some right not to be held hostage in this way. (And the same is true for innocent Russians threatened by our government.) So we could, if we wished, raise a good moral objection to the threat against us. It does not follow from this (although I believe it to be true) that the threat is morally unjustified overall. Our good objection might be outweighed by some obligation to submit to the threat for the sake of others. But if the threat is justified it must be over our good objection, that is, because the wrong to us is outweighed by the reasonable hope of averting great evils.

But what about Brook's prudential point? If we were really made safer by the Russian threat, could we still have a good moral objection to it? I very much think so. Notice that Brook's argument presupposes that to retaliate against innocents is to wrong them. So it follows that the chief benefit we receive from the Russian threat is protection from wrongful Russian retaliation (since whatever reduces the danger of an American first strike also reduces the danger of a Russian backlash). We are also protected, of course, from the bad effects (for example, drifting radiation and economic disturbance) of an unretaliated first strike by our own government. But that unthinkable act would be just as clearly wrong. So we are protected by the threat against us only because the governments who control our fate would otherwise be more likely to indulge in crimes against humanity, crimes that would clearly wrong us and others. But if this is how we benefit, then surely we have a rock-solid moral objection to the threat against us even if, prudently, we do not give it voice. To deny this is to suppose we can be deprived of a good objection to some form of ill treatment by the fact that otherwise we would be treated even worse. If a kidnap victim senses that she will be killed if she does not quietly submit to rape, she may be wise to submit. But it would be preposterous to argue that she therefore has no moral objection to it.[5]

It may be tempting to think that I have just picked the wrong kind of example, and that we could, with enough ingenuity, find

5 And if she thought that her tormentor was more likely to kill her if it did not occur to him to abuse her, she might even welcome (and possibly encourage) the abuse. But this would hardly show that she was not gravely wronged by it.

a convincing case in which innocent people benefit from being threatened by someone who threatens *only* to provide that benefit. In a footnote, Brook describes a very odd situation in which in order to prevent a madman from exploding a bomb that will (as he refuses to believe) almost certainly kill his children, you must convince him that *you* will kill them if he explodes the bomb. Naturally, you would try to do so by bluffing, but then you would not be creating a threat in my special sense. So perhaps Brook is thinking of a Parfit-type case in which you will be convincing only if, for example, you take some convenient drug that actually causes you to form the conditional intention to kill any of the children who survive the blast.

Of course the drug might also take away your free will. If so, it would seem to place you outside the reach of moral criticism, and so deprive the children of a strictly moral objection either to your having the conditional intention to kill them or to your actually killing them. But then the case could not serve Brook's purpose. We must therefore suppose that the drug would merely corrupt you in a way obvious to others, making you hate the thought that any of the children might survive the explosion, and consequently making you wish to kill any who do. But the children surely have a general right not to be the object of such murderous intentions. So if they do not waive this right, they would have a good objection to your conditional intention to kill them. And this could be true even though the intention serves to protect them. For it protects them, after all, only because of the morally deplorable situation they have fallen into. They hope that your newly acquired viciousness will cancel the villainy (or crazy recklessness) of their father. In this respect they are rather like hostages who hope that the moral outrageousness of some of their captors will so appall other captors as to set the two factions to squabbling and so offer a chance of escape. It would be absurd to say of such a case that because the hostages expect to benefit, they have no good moral objection to the provocative actions and intentions of their more wicked captors. Again, in morally bad situations we may hope to benefit from intentions that clearly wrong us.[6]

6 In other situations too. Imagine someone who, from a distance, sees his child running toward the street to get a ball and realizes that unless the child is stopped, it will be run over by some unsuspecting driver. The father also sees the neighborhood bully, who is completely unaware of the traffic, running toward his

What about the act of taking the drug? Your intermediate end in this act would be to have a murderous intention toward the children, an intention that would clearly wrong them if they have not waived their right to be free from it. But a good moral objection to an end transfers to the sufficient means. So the children must have a *derived* right that you would infringe in taking the drug without their effective moral permission. To deny this is to deny that they would have any right to demand that you *not* take the drug, should that be their inclination. But surely it is very much their business whether you may try to protect them in this highly questionable way. So you may take the drug without moral scruple only if they can and do waive this derived right.

Of course we are supposing that they do want you to take the drug. So they presumably would wish to waive this right. But can they waive it? The trouble is that it derives ultimately from their right to life, and it is far from clear that they can waive *that* right, even to protect themselves. But if they cannot find a way of waiving the derived right, then even if they wish you to take the drug, they cannot fail in my sense to have a good moral objection to your taking it.

But suppose they *can* waive this right. Can they do so *and* retain a right not to be the object of the murderous conditional intention that the drug will produce in you, the very thing that makes taking the drug problematic? I do not see how. And can they waive this second right but retain a right not to be murdered by you if the condition is satisfied? Again I do not see how. Suppose they say, "We waive the right that you would otherwise infringe in taking the drug, but we certainly do *not* waive the right that you will infringe in conditionally intending to murder us." You would be foolish to regard this as a significant moral concession. What the first part of their statement gives, the second part takes back. As far as waiving is concerned, the two rights seem tied together. But suppose they say, "Yes, we waive any right you would otherwise infringe by intending to kill us under a certain condition, but we retain the right that you would infringe by actually killing us should the condition be satisfied." This seems to me equally empty. For waiving one's rights is giving moral permission, and I do not see

child with the possible malevolent intent of knocking him down and kicking him. Surely the parent will hope that that is indeed the bully's intention.

105

how a person can give you permission to intend or to decide to do something without giving you permission to do it as intended. So if the children actually manage to waive the right you would infringe by taking the drug, they *eo ipso* waive the right that you would infringe by killing them as a result of the intention they know you will acquire.

Now I rather doubt that they have the moral power to waive any of these rights. But if they do, they must waive them all. And then your killing them, however wrong on other grounds, will not violate their rights. And so the case is not a counterexample to my defense of the right to punish. For in that defense I claim only that if someone's rights are not infringed or violated by creating the prospect of your harming him under certain conditions, they are not infringed or violated by your actually harming him under those conditions.[7]

I do not think that any of these alleged counterexamples can succeed. It seems to me obvious that we to some extent wrong an innocent person whenever we deliberately, without his effective moral permission, hold him hostage to a threat designed to influence the behavior of others – even if we do so only in order to protect him. This seems to me to follow from the obvious limits of our authority over one another, something that only an unpalatable consequentialism could obscure. Of course, if someone can validly permit us to subject him to such a threat, then we may do so without infringing his rights, but only on the assumption that we have been permitted to do what we have been permitted to intend.

The other two objections are less important and can be dealt with more quickly. Brook thinks that I claim that some people are morally immune from threats of civic punishment – for example, innocent third parties and the insane. But this is true only if we understand the threats in a certain way. As I see it, *everyone* is under threats of punishment for voluntary crimes done with the knowledge that they are punishable. I argued, and still believe, that third parties may not be threatened in order to influence the behavior of *others*. But this leaves them under threats of punishment for crimes they themselves commit. As to the insane, I argue that they may

---

7 As I say on p. 54 of my article (essay 3 of present volume), my central thesis concerns the specific question whether punishment violates the punished person's *rights*.

not fairly be brought under threats that they cannot appreciate. But this leaves them fully under any threat that they can appreciate. Contra Brook, even those too good ever to commit crimes are, in my view, under the force of the threats. So I do not see that there is any basis for saying that general threats of punishment discriminate between those who have and those who have not forfeited some right. On my view, there is no initial right not to be brought under proportionate and properly formulated self-protective threats.

As to the last objection, I cannot see any plausibility in the thought that proper threats of punishment use people. I objected in my article to the idea that punishment can be justified by the deterrent effect one person's punishment has on others – by the general example we may hope to make of someone's pain and degradation. But my justification for placing people under threats of punishment makes no such dubious appeal. As I see it, deterrent threats against a person are justified solely by their expected effects on *his* behavior. So Brook is right to say that we use threats of punishment to get people to behave themselves. But he is wrong to suggest that we therefore use people by threatening them. The slide from the idea of using a threat to the idea of using the person threatened is certainly illicit.

Before concluding, I should like to address an *ad hominem* objection raised by Daniel Ellsberg at a symposium in which I, rather carelessly, invoked the principle of wrongful intentions – the principle that it is wrong to intend that which it is wrong to do. This principle seems to me attractive, and although I have not asserted any version of it in print, I would like to accept some form of it. But as Ellsberg pointed out, I cannot, consistently with my views about punishment, accept the usual reading of the principle in which the moral acceptability of an intention *presupposes* the moral acceptability of what is intended. For that would imply that the acceptability of a sincere threat of punishment presupposes the acceptability of the punishment. And this is just what I wish to deny.

But there seems to be a more complicated yet still substantial reading of the principle of wrongful intentions that is compatible with my views on punishment. If a future action would be wrong when considered apart from any moral case that could be made for the present intention to do it, then that intention is wrong *unless* it can be justified in a way that would carry the justification forward to the act itself. Conversely, any alleged direct justification of an intention that would not carry forward to the thing intended cannot be a sufficient justification even of the intention. This, in effect, is to deny that the moral status of the intention and the act can come apart. And that is what I find most plausible in the traditional principle.[8]

What I cannot accept is the further claim that the justification of an intention always *follows* from the anticipated justification of its object. Typically this is so. But not, on my view, in the case of punishment.[9] There the fact that someone lacks a right not to be placed under society's self-protective threats of punishment implies that he lacks a right not to be punished if, freely and in face of the threat, he commits a crime. This particular kind of justification of the threat – its not violating any right of the threatened party – carries forward, as I argue in my article, to establish the same kind of justification of the punishment. This is patently not the case in any purported consequentialist justification of sincere threats against innocent third parties, including threats of nuclear deterrence. I am therefore inclined to accept the implication of the principle of wrongful intentions as it applies to these cases and to condemn not only the carrying out of such threats but also the threats themselves.

8 Although this reading of the principle seems to me compatible with all my central claims and arguments about punishment, it is incompatible with my assertion on p. 87 that "a case that prescinds from any consideration of how one will later be justified in punishing and concentrates exclusively on what is to be said for and against the creation of the real prospect of punishment for crime . . . can be sufficient to establish the right to the threat of punishment." I should have said "a case that prescinds from consideration of how one will later be *nonderivatively* justified in punishing. . . . "
9 Or, as I argue on pp 89–90, in certain cases of promising.

5

Truth and explanation in ethics

In the last half century, moral philosophers who oppose the idea of objective moral truth have tended to rely on two kinds of argument: the internalist charge that no objective judgment (other than a report of one's existing motivations) could have the kind of guaranteed relevance to decision that moral judgments have;[1] and the relativist charge that basic moral disagreement is unresolvable.[2] But both of these objections have, by now, been made and answered in so many ways that it is hard to assess their force. To remind us of a different, and perhaps more decisive, challenge to the possibility of objective moral truth could therefore be a service. And that is why the opening two chapters of Gilbert Harman's *The Nature of Morality* deserve our serious attention.[3]

Harman develops there a forceful empiricist argument. He holds that moral claims must remain problematic and open to skeptical doubt unless they can be observationally confirmed or unless moral facts can be reduced to facts that are observationally confirmable. He also holds that hypotheses, moral or nonmoral, are observa-

From *Ethics* 96 (April 1986):524–544. Copyright © by The University of Chicago. All rights reserved.

Thanks for helpful suggestions to Dorit Bar-On, Tyler Burge, Ronald Condon, Alan Nelson, Keith Simmons, and especially Rogers Albritton and Michael Thompson.

1 This charge, descending from Hume's famous remarks in *A Treatise of Human Nature,* ed. L. A. Selby-Bigge (Oxford: Clarendon Press, 1888), pp. 456–457, is developed by Charles Stevenson among others. See, e.g., his discussion of the magnetism of value judgments in "The Emotive Meaning of Ethical Terms," *Mind* 46 (1937): 14–31. It is also present in John Mackie's recent denigration of "objective prescriptivity" in *Ethics: Inventing Right and Wrong* (Harmondsworth: Penguin Books, 1977), pp. 38–42.

2 See, e.g., Edward Westermarck, *Ethical Relativity* (New York: Harcourt, Brace & World, 1932). Also see Mackie, pp. 36–38, for an updating of the objection.

3 Gilbert Harman, *The Nature of Morality* (New York: Oxford University Press, 1977), pp. 3–23.

tionally confirmed only if they help explain the *occurrence* of the observations that confirm them.[4] But it seems clear to him that moral hypotheses never help explain why we observe anything. And he finds it far from obvious that this failure could be set aside by finding some reduction of so-called moral facts to observationally confirmable facts.[5]

In this paper I shall present and examine a version of this argument that will be more explicit and less guarded than the original and that will throw into greater relief what I take to be its really interesting core idea. This idea will emerge as a single epistemic principle that I shall call the *explanatory requirement*. The revision has other motivations as well. Harman appears to think that we could establish the genuineness of a disputed fact by showing that it reduces to obviously respectable facts.[6] But this seems to me implausible. He also implies that moral hypotheses never even seem to help explain our observations.[7] And here I think that he has overstated his case. I hope to expose both mistakes and free the argument from them. My other motivation is strategic. Since Harman's argument is most interesting if it stands as an independent line of attack, I seek a version of it that at no point could be thought to depend on the familiar relativist and internalist objections mentioned earlier. The argument, thus amended, will be presented in Sections I and II. In Section III, I shall consider an important ob-

4 Ibid., p. 6. He usually speaks of the explanatory role in one of two ways: (*a*) that a hypothesis is *relevant* to an explanation of something or (*b*) that a hypothesis *helps* explain something. Although it would not be very natural, someone might take the first formulation to convey something weaker than the second. The difference can be illustrated in case a particular hypothesis h falls under a general theory T. Someone might take h to be relevant, in a rather artificial sense, to the explanation of some event e if, assuming the laws or principles of T, e or something contained in the explanation of e implies h. But whether or not h helps us explain e, or has a role to play in explaining e, would naturally be understood to depend on whether our explanation would be undermined or made less good if deprived of h as a premise, background assumption, or inference rule. When Harman speaks of something as relevant to an explanation, I think he has the latter in mind.

5 Ibid., pp. 14–17, 21–23. Note also that, in the end, these skeptical remarks about the reducibility of the moral are shown to apply only if moral facts are taken to be absolute. Harman's own moral theory treats them as relative and conventional, and therefore reducible to various psychological facts about the conventions we have accepted. See pp. 131–133.

6 Ibid., pp. 13–14. Here Harman suggests that we might be able to overcome the doubt about moral hypotheses raised in the first chapter by showing how moral facts might reduce to naturalistic facts.

7 Ibid., pp. 7, 10.

jection to it that seems to me misplaced. And in Sections IV–VI
I shall develop criticisms of my own.

I

Apart from the possibility of reductions, Harman's argument often
seems to suggest that it is reasonable to accept a hypothesis only
if it helps explain (if only very indirectly) the occurrence of one or
more of our observations.[8] This idea seems to come from two
sources: One is the traditional empiricist idea that nonanalytic
claims are credible only to the extent that they are observationally
confirmed. The other is the more recent idea, championed by Harman, that confirming something is a matter of inferring it as part
of a good explanation of our evidence.[9]

Earlier empiricists thought we could secure nonproblematic data
in a transparent language of observation free from theoretical input
and controversy. They also thought that certain statements were
analytic and, therefore, true a priori. The idea of a theoretically
innocent observation language has been largely abandoned, and
analyticity has come under serious attack; but the more basic picture
of confirmation only by observation remains alive and, to some,
attractive. Perhaps an updated version of this picture could do without analyticity, but the idea of a pure observation language had a
function that might seem essential. For if our observational judgments always involve theoretical concepts, it seems that these judgments might be subtly biased in favor of the theories they
presuppose. Although Harman doesn't explicitly address this general problem, he seems to have found an ingenious kind of solution
to it: assign the ultimate confirming role not to what we judge
observationally (since bad theory may make that false or even incoherent) but to the *occurrence* of these judgments.[10] This switch

---

8 Harman never says this outright. The most explicit statement of the major premise of his skeptical argument is on p. 13: "We can have evidence for hypotheses
of a certain sort only if such hypotheses sometimes help explain why we observe
what we observe." His use of the plural "hypotheses" leaves it uncertain whether
he wants the claim to distribute over individual hypotheses. But he never denies
this interpretation, and it is a natural way to understand him.

9 Gilbert Harman, "Inference to the Best Explanation," *Philosophical Review* 74
(1965): 88–95.

10 Harman, *The Nature of Morality*, pp. 6–8. And note that the special place he
assigns to the occurrence of judgment does not imply that explanatory science

111

from what is observed to the observing of it recaptures some of the advantages of an observation language. For someone observes that p, in the sense here intended, just in case he makes a fairly immediate, that is, not consciously inferred, judgment that p on the basis of observation.[11] And since a claim that someone observes that p, in this sense, is noncommittal about the truth of p, it will tend to be relatively free of theoretical preconception and, therefore, relatively noncontroversial.

One natural combination of this elegant revision of empiricism and the plausible conception of confirmation as explanatory inference gives us the following epistemic principle: we should accept a claim about anything (other than the occurrence of observation) as factual, that is, objectively true, only if assuming it in some way helps us explain, or enhances our explanation of, the occurrence of one or more of our observations.[12] Assuming that the help in question can be very indirect, as that provided by the background assumptions of mathematics and logic, and still ignoring complications about reduction, this principle seems a plausible expression of a kind of contemporary empiricism. There is one way, however, in which it must obviously be qualified. If we may accept a set of claims $p_1 \ldots p_n$ as factual in light of the principle, and we see that they entail q, then surely we may accept q as factual whether or not it helps explain anything. And we are also surely entitled to accept any hypothesis r that $p_1 \ldots p_n$ make very likely, even if we do not expect to be able to confirm r observationally. The principle, with these additions, is what I shall call the *explanatory requirement*.

Is this requirement satisfactory as its stands? Harman might not think so. He seems to recognize reduction as an independent way in which statements might be validated.[13] Let's look into this. Sup-

---

must always, or even typically, focus on such events. This is because the immediate explanation of why we observe such and such is often obvious.

11 This seems more or less in accordance with Harman's use (ibid.) on pp. 5 and 6.

12 An assumption might enhance an explanation of the occurrence of an observation without, in some natural sense, helping to explain the occurrence if it, e.g., effected a desirable simplification in our explanatory theory. For purposes of brevity, I shall usually omit explicit reference to this necessary qualification. The reader should take it as understood.

13 See *The Nature of Morality*, p. 13, where Harman cites facts about the average American as an example. This example is not, however, entirely convincing.

112

pose, on reflection, we find that the statements of some familiar theory T1 do not help us explain, or do not help us explain well enough, the existence or character of any observations, and do not follow from anything that does. Then whatever our attitude toward T1 in everyday life, as good Harman-style empiricists, we must see that, so far, we have no reason to regard T1 as genuinely factual. Now suppose someone claims, as a reductive hypothesis, that the statements of T1 actually pick out the very same facts picked out by statements in another theory T2, where there can be no doubt that the statements of T2 satisfy the explanatory requirement. How might we be justified in accepting this hypothesis?

Perhaps we could regard it as analytic. But the Quinean spirit of Harman's enterprise makes this somewhat awkward. Moreover, we have a good strategic reason to keep clear of the possibility of analytic truths. If it is admitted, the present argument will tend to slide into the older debate whether morality rests on conceptually true foundations.[14] And those philosophers who, like Foot, have argued that certain moral claims cannot sensibly be denied could regard these parts of moral theory as unthreatened. But if the reductive hypothesis is not analytic, it seems that it should be subject to the same standards we apply to other statements – standards that include, for present purposes, the explanatory requirement. But what might the reductive hypothesis help explain, or how might it enhance our explanations? In textbook cases of reduction in sci-

---

The fact that the average American drives a car can certainly help explain my observation, as I cross the country, of the proliferation of freeways.

14 The older controversy I have in mind is perhaps most clearly represented by that between Richard Hare, who in *The Language of Morals* (Oxford: Clarendon Press, 1961), pp. 41–43, argues just that one may always reject any moral claim (not an instance of a truth of logic) without necessarily falling liable to a charge of having misunderstood it, and Philippa Foot, who in "Moral Beliefs," *Proceedings of Aristotelian Society* 59 (1958–59): 83–104, argues that it would be nonsense to reject certain moral claims. Note that the slide into the older dispute would not be prevented by ruling out the possibility that substantial moral principles could be analytic but allowing that reductive claims about morality might be. For these reductive claims would have just as much real practical force as moral principles properly so called. Indeed, since morality is already a theory that links moral and nonmoral properties, it is difficult to see how one could justify the claim that one had discovered a reductive principle linking morality to some nonmoral theory rather than a principle of morality itself. (This difficulty is surely implicit in Moore's "open question" argument.) The reduction of the moral to the nonmoral thus seems significantly unlike the reduction of one scientific theory to another.

113

ence (e.g., thermodynamics to statistical mechanics) the chief function of reductive hypotheses is, not surprisingly, to reduce the number and kinds of different facts and properties needed in our overall theory. This, however, presupposes that the reduced theory is already established as factual, something we, as yet, have no reason to believe about T1.

Perhaps the reductive hypothesis explains why we tend, supposing we do, to make certain T1 judgments just in case we are in the presence of certain T2 facts. But this seems to be explained not by the reduction itself but by its implication that T2 facts have the causal power to elicit T1 judgments from us. And this causal claim, suitably elaborated, seems a good enough explanation by itself. How would it be enhanced by the further step of positing real T1 facts? This supposition would, of course, imply that we were right in our everyday, precritical, trust in the objective truth of T1. But to count this trust as, in itself, reason to posit T1 facts would be to throw the whole skeptical argument against morality into doubt. For most of us, precritically, trust the objective truth of large parts of commonsense morality. I am, therefore, inclined to think that reduction cannot be a legitimate way of establishing the credentials of statements that do not already satisfy the requirement in its present form.[15]

A similar point holds about supervenience. The claim that the distinctive predicates of T1 supervene upon the indisputably objective predicates of T2 may be taken to assert only that *if* the claims of T1 are objectively true, they will fail to distinguish objects that

15 There are two other ways one might try to evade this conclusion. First, it might be suggested that the reductive hypothesis could, without presupposing the objective truth of T1, describe the way we use the *terms* of T1. But the idea that some reductions are covertly metalinguistic raises difficult questions. For one thing, how is the segregation of apparently object-level statements into those that are genuine and those that are covertly metalinguistic to be accomplished? The second possibility is this: suppose that the claims of T1 do not help explain our observations well enough to satisfy the requirement but do provide weak explanations of them. Could the reductive hypothesis then satisfy the requirement by giving a good account of the weak explanatory force of TI? I doubt it. The reductive hypothesis would seem to explain this weak force only because it implies that we tend to make certain T1 judgments just in case we are in the presence of certain genuinely explanatory T2 facts. But this correspondence is explained not by the reductive hypothesis itself, but by the hypothesis that certain T1 judgments are causally provoked by the presence of certain T2 facts. And for reasons given above, this explanation would not seem to be enhanced by positing T1 facts.

114

are indistinguishable with respect to T2. Or it may be taken to assert this together with the claim that T1 is objectively true. The weaker claim does not entail the objective truth of T1. And the stronger claim entails the truth of T1 only because it presupposes it. Claims about supervenience cannot, therefore, be used to establish the acceptability of T1.

We must now consider one further question that will be crucial to the later argument: suppose a theory plays a role only in explanations of our observations that are inferior to the best explanations we possess. What characteristics must these inferior explanations have for the theory to satisfy the explanatory requirement? Harman might regard this question as beside the present point. For he seems to think that we could never sensibly explain the occurrence of any observation by reference to moral facts. But I think he is mistaken. A rather bad man might strike us as more or less decent because we see him always surrounded by villains who, by contrast, make him look better than he is. This explanation is, in fact, reminiscent of one that Harman puts forward for our approval, namely, something's looking green because it is yellow but seen in blue light.[16] The problem this raises is important and unavoidable. We want, with Harman, to regard certain everyday empirical theories and certain earlier theories of modern science as factual even though we have better explanations of everything they can explain. Indeed, we may want to reduce the facts these theories describe to facts expressed in our best explanatory theories. But, as we have seen, reductions presuppose that the reduced theories are factual. So we need a requirement liberal enough to let these theories in. On the other hand, we are trying to construct a case against morality that rests on its alleged explanatory weakness. So we need a requirement strict enough to rule morality out.

Certain ways in which we might try to draw the line between morality and the admissible theories would depend on the classic objections to moral realism. We might disallow moral explanations on the relativist ground that, because we cannot resolve disagreement over moral principle, we cannot determine which moral explanations are correct. Or we might say that the practical or expressive character of moral judgment disqualifies it for the cognitive work required by genuine explanation. But on either strat-

16 Harman, *The Nature of Morality*, p. 22.

egy, the present argument clearly collapses into more familiar ones. Since we want to avoid this, we must try to draw the line in some other way.

Fortunately, a plausible strategy remains. For even if we may sometimes use moral hypotheses to explain the occurrence of an observation, it seems plausible to think that we never *need* to use them. An intelligent and reflective explainer can always replace them with nonmoral hypotheses about the world together with psychological hypotheses about people's moral beliefs and attitudes. And in doing so, he gets a more informative and powerful explanation. The man in my example seemed decent enough in the presence of the other men because he had fewer of the qualities we regard as vices. The allegedly explanatory moral fact about comparative badness is here replaced by a psychological fact about our moral beliefs. This kind of move is not always available, however, when we consider explanations provided by the everyday empirical theories that we wish to endorse as factual. Consider, again, the case of color. Even if scientists came eventually to possess definitional reductions of color facts, color explanations would, as Harman points out, be indispensable to ordinary people. And color explanations would have been, in times past, needed by everyone. This is because the better scientific explanations of color observations involve scientific concepts and knowledge that ordinary people, who explain things by reference to color, lack. The better explanations that may always replace our moral explanations can, on the other hand, be fashioned from concepts that the intelligent moral explainer must already have because his own application of moral principles depends on them. Moral theory, in presupposing a rich supply of naturalistic concepts, contains the full-blown means by which its own explanations may be put aside. The less than best theories that we wish to validate by way of reduction to later and better theories may contain the seeds from which these later theories grow, but they do not contain the means of their own supplanting.

II

The argument against moral objectivity based on the explanatory requirement can be laid out most clearly if we adopt some simple terminology. Moral judgments that we accept but do not consciously infer from other moral judgments will be called *moral intuitions.*[17] Intuitions about particular situations that we actually observe will, following Harman, be called *moral observations.*[18] Intuitions not about particular cases but of theoretical principles will be called *theoretical intuitions.* Those theoretical moral judgments that we do not intuit but consciously infer as part of the best overall account of our various intuitions will be called *inferred moral theory.*[19] A person's inferred theory has the function of explaining, in the sense of discovering a plausible general pattern in, what he intuits. There is, however, another quite different kind of moral theory that must also be considered. In the attempt to explain why a person forms his particular moral intuitions, we may be led to suppose that he is guided by an *implicit moral theory* in something like the way in which certain linguists think we are guided in our grammatical intuitions by implicit grammars. In positing such a theory to explain a person's moral intuitions, we need not suppose that its moral contents are true. We may think of it as a set of deeply held but unarticulated moral beliefs from which the person unconsciously draws conclusions. Or, more cautiously, we may think of it as no more than a set of tendencies (or the structural features underlying a set of tendencies) to form intuitions in a coherent and intelligible manner, as if he were inferring them from certain principles. Whichever interpretation we select, it will be convenient to mark the difference between implicit and explicit theory by reserving "belief" or "acceptance" for the latter and using "tacit belief" and "tacit acceptance" for the former.

Let me begin the argument.[20] We might validate morality in two different ways. We might be able to show that certain moral principles satisfy the requirement without bringing in reference to their

17 Moral intuitions, in this sense, do not have to be true. And they do not have to be accepted without reflection. Not all reflection involves inference. Note also that this use of "intuition" has nothing to do with the metaethical theory of intuitionism or its claims of nonnatural properties and special moral faculties.
18 Harman, *The Nature of Morality,* p. 5.
19 If we intuit certain general moral principles, these become prima facie parts of our explicit theory, the rest of which will no doubt be inferred as the best account of our intuitions about particular cases given our theoretical intuitions. It is possible, however, that we may discard from our considered inferred theory some principle(s) that we once intuited. Not all of our intuitions (either particular or general) may be consistent with the theory that best explains the most important of them.
20 In the first part of the argument I try to follow at least the general lines suggested by Harman. Later I go more my own way.

particular implications. If so, the moral claims about particular objects that follow from the conjunction of these principles and other nonproblematically objective claims would also satisfy the requirement. Alternatively, we might be able to show that certain moral claims about particular situations satisfy the requirement without bringing in reference to the moral principles that imply them. If so, these principles would then qualify, less directly, by furnishing good explanations of the specific moral facts. These seem the only two interesting possibilities.

Perhaps we can begin by validating certain moral claims about particulars. But how could the truth of these claims help explain the occurrence of any observations? Surely not indirectly, by way of explaining the merely physical aspects of what we observe. Could it be by way of explaining certain observable human actions or attitudes? Not according to Harman. For he holds that even when, for example, we punish wrong actions or act in moral perversity, our choices can be fully explained by our moral beliefs and attitudes. In such cases we do or punish the wrong action not because it is wrong but because we think it wrong. And our moral emotions and attitudes are best explained in a similar way, by our moral convictions and training rather than by moral facts.

Perhaps certain moral facts about particular situations directly explain the occurrence of observations. But which observations? Surely the most likely candidates are those moral observations in which we might be thought to recognize these facts. But here the argument, as we have already seen, makes its pivotal move. It asserts that the occurrence of our moral observations is best explained not by the truth of what we intuit but by the operation of our implicit moral theory as it interacts with our nonmoral perceptions. Our observation, in Harman's example, that the boys we see setting fire to a cat are acting very badly is best construed as a kind of unconscious application of our own humane moral principles to what we see, in the ordinary sense, is happening.

Since so-called particular moral facts don't help explain the occurrence of our observations, the capacity of moral principles to explain these facts is of no avail. It seems, therefore, that if any moral claims about particular objects and situations satisfy the explanatory requirement it is because they follow from moral principles that satisfy it independently. But how might the principles do this? It seems unlikely that we could derive them from anything still more basic. But how else might they qualify? The only remaining live possibility seems to be this: that we might need to assume them in order to explain the existence of the general moral beliefs of our tacit moral theories, general beliefs that play a causal role in the genesis of our moral observations.[21] For then the principles in question would, indirectly, help explain the occurrence of our moral observations. But, against this possibility, it is very tempting to think that we already see, in at least rough outline, how our underlying moral principles are to be explained.[22] Surely most of them are, in one way or another, built into the fabric of our common culture and, even, our common language. Some may be emphasized and others abandoned, of course, under the influence of particular associations. When people strike us as admirable and extraordinary we tend to pick up their particular ways of thinking. And when they strike us as base and fraudulent we tend to lose what we have previously had in common with them. Apart from such armchair moral psychologizing, plausible though it may seem, there is another difficulty with the idea that we might need to assume the truth of moral beliefs to explain our deepest moral convictions. For it is very hard to see how this assumption *could* help us explain them. Plato, of course, in his theory of recollection, thought he saw otherwise. But Plato's kind of explanation is plausible neither to common sense nor to modern science.

This completes my sketch of the argument. Its most interesting and controversial claims are, I think, these: First, the explanatory requirement itself. Second, the claim that moral hypotheses about particular situations could not satisfy the requirement by way of

21 Someone might argue that even though general theoretical intuitions have no role in the formation of our immediate moral observations, we should regard morality as validated if we see that general moral assumptions are needed to explain the occurrence of these general intuitions. But Harman's argument might be extended to cover this case. For the occurrence of a theoretical intuition might seem best explained not by the truth of the intuited principle but by the fact that it resembles something found in our implicit theory. The sense we sometimes get of a principle's intuitive rightness (the confidence not arising from our recognition of its capacity to explain other intuitions) might be no more than an echo from our moral deep.

22 Richard Werner, in "Ethical Realism," *Ethics* 93 (1983): 653–679, seems to think that there may be conversions of what I am calling tacit moral belief that may defy morally neutral psychological explanation. Since the relevant parts of moral psychology are as yet very underdeveloped, it is difficult to know whether there are, at the very deepest level, such conversions and what the best explanation of them might be.

helping to explain people's behavior or attitudes. Third, the claim that the occurrence of a moral observation, or any other particular intuition, is to be explained not by reference to its truth but by reference to the contents of one's implicit theory. And fourth, the claim that there is no plausible way in which the truth of one's implicit moral theory could be part of the best explanation of one's holding it. If these claims are true, we may be forced to conclude that moral statements, in failing to satisfy the explanatory requirement, compare unfavorably not only with the empirical claims of science and everyday life but also with the formal statements of logic and mathematics.[23]

III

In a very interesting and wide-ranging recent paper, Nicholas Sturgeon offers two counterexamples in which moral statements about particular persons, actions, or practices seem to have impressive explanatory force.[24] In these examples, our public behavior seems to be explained in part by moral facts about the world around us and in part by moral facts about our own characters. Since we often correctly observe people's behavior anything that helps explain it will also help explain the occurrence of these observations. Sturgeon directs his examples at Harman's original argument. But they might also be counterexamples to my version. For they might be cases in which moral hypotheses are needed, prior to various scientific advances, to explain why we observe what we do.

In one example Sturgeon cites the historical fact that abolitionist movements were more vigorous in English- and French-speaking America than in other parts of the slave-holding world.[25] A good explanation of this difference might lie, he claims, in the fact that slavery in that part of America was morally worse than slavery elsewhere. I agree that this does suggest a good explanation. But it remains to be seen whether the moral evaluation Sturgeon cites

---

23 Although Hartry Field, in *Science without Numbers* (Princeton, N.J.: Princeton University Press, 1980), argues that scientific accounts of the world do not require that mathematics actually be true. For reasons reminiscent of Harman's, he finds skepticism about mathematical truth to be appropriate.
24 Nicholas Sturgeon, "Moral Explanations," in *Morality, Reason and Truth,* ed. David Copp and David Zimmerman (Totowa, N.J.: Rowman & Allanheld, 1984), pp. 49–78.
25 Ibid., pp. 64, 65.

is a necessary part of it. For the explanatory force we sense here may, after all, come exclusively from what we know about the nonmoral features of our past form of slavery and about the moral views and attitudes of those who had to live with it. Now the main moral reasons why slavery in our part of the world seemed particularly repugnant were, I suppose, that it went especially far in making slaves suffer and in denying them self-respect. The question is, therefore, whether an explanation that appealed only to such features as these and to contemporary moral and nonmoral reactions to them would capture all the power of Sturgeon's explanation.

I think it would. If Sturgeon's account does not presuppose some such nonmoral explanation – if it simply asserts that our form of slavery was morally worse in whatever respects happened to make it so – then it is considerably less informative than it at first seemed. It is also much weaker. For it is possible that people would not have objected so strongly to other ways in which our form of slavery might have been especially bad. Abolitionism was a response to more or less specific information that provoked moral disgust and the desire for change. On the other hand, if the moral explanation does presuppose what our past form of slavery was like and how it was regarded, why does it also need to include our present moral evaluation? Surely it was the abolitionists' verdict on slavery, and not ours, that explained its demise.

Sturgeon's other example concerns moral character as an explanation of behavior and, indirectly, the effects of behavior.[26] In a book about the tragic Donner party of 1846, Bernard De Voto alleges that the vain, cowardly, and incompetent performance of Selim Woodworth, leader of the rescue expedition, caused many to perish who might otherwise have been saved. De Voto concludes that Midshipman Woodworth was "no damned good." Sturgeon cites this as a clear inference to a reasonable explanation and thus calls our attention to the central role that psychological characterizations (descriptions of us rather than of our acts) play in explanations of behavior. But even here we must ask whether the moral properties mentioned in such accounts contribute to their explanatory force.

Accounts of the very general kind that De Voto invokes, appealing to the fact that someone is "no damned good," seem rather

26 Ibid., p. 63.

121

crude as explanations of particular acts. It might be thought, how-ever, that they could illuminate wide-ranging patterns of behavior, for example, that someone has been repeatedly cruel, has told many lies, *et cetera*. But even if someone were badly behaved in every way – and no one in real life ever is – it would seem odd to think that this could be better explained by saying that he was no good than by saying that he happened to have all the particular vices. For a reference to his general badness would in no way help us understand the odd coincidence of his bad qualities. We would surely look to his earlier exercises of free choice or to some unusual features of his upbringing or physical constitution for the real explanation.

This suggests that Sturgeon's best case might lie not in general praise and blame but in the deployment of a more specific, but still distinctively moral, vocabulary of character – for example, in claims that someone is cowardly or unjust. We must first decide, however, whether a specific character term is properly moral or whether it is a nonmoral term for a trait whose possession moral theory de-clares to be good or bad – as, for example, it might declare harshness toward students to be bad in teachers. If it is the latter, its explan-atory role is beside the point. (No one would suppose that because someone's harshness can explain things it follows that the badness of his harshness can also explain things.) But I cannot see how a specific term could be both psychological *and* moral unless in ap-plying it to someone we both assign a certain psychological trait to him and judge him to be morally good or bad in respect of having that trait. Suppose, for example, that "coward" is such a term. To call someone a coward would then be to ascribe to him a certain psychological trait involving fear and to make a negative moral judgment about his possessing that trait.[27] On this picture, the moral aspect of the attribution lies in its second, evaluative, element. A speaker who did not wish to make this judgment might, however, ascribe the trait, under a purely nonmoral description, to people. And such ascriptions would have all the power to explain behavior that the more typical, moral ascriptions have.[28] The cow-

---

27 We therefore seem forced to claim an analytic connection between "cowardice" and "moral badness" (or "moral vice") in order to establish the former as a distinctively moral term.
28 Sometimes we can find a nonmoral description that seems to capture the basic structure of a psychological trait picked out by what seems to be a specifically

ard, after all, flees from danger because he is in the grip of a certain kind of fear and not because his condition reflects discredit on him.

At this point someone will object that a person's being morally bad just is, that is, reduces to, his possessing some complex of psychological traits, and that the bad-makingness of a specific vice such as cowardice just is its inclusion in this complex.[29] But we have already seen reason to doubt that reductive claims provide a way around the explanatory requirement. The objective truth of ascriptions of moral badness would have to be established before we could accept the proposed reduction. Moreover, we have a special reason to be skeptical about the possibility of reducing the moral to the nonmoral. Such reductions would not, presumably, be offered as analytic. And it is far from obvious that they can be modeled on familiar synthetic property reductions in the physical sciences, for example, that of heat to molecular energy. In these familiar examples, the informativeness of a reduction is explained by claiming that our everyday concept identifies the property in question by way of its nonstructural phenomenal features. We locate the presence of heat by the way it feels to us, a manner of identification that does not reveal anything of heat's fundamental structure. The parallel claim for moral badness would be that we recognize its presence by the way it feels or appears to us, its fundamental nature lying elsewhere. But what could these phenomenal features of moral badness be? That it is undesirable or

moral term. We might, e.g., think that cowardice is fearfulness that interferes with the vigorous pursuit of one's own good and one's own ideals. Then it will be easy to see that the trait's explanatory force owes nothing to its moral goodness or badness. But sometimes we may be unable to find any adequate nonmoral characterization of such a trait. Even in this case, however, we can refer to it as "the trait picked out by such and such moral term." This description can be used by a speaker who wishes to ascribe the trait but not to make the usual moral judgment. Its use indicates that while the speaker has not yet found an adequate nonmoral characterization of the trait (and may never find one), he does not regard its essence to be moral. This roundabout description enables him to pick out the trait without presupposing the existence of moral properties and seems to give him everything he needs for explaining behavior. If, contrary to what I am supposing, the essence of a specific trait does seem to be moral – if, e.g., we think cowardice is simply *morally excessive* fearfulness – then it becomes much less plausible to think that reference to the trait really helps us explain behavior. The recruit flees because he is too fearful to stand his ground and not because he is too fearful to be morally good.

29 Not Sturgeon, however, who doubts that there is a reduction of the moral to the nonmoral and denies that such a reduction is needed for moral objectivity. See pp. 59–63.

something to be avoided? But surely these features are at the heart of moral theory. If they are appearances, then it is the appearance of moral badness and not badness itself that we mean to be talking about.

Sturgeon has one further objection that is more theoretical in character and which threatens to undermine our argument where it seems intuitively strongest. Harman, as we have seen, thinks that the rightness or wrongness of a particular act has no explanatory force. Sturgeon responds by proposing a criterion of explanatory relevance. According to this criterion, a statement p is relevant to the explanation of another statement q if p's having been false would mean that q also would have been false or that q would have had a different explanation.[30] Sturgeon immediately notes, however, two exceptions.[31] The first concerns collateral effects of the same cause. Striking a match produces heat as well as light. But while the light would not have occurred had the heat not also occurred, the heat is not, in the desired sense, relevant to the explanation of the light. The second disclaimer concerns larger aspects of the setting in which a particular effect occurs. When a whole described by p (e.g., winning the decathlon) is such that if it had not occurred it would have been because some part described by q (e.g., winning the javelin toss) had not occurred, then p will not necessarily be relevant to the explanation of q.

In noting these exceptions it is natural to suppose that Sturgeon must be thinking that for p to be, in the required sense, relevant to the explanation of q it must have a role to play in it. But if so, then other exceptions to the counterfactual criterion must be added. When an explanatory condition p is not only necessary but sufficient for the state of affairs q that it explains, q's being false would mean that p was false. But it would hardly follow that q had a role to play in the explanation of p. Moreover, highly general entailments of genuinely explanatory factors may fail to be explanatory. That Jones finished first in the race explains why he got the prize. But that Jones finished at some position or other in the race (which is entailed by his finishing first) does not explain why he got the prize.

For a similar reason, an action's highly general supervening qual-

30 Ibid., p. 65. For present purposes we may ignore the last condition. Sturgeon's argument depends only on the claim that p is explanatorily relevant to q in case q would not be true if p were false.
31 Ibid., p. 75, n. 21.

ities, such as moral wrongness, often fail to explain what the action itself explains. Suppose we see that somebody is doing something wrong, as in Harman's example of the boys who set fire to a cat. Sturgeon wants to claim, quite plausibly, that if the boys were not doing anything wrong they would not be igniting the cat and, equally plausibly, that if they were not igniting the cat we would not, observationally well positioned as we are, think that they were doing anything wrong. And he wishes us to infer from this and from his criterion of explanatory relevance, if I have understood it correctly, that the wrongness of their act plays at least some role in the explanation of our thinking it wrong. But suppose it is also the case that if the boys were doing nothing wrong they would be playing ball and not igniting anything. By Sturgeon's criterion, it would then follow that the wrongness of their act plays a role in explaining why someone else, who is too far away to see the cat, sees them to be igniting something or other. But this would be to assign to a moral fact the unlikely role of helping to explain a straightforwardly perceptual judgment. Sturgeon may, of course, fall back upon a technical sense of "relevance" to show that the moral fact is relevant even here. But I cannot see why someone committed to the explanatory requirement should think such a technical sense matters.

IV

If morality fails to satisfy the explanatory requirement, it is not, perhaps, without respectable company. The kind of argument we have constructed to cast doubt on the objective truth of moral claims can also be used to cast doubt on the objective status of many of the classifications of ordinary life not used in the natural sciences. This includes many statements about natural objects (e.g., that my garden is full of weeds) and perhaps most statements about ordinary artifacts. Take my judgment that the object beneath me is a chair. Is the truth of this claim part of a good explanation of anything else that exists or happens in my vicinity? That the object in question makes a certain noise when dropped, burns when ignited, will not fit through certain spaces, *et cetera* are facts best explained by its material consistency, weight, size, and shape. Perhaps its coming from a certain kind of store, its occupying a certain space in my office, and its frequently being sat upon are best explained by its status as a chair. But any explanation of this kind would seem to presuppose certain principles that classify objects having certain histories and uses as chairs. And, as we shall see in a moment, it is not clear that such chair-theoretical principles deserve a place in explanations of any empirical phenomena.

Perhaps the so-called fact that there is a chair under me satisfies the explanatory requirement directly by helping to explain why I observe that there is. The presence of the chair might be thought to explain various stimulations in my nerve endings, which in turn explain various events in my brain, which in turn explain my perceptual judgment. But, as in the case of morality, we do not have to turn to special technical concepts and knowledge to find a better kind of explanation that deals in a quite different way with the classification of the object beneath me. Suppose someone explains my observation, not by claiming that I am affected by and as a result perceive a chair, but by claiming merely that I am affected by an object of a certain general shape and construction. And suppose that he brings in the term "chair" only as it occurs in my system of beliefs. According to such an explanation, I first interpret the tactile and visual sensations produced by the object beneath me in ordinary terms of shape and construction and I unconsciously infer from this, by way of my implicit theory of furniture (or, more precisely, my implicit theory of chairs), that it is a chair.

Someone who offers this kind of explanation, whether he agrees with my judgment or not, remains officially uncommitted to chair-facts. Filling out the explanation would require detailed attention to the respects that make me classify various objects as chairs and non-chairs. (As the replacement of moral explanations would require detailed attention to how we sort things into good and bad or right and wrong.) The result would, in this respect, have the form of the explanations now sought in cognitive psychology. But it should not require special concepts or special experimental equipment. Despite its refinement, it would be continuous with explanations we give in everyday life, for example, an explanation of why someone mistook something for a chair. Moreover, it is very likely that I and the person giving the explanation of my observation would disagree on the classification of certain objects as chairs. In these cases, explanations that appeal to chair-facts will clearly have something against them. So the kind of explanation in the original case that does without such facts has the virtue of greater generality. Most important, it is natural to think that an intelligent adult who distinguishes chairs from non-chairs must have in the implicit theory that he uses to do this all the concepts needed to replace explanations that posit chairs with better explanations that do not. The theory of chairs is in this respect like the theory of morality and unlike the ordinary theory of color or the superseded theories of modern science.

If this is right and if we continue to follow the plan of the earlier argument against morality, it appears that claims about particular chairs will satisfy the explanatory requirement only if the principles of chair-theory that imply them satisfy the requirement independently. For convenience, suppose that the only relevant chair-principle is this: that any object made to seat a single person, off the floor and with support for his back is, if its manufacture is reasonably successful, a chair. Now how might this principle be validated? It obviously has a direct role to play in explaining why the object beneath me is, as we say, a chair. But this matters only if the object's being a chair helps provide a good enough explanation of the occurrence of some observation, something we have seen reason to doubt. So if the principle does satisfy the requirement, it must do so by way of explaining something else. And of all such things that it might explain, none seems a likelier candidate than our tacit acceptance of the principle itself.

How could the truth of the principle be thought to explain our belief in it? Someone might argue that since the human community has, for ages, tacitly accepted the principle, its acceptance must be useful. And he might argue further that only the truth of the principle could account for this utility. But this second claim is debatable. Accepting the principle would seem to be advantageous because it tends to guarantee that someone who accepts it will easily recognize objects made to seat a single person off the floor, *et cetera* as constituting a distinct kind of thing, which he may then put to good use. But that someone recognizes this category and puts its members to good use does not imply that it is, or that he takes it to be, the category of *chairs*. (We are, remember, doing without the possibility of analytic and, therefore, trivially true claims.) Agnosticism about chairs would, like agnosticism about right and wrong, be odd. But it would not interfere with the agnostic's ability to find suitable objects to sit on. The truth of the principle does not, therefore, seem to be an essential part of the explanation of the utility associated with acceptance of the principle.

Perhaps the best explanation of our accepting the principle would refer to the ways in which we acquired it in childhood from our parents and teachers. This kind of explanation would, if repeatedly applied, take us back to the people who invented chairs. And perhaps it will be suggested that the truth of the principle then had a genuinely explanatory role to play. But, again, what would it have explained? The principle, in one or another possible translation, might then have served as a stipulated definition of a new term. But it is hard to see how such a long-forgotten act of definition, if it ever occurred, could account for the present truth of the principle. Statements introduced by stipulation soon take on linguistic lives of their own. And if we continue to reject the idea that they might become transformed into ordinary, nonstipulative, analytic truths and if we continue to accept the explanatory requirement, it would seem that they must remain true, if they do, on their explanatory merits. But these merits have, in the case of the chair-principle, eluded us. If we reject the appeal to analyticity in accounting for the truth of such basic beliefs, it is far from obvious that we can replace it with an appeal to explanation.

V

Since I feel more certain that the object beneath me really is a chair than I do of any proposed philosophical criterion of objectivity, I am inclined to think the case of artifacts is a serious counterexample to the explanatory requirement.[32] But philosophy itself seems to be another area on which the requirement casts grave doubts, in this case doubts that must apply to the requirement itself.[33]

Suppose that a certain philosopher intuitively classifies statements brought to his attention as objective or nonobjective in accordance with the explanatory requirement. He therefore can "see," philosophically, that moral claims are nonobjective. How would we account for the occurrence of these philosophical observations? Would we explain them as so many particular truths that the philosopher is clever enough to discern? Or would we explain them

---

32 Some philosophers will, no doubt, be content to exclude artifacts from the class of real objects. I, however, cannot see any natural sense of "real" according to which this exclusion would be plausible.

33 It occurs to me that the objection I am about to raise is reminiscent of an earlier objection to logical positivism.

as inferences from his tacit knowledge of the explanatory requirement? Surely we would be more cautious, proceeding as Harman does in the moral case. We would bring in the explanatory requirement as something the philosopher tacitly believes, setting aside its truth as irrelevant to the explanation. And we would proceed in this way even if we ourselves accepted the requirement. For accepting it is one thing and forcing it into explanations that do not need it is another. As responsible investigators, we would surely try to remain as neutral as possible in the presence of philosophical speculation or controversy.

Similar considerations apply to attempts to explain why a philosopher tacitly or explicitly accepts the explanatory requirement. Of course, if we assume that the requirement is both objectively true and known by the philosopher, then our explanation of his acceptance had better be compatible with his knowledge. If we decide that he accepts the principle only because he unconsciously wishes to intimidate others with it, then we would not be able to say that he knew it. But there are possible explanations that would be compatible both with his knowing and not knowing it. Perhaps he tacitly accepts the principle because it was implicit in his training. Or perhaps he explicitly accepts the principle because his philosophical outlook makes it seem more plausible to him the more he reflects on it. Such explanations, which seem to me to capture the origin of many of our philosophical convictions, appear compatible with either the presence or absence of knowledge. Whether the philosopher really knows the principle depends on the virtues of his training, outlook, and reflection.

Of course, it remains possible that the truth of the explanatory requirement either helps us explain the occurrence of other, perhaps nonphilosophical, observations or follows from what does. No doubt the requirement is satisfied by the best hypotheses of empirical science. But how could that be thought, without begging the question, to imply that it holds everywhere?

VI

The explanatory requirement attracts us for two reasons that do not, I think, hold up. The first begins with the claim (which I will not here dispute) that where a given judgment constitutes knowledge, the occurrence of the judgment must be some *evidence* for, that is, must tend to *support,* that which is judged to be true. If we can safely assume that all our knowledge is either itself observational or in one way or another affects our observations, and if we can safely assume that p tends to support q only if q (or something that implies q) helps explain p, then it follows that anything we know satisfies the explanatory requirement. The second assumption is, however, false. The presence of a cause might support an inference to its usual effect, but the effect would not explain the cause. And if we rule out the possibility that the cause might be self-explanatory, it could be true that nothing that implies the effect explains the cause. Still, in the case of knowledge, it might seem that the second assumption does hold. For it is natural to think that one who knows p must be *reliable,* either about the general subject matter that includes p or, at least, about p itself in various counterfactual situations in which it does or does not hold. And it is tempting to suppose that this reliability must result from the fact that the knower's faculty of judgment tends to be affected in the right way by the kind of thing he knows, or to what implies it. The truth of what he judges is thus assigned a distinctive causal role in explaining the occurrence of his judgment.

Such a conception must fit the cognitive virtues (intelligence, sensitivity, good sense, penetration, etc.) and cognitive plausibility somewhere into the causal picture. These virtues would, presumably, be various mental features of certain people that enable them, for reasons we should eventually be able to understand in empirical detail, to receive accurate impressions of fact. And plausibility would be the felt attractiveness that, by way of an empirically determinable mechanism, fact conveys to hypothesis in the mind of an intelligent investigator. The model is, of course, the senses, with the intellectual virtues likened to various powers of sight and plausibility likened to the reliable subjective impression that an object is clearly seen. But it is far from obvious that this model is appropriate to the kinds of inquiry we are here considering. Perhaps philosophical or moral plausibility and the virtues of philosophical or moral thought are not aspects of a causal chain leading from fact to true belief. But if they are not, then we must continue to identify excellent philosophical or moral thought and plausible philosophical or moral views without supposing that a perfected naturalized epistemology could someday show why we were correct or, perhaps, mistaken.

If these identifications do not presuppose some empirically discoverable causal role for philosophical or moral fact, then we can explain the reliability of someone who knows something philosophical or moral, and, therefore, the fact that the occurrence of his judgment supports its claim to be true, without supposing that what he knows must be brought in as part of the explanation of his knowing it. He is reliable because he thinks so well about the relevant part of his subject matter that what there seems plausible to him is generally what would seem plausible beyond doubt to the best human reflection. Such an account of moral or philosophical truth might or might not be, in Dummett's sense, antirealist. But even if it were, one might adopt it and still hold the kind of truth in question to be fully objective in any ordinary sense.[34] Someone who wishes to turn the premise about evidence into the conclusion about explanation must, therefore, first take on the very large philosophical task of showing that the knower's reliability cannot be understood in some way that fails to assign explanatory significance to what he knows.

The second problematic reason why the explanatory requirement attracts us is that systems of thought that fail to satisfy it may seem liable to certain kinds of undetectable and, therefore, uncorrectable error. For example, most people until recent centuries "saw" that the earth was flat. Their error was revealed, however, by the fact that when pressed into explanatory service, the hypothesis of the earth's flatness did not explain many events as well as the supposition that the earth was spherical. So we were disabused of this natural but serious error by the fact that a given perceptual claim must enter into complex explanatory relations with a host of empirical events. But if our moral intuitions about particular objects have no empirical explanatory force, then they are not subject to this kind of check on their accuracy. The intuition that it would be gravely wrong to seize this innocent person to get bodily parts to save these five others arises in us just as strongly and naturally as did our previous judgment that the earth was flat. But if moral facts cannot help us to explain anything that happens, how shall we ever know whether intuition is just as mistaken?

34 In "Realism" in *Truth and Other Enigmas* (Cambridge: Harvard University Press, 1978), Michael Dummett makes it pretty clear (despite a misleading remark about Kreisel on p. 146) that he does not regard the issue between the realist and antirealist to be over the objectivity of the truth of the disputed statements (see p. 147). Note also his remarks at the end of "Truth," p. 18.

Of course, the error about the earth's shape would not have been detected and corrected if our physical and mathematical theory had not been fairly reliable or if our other perceptions had not been generally correct. The explanatory check depends on the adequacy of theory and perception and is no safeguard against widespread error in either. If we had mistakenly "seen" ships falling off the "earth's edge" or if our plane geometry had tolerated the return of a straight line to its starting point we might never have been the wiser. The adequacy of our theory is especially important to the checking. Perceptual judgments about different objects or events are inconsistent only in the presence of theory that shows them to be. And bad theory will fail to reveal genuine incompatibilities or, if it does, will suggest the wrong resolutions. Still, given the right background, the complex web of explanatory interconnections among our perceptual judgments provides us with a rich supply of potential checks missing in the case of morality.

It is a mistake, however, to think that morality is without re-sources for significant checking of its own. If our moral intuitions are generally correct, if our moral theory captures the truth in those intuitions well enough, and if (as is plausible to suppose) the best moral theory would reveal all correct intuitions to be systematically and intelligibly interconnected, then mistaken intuitions will tend to be in tension with theory. Any conflict between intuition and theory will, of course, require choice. Perhaps theory can be im-proved in a way that will accommodate intuition, or perhaps in-tuition will have to give way. A correct sense of the better resolution is essential. But this is also true in the empirical case. The kind of checking we find in morality is not, as we have seen, a matter of what is intuited explaining, courtesy of a more or less adequate theory, what happens in the world; rather it is a matter of a theory that more or less adequately captures the general correctness of our intuitions failing to sustain a particular intuition. But the check has comparable force and is grounded in similar basic assumptions.

Someone may object that empirical schemes have the special advantage of enabling us to explain how a particular observational error arose, so that in the end we are not left with something like an inexplicably dangling intuition. After we learn that the earth is round we can easily see why its size would make it appear flat. But something similar happens when moral theory is supplemented with other knowledge about human liabilities to error and confusion. We can be brought to see how the relevant empirical features of a heretofore incorrectly evaluated moral situation would have escaped our notice or how a certain false moral principle could have been easily mistaken for a true one. Such explanations in no way imply that moral facts themselves help explain our recognition of them. They simply invoke the general ways in which we are prone to get things wrong.

One final reflection: while empirical schemes, in which facts about particular objects must help explain a variety of occurrences, are protected against local error in the way we have seen, it is doubtful that any additional protection is conferred by the specific requirement that such facts help explain occurrences of human observation. For neither ordinary nor scientific explanation of the occurrence of observation is well suited to the task of double checking the truth of what we already believe. This is because in our psychological explanations of observation we must posit a world impinging on our senses, and in doing so we must rely on a picture of the world that we have already developed quite independently. The job of cognitive psychology is to explain how such a world could have provoked our observations of it. If psychological speculation should suggest that we could not come to know about some empirical state of affairs we already take to be perfectly objective, it is the psychological speculation and not the state of affairs that must be questioned.[35]

And even if I am wrong, and cognitive psychology can serve as a significant check on our independent beliefs, it will do so by showing that things are better explained by assuming a given belief to be false and not simply by going about its business without affirming or denying the belief. This theory, like any other, will be more powerful and interesting the less it needs to assume. But to suppose that the world as cognitive theory might be able to pare it back is the only real world, that all else must be consigned to some noncognitive scrap heap, would be to assign a metaphysical significance to the empirical explanation of observation that we have seen good reasons to reject and, so far, no compelling reasons to accept.

---

35 This point does not hold, of course, if the state of affairs in question presupposes some psychological theory.

6

Reflection and the loss of moral knowledge: Williams on objectivity

In *Ethics and the Limits of Philosophy* Bernard Williams surveys a wide variety of important moral topics.[1] He looks back to Aristotle and Kant, freeing their views from various controversial metaphysical assumptions and examining what remains plausible in their grand attempts to ground morality in reason. He casts a critical eye on the most influential contemporary views, utilitarianism (chiefly as developed by Hare) and Rawlsian contractualism. And he raises important general questions about the proper nature and limits of moral theory – its form, its relation to pretheoretical intuition, and the role that linguistic analysis can play in it. In all this, Williams is largely skeptical. Of the great historical projects, he thinks only the Aristotelian might be successfully completed, and even here he regards the chance as slim. He has, moreover, little hope for the kind of streamlined ethical theory that contemporary moral philosophers hanker after and as little confidence in linguistic analysis as a moral methodology.

The culmination of this line of critical thought comes in Chapter 8, "Knowledge, Science and Convergence." There Williams argues, *pace* Socrates, that philosophy not only cannot create new moral knowledge of its own, it actually destroys the only real moral knowledge that human beings can have. That is the knowledge they inherit as members of particular traditional cultures, or of modern cultures in which certain traditional moral notions have survived. In short, ethics is objective only when it is philosophically

From *Philosophy and Public Affairs* 16:2 (Spring 1987) 195–209. Copyright © 1987 by Princeton University Press. Reprinted by permission of Princeton University Press.
1 The book discussed in this review essay is *Ethics and the Limits of Philosophy* (London: Fontana Books/Collins, 1985).

naive.[2] This is because unreflective, traditional man thinks in concrete, or as Williams puts it "thick," ethical terms (such as "courage" and "gratitude") while reflective, philosophical man thinks much more abstractly. The thickness of traditional thought enables it to capture genuine differences in things – the difference, for example, between people who are brave and people who are not – while the thinness of critical thought, with its anemic concepts of right and wrong or good and bad, removes it too far from the realities of the social world.[3] Even if we came to apply these thin concepts to just the same things, our agreement would lack the right kind of responsiveness to the way things are, and our common opinion would therefore fail, in some important sense, to be objective.

This unflattering comparison between philosophy and traditional culture is, if true, of the very greatest significance. But is it true? In this essay I shall try to show why I remain far from convinced that it is. But before I can begin my criticisms, we shall have to look more closely at Williams' arguments.

I

He begins the discussion in Chapter 8 with the familiar metaethical contrast between moral and nonmoral disagreement.[4] But rather than focusing on the implications of disagreement itself, he finds it more profitable to consider what we should say about the way in which reflection might resolve it and lead to a convergence of belief. In the case of science such convergence is sometimes guided by the way things actually are. Williams doubts, however, that we could thus hope to understand reflective convergence in the application of thin ethical concepts. Of course philosophers do not now agree about the abstract fundamentals of ethics. But even if their views came to converge – and Williams does not rule out the possibility – he thinks we should have to explain the convergence by reference to certain contingent social or historical forces and not

2 Williams qualifies this claim in order to allow for the possibility that the Aristotelian project might succeed. See footnote 10.
3 "Thick" is Williams' term, the usefully contrasting "thin" is mine.
4 Williams reserves "moral" and immediately related terms for a particular kind of ethics. We need not follow him in this idiosyncratic usage.

by reference to a shared sensitivity to the way the world anyway is.

Williams considers an obvious objection to the idea of the way the world really, or anyway, is.[5] How, it might be asked, could we form such an idea? If we determine the world by reference to our actual beliefs, we shall have to locate in it all the properties, including moral properties, that we normally ascribe to things. But what is the alternative? We cannot coherently hope to determine the world as it is prior to our conception of it. Williams responds to this dilemma by introducing his idea of *the absolute conception of the world*.[6] This conception has two features. It is *nonperspectival* in representing the world in "a way to the maximal degree independent of our perspective and its peculiarities."[7] And it constitutes the best *total empirical explanation* of all our beliefs and perceptions, explaining not only our acceptance of the absolute conception itself but the origin of all our perspectival representations. Williams seems to see in these two features a way of giving content to the challenged idea of the way the world really is. The real world, at least for our purposes, is the world as represented by the furthest development of the absolute conception.

Justified beliefs included within this conception have, naturally, the strongest form of objectivity. But Williams does not want to exclude the possibility that perspectival beliefs – for example, about colors or tastes – might be objective in a different way. Here the story becomes somewhat less clear and certainly more complicated. Perhaps Williams thinks this kind of perspectival objectivity derives from the objectivity of the absolute conception. That conception explains, as we have seen, how and why our perspectival judgments arise. And in the course of these explanations it might show us that in using certain perspectival concepts we are actually distinguishing between things that are, in some way that our peculiarly human perspective does not fully disclose, really (that is, absolutely) different.

Williams, however, does not explicitly give this account of perspectival objectivity. What he actually says is that perspectival con-

5 Williams, p. 138.
6 Ibid., pp. 138–140.
7 Ibid., p. 139. By "our perspective" Williams means to pick out what is peculiar to the outlook of human beings. Our representations are nonperspectival when we would expect any sufficiently intelligent nonhuman observer to share them.

cepts are objective when their application is *world-guided,* that is, "controlled by the facts or by the user's perception of the world."[8] But if world-guidedness is not to be traced to the absolute conception in the manner just described, how exactly is it to be understood? Here are two possibilities, each suggested by parts of the text: According to the first, our application of a perspectival concept to an object is world-guided just in case there is some kind of substantive empirical explanation *not* belonging to the absolute conception that traces our judgment to the fact that the world is as the judgment represents it. We think the object falls under the concept in part because it does. It is essential, however, that such an explanation be substantive and illuminating. For Williams appears to think that an unilluminating explanation of this form may be trivially available for any belief.[9] (One finds the picture beautiful because, of course, it is beautiful and one sees that it is.)

According to the second account of world-guidedness, the fact that a world-guided perspectival concept correctly applies to an object need not be part of any substantive explanation of our judging that it applies. It is enough if the explanation of our judgment (a) makes reference to other objective facts about the object and (b) makes *no* reference to *certain* facts about us. This account would distinguish between classificatory dispositions that are worthy of epistemic respect and those that are not. If, for example, we apply a concept simply because we have been trained or programmed in a certain way or because we have come to have certain historically contingent tastes, our applications would not be world-guided. But if, for example, we apply it because we are responding to the world in ways fixed by the physical structure of our senses and nervous systems, our use would be world-guided. Perspectival concepts whose use depends largely or entirely upon epistemically favored dispositions would, on this account, be objective.

However world-guidedness is to be understood, Williams is clear that thick ethical concepts such as those of chastity and usury, although perspectival, can be world-guided and objective. But he finds no reason to think the same of the philosopher's thin value concepts of good and bad or right and wrong.[10] And it is this tension

8 Ibid., p. 141.
9 See Williams' discussion of beliefs about grass, p. 138.
10 As already indicated, Williams allows that thin ethical concepts might come to have a weak kind of objectivity that he describes as "within the perspective of

that leads to his paradoxical conclusion. For in beginning to reflect on a customary scheme of thick ethical concepts, we must raise the question whether action encouraged by that scheme is really right. And once that question is raised, we are committed to seeing the scheme as having implications about right action – implications that, if Williams is correct, cannot be objectively true.[11]

II

This completes my sketch of Williams' view. His assumption that objectivity, in some or all of its forms, depends on the empirical power of what we believe to explain our believing it seems to be gaining a certain currency in contemporary metaethics.[12] Since this assumption seems to have a sharply skeptical cutting edge, it is worth our close attention. My own view is that objectivity in general depends not on this kind of explanatory connection, but rather on our best efforts to think well about a subject matter, relying on each other for correction and stimulation. Put crudely and without needed qualification, a belief is objectively true if conscientious and intelligent investigators with access to all the relevant data and arguments would, in the end, accept it. The truth of such a belief may or may not have a role in a substantive empirical explanation of how we come to know that it is true. This is not to deny that the empirical explanation of our apparently coming to know something must be compatible with our knowing it – that we not come to believe it through intimidation or prejudice. But it is to deny that explanations compatible with genuine knowledge

practical reason" (p. 132). This form of objectivity can be enough for knowledge (p. 154), and must also be enough for truth. But the truth in question is apparently not to be thought of as correspondence to fact, or at least not to any kind of fact that can itself have an influence on the mind. Such knowledge would not be world-guided (p. 152). The only hope of it lies, Williams thinks, in the unlikely possibility that the Aristotelian teleological project proves viable. The arguments I am considering here do not concern this form of objectivity.

11 Williams denies, however, that such implications hold *before* we think critically about the scheme. In denying this he adopts what he calls a "nonobjectivist" model for these concepts (p. 149).

12 See, for example, Gilbert Harman, *The Nature of Morality* (New York: Oxford University Press, 1977), pp. 3–23, and Nicholas Sturgeon, "Moral Explanations," in *Morality, Reason and Truth*, ed. David Copp and David Zimmerman (Totowa, NJ: Rowman and Allanheld, 1985), pp. 49–78. I develop more elaborate criticisms of these ideas in "Truth and Explanation in Ethics," *Ethics* 96, no. 3 (Spring 1986):524–544.

must make reference to the fact known as one of the explanatory conditions.[13]

I suspect that some nonexplanatory idea of objectivity gives substance even to Williams' notion of the absolute conception of the world. To see this, consider that most of our best physical science has not been developed in order to explain what goes on in our heads. Modern physics, chemistry, and even biology try to explain nonmental phenomena of the world around us – the attraction of bodies, the reactions of chemicals, the origin of species, and the like.[14] The cognitive sciences, such as we have them, begin their explanations by reference to proximate stimuli described more often than not in ordinary terms – emissions of light or sound in a perceiver's local environment. The accounts that cognitive psychology provides of our beliefs and perceptions are to a considerable extent indifferent to the precise nature and cause of these external stimuli. These accounts would go through whether, for example, elementary particle physics turns out one way or another, even where the alternatives are of the very greatest importance to physics. If this is right, then our scientific belief that the world is one way (represented by one possible development of elementary particle physics) rather than another (represented by an alternative development) will not be confirmed by its contribution to the empirical explanation of our beliefs and perceptions. It will be confirmed by the experimental methods of physics itself – as part of the best theory of physical events around us. And insofar as we aspire to complete empirical explanations of our beliefs and perceptions, we simply add the best results of physical science to the specific accounts of

13 On my second interpretation of his use of "world-guided," Williams could accept this denial as it applies to the objectivity enjoyed by perspectival concepts. He would not, however, accept its application to scientific objectivity. For on p. 152 he says that "convergence on a body of ethical truths which is brought about and explained by the fact that they are truths" would give ethics an objectivity strictly analogous to scientific objectivity. This seems to show that, for him, scientific objectivity depends on the capacity of the thing believed to help explain our acceptance of it.

14 Of course, we perceive many of these phenomena and our perception of them is, we naturally suppose, to be explained by the way in which they affect our sense organs. But this does not mean that in trying to explain the phenomena we are ultimately trying to explain our perceptions of them. A serious chemist, for example, could be utterly indifferent to the contribution he may be making to the ultimate explanation of our *seeing* chemical reactions. Moreover, the objectivity of physical science would surely remain secure even if the causal (and hence explanatory) theory of perception proved unsatisfactory.

139

psychology. But this means that the major part of the absolute conception of the physical world, as Williams presents it, will have no greater claim to objectivity than this: that it is the conception of the world that good scientists, conscientiously applying scientific method in order to understand the world around them, have converged on. That this picture can be called on to complete the explanations of an empirical psychology, is not, so far as I can see, our ground for regarding it as objective.

It may be said that I am thinking too exclusively about explanations of our prescientific beliefs and perceptions. What about the explanations of the theoretical beliefs the physical scientist reaches in the course of his investigations? It might be thought that in this special case cognitive science could actually confirm the results of physics by showing that the mental event in which the physicist draws a theoretical conclusion is best explained by reference to the truth of that conclusion. But to think this is to think that the methods of physics might, in a curious way, be replaced by the methods of psychology – that instead of having physicists discovering the truths of physics we might have them discovered by cognitive scientists experimenting on working physicists. But this seems incredible. Even where psychology sets out to explain the cognitive dynamics of particular scientific investigations, it could conclude that a physical theory is accepted because it is true only by deferring to the independent authority of physics that the theory is true.

Something similar holds, I think, if we consider not cognitive science as such, but neurological science – the physical science of the central nervous system and its interactions with the external world. The neurology of sight, hearing, and touch may well turn out to have little or no capacity to confirm or disconfirm physical theory about the rays we see, the waves we hear, and the minute physical structure of the objects we touch. Nor should we expect the physiology of the brain, as complex as that science may become, to be a testing ground for physics. It seems more likely that brain physiology will concern itself with matter at some level less refined than that at which the experimental physicist works. Physical events in the brain, like physical events in the laboratory, will have explanations that end in the ultimate accounts of matter provided by physics. But it is no more an urgent project of physics to explain atomic events in the brain than to explain atomic events elsewhere.

And there is no special confirmatory significance to be assigned to experiments performed upon the microstructure of brain matter.

I am therefore inclined to think that what really motivates the thought that science gives us a picture of the way the world really is (in itself) is not the specific capacity of science to explain the origin of our conception of the world, but the general power of its experimental methods of confirmation and disconfirmation. It is hard, though not impossible, to continue to put forward a physical theory in the face of repeated experimental failure. But it is all too easy to continue to put forward an ethical theory that does not hold up to the most searching critical scrutiny. The disciplines in which suspicions about objectivity most naturally arise are just those in which empirical confirmation has little or no application – fields in which we have nothing other than intelligence, concentration, industry, and good sense to keep us on the rails.

But even a version of the absolute conception that banks wholly on the power of scientific method faces a serious problem. At some of its advance outposts, it is unclear that physics gives us anything we could describe as a *conception* of the world. For that we seem to need some interpretation of what the physical theory in question can possibly mean. This is notoriously true of quantum mechanics. Its equations enable us to operate upon the world but scarcely give us any kind of coherent understanding of what the world is like. That understanding, insofar as it is possible at all, must consist in an interpretation of the basic theory. And the superiority of one interpretation over another may not be empirically testable. It may be something we will be able to recognize only by comparing its inherent plausibility with that of other interpretations. The completion of our empirical picture of what the world is really like may thus depend on the same kind of anxiety-producing trust in our powers of pure thought that we need to summon in the case of philosophical ethics.

III

I turn now to Williams' distinction between those *perspectival* concepts that can apply objectively and those that cannot. He assigns thick ethical concepts, such as that of courage, as well as concepts of various secondary qualities, such as colors, to the first category. And he assigns the philosopher's thin ethical concepts to the second.

It must be noted, however, that Williams never makes perfectly clear the exact character of the distinction between thick and thin ethical concepts. Sometimes the difference is said to be a matter of level, with thick concepts applying to actions and people and thin concepts applying to ethical schemes made up of thick concepts.[15] But more often the distinction seems to be a matter of generality, the thick concepts having what prescriptivists would think of as greater descriptive content but what others might think of as more specific evaluative content.[16]

This ambiguity may be important. For if thinness is a matter of level rather than generality, then such ethical concepts as that of a good man, good woman, good parent, and good friend are thick. And this would undermine Williams' central contention that where unreflective traditional societies have convergent ethical beliefs they also have ethical knowledge. For surely most traditional societies have their own criteria for the application of just such concepts – criteria that even the most indulgent outside observer must sometimes reject. (Assuming, as I do, that the observer could identify these familiar concepts in a moral culture that rejects some of his general beliefs about how the concepts are to be applied.) More important, an observer would ascribe truth to some of a society's substantive ethical views about good men, women, and the like (as he surely must given that he interprets its language as expressing these concepts) not because he assumed that traditional moral views must be correct, but because he found these particular views congenial to his own ethical outlook.

A second problem should also be mentioned. It is essential to Williams' view that while an outside observer may know that what the natives say is true when they correctly apply one of their peculiar thick ethical terms "E," he cannot know what *they* know. That is, he cannot know that such and such really is E. For he is critically reflective about their ethical scheme, and sees the application of "E" as having various thin ethical implications that he cannot wholly accept. So if he knows what they know, this kind of critical re-

---

15 Williams, p. 146.
16 Ibid., p. 152. Williams, however, should not be content with an explanation that refers to degree of descriptive content. For he explicitly rejects the prescriptivist assumption that thick ethical concepts can be prized apart into descriptive and prescriptive elements. It may be, however, this rejected model that really motivates the distinction.

flection could not be thought to destroy the possibility of moral knowledge. Williams is thus committed to the view that an observer can know that the sentence "x is E" is true but cannot know that x is E. To explain this, he appeals to familiar facts about indexical language – in particular terms connoting that a speaker has some special status. He gives the example of schoolboy slang in which only pupils, and not teachers or parents, may refer to a certain building as "Weeds." Williams seems to think that thick ethical terms behave in a somewhat similar way. Saying that "such and such is E" connotes membership in the particular ethical culture that uses "E." An observer coming from a different moral culture is therefore barred from using the sentence sincerely.[17] Williams seems to call on this fact about usage to block a claim about knowledge. It is because the observer cannot say that something "is E" that he cannot know that it is E. The trouble with this idea is that in no other case does an indexically generated restriction on what we can say imply such a restriction on what we can know. This can be seen from the point of view of the group or person entitled to use the special term. Williams' schoolboy will have no trouble acknowledging that his teacher "knows that Johnny is at Weeds." And what the boy acknowledges may certainly be true despite the restrictions on what the teacher may say. In the same way, it may be perfectly true that Jones knows that I am here even though Jones could not express that piece of knowledge by saying "I am here."

Let us put these troubling difficulties aside and move to the main point. Suppose that in the distant future the pursuit of philosophical ethics leads philosophers to agree on a certain scheme of thick ethical concepts as the best such scheme for human life. (The situation I am imagining is one in which these future moral philosophers have a lively and accurate sense of the history of ethics, including that of our own period, and see this history as having led, by fits and starts, to a position in which it is finally possible to discern the basic ethical truths clearly.) For Williams, this philosophical agreement would be quite different from ordinary agreement about someone's bravery or something's color. He thinks that we could not explain the philosophical convergence in the cognitively favorable way in which we can explain these more familiar conver-

17 Williams does not note that the observer may have to use it somewhat insincerely in the process of learning the new moral language.

gences. But, admitting that there would be many differences between these explanations, it is not clear to me that there must be
among them a difference that casts a shadow on the objectivity of
the philosophers' agreement.

We could, of course, explain our finding some person courageous
by reference to the fact that he *is* courageous and that we can *see*
that he is. But this would be an appeal to the kind of insubstantial,
unilluminating explanation that Williams has rejected as irrelevant.
If we seek a serious empirical explanation, we shall have to refer
to what we know about the person's actions and motives and to
our understanding of what it is to be courageous. And this kind of
serious explanation would also be available, it seems, for the philosophers' agreement. They could explain it by pointing to the
features they find present in the ethical scheme they think best and
to their understanding of what it is to be a better or worse ethical
scheme. It is far from clear to me, therefore, that the relevant
difference shows up at this level of explanation. But perhaps it
appears when the absolute conception is invoked.

It would certainly be embarrassing to the philosophers if there
could be *no* explanation in terms of the absolute conception for
their common ethical belief. But this is hardly likely. One would
think their agreement empirically inexplicable only if one thought
it empirically impossible. And Williams does not think this, or at
least he does not put it forward as part of his argument. So some
good explanation, we may assume, could be found. Is it then that
their agreement would be explained by reference to psychological
and cultural features that favorably dispose them toward the approved ethical scheme, while our agreement about courage is ex-
plicable without reference to such factors? But surely a psychology
and anthropology of favorable and unfavorable responses would
have to enter into both explanations.

Someone might think, however, that they would enter in two
quite different ways. In the case of the philosophers, culture and
psychology might be thought to come in as the *complete* explanation
of their convergence – there being nothing about the preferred
ethical scheme itself (that is, nothing at all naturally outlined within
the absolute conception) to which they can be thought of as responding. While in the case of our agreement over someone's courage, reference to psychology and culture would come in only by
way of explaining why we react favorably to something about the

person that might be noticed quite independently of our reaction. Such a difference would clearly motivate the thought that the philosophers' agreement must be less objective than our agreement over courage.

The trouble is that Williams is in no position to accept this account of the difference. For he denies that thick ethical concepts need be perspectival echoes of independent nonperspectival concepts, different but congruent ways of mapping the same terrain. Thick ethical concepts may, he argues, bring something new to our capacity to organize the world. And surely he is right to hold out for this possibility. To master a certain thick ethical concept, an intelligent outside observer may first need to grasp what Williams calls the *point* of the ethical system in which the concept occurs. But, of course, the philosophers may wish to say something similar. They may deny that the difference between better and worse ethical schemes can be grasped through other concepts, even those of the absolute conception. All that can be demanded of an ethical concept by way of a connection with the absolute conception, they will say, is that the ethical concept supervene on the absolute conception – that there be no ethical difference without an absolute difference. For supervenience is itself a kind of discipline, a guarantee that the supervening concept is not, relative to the concepts on which it supervenes, applied arbitrarily. And once the philosophers have reached agreement, their thin ethical concepts (as they then apply them) *will* be supervenient.

A skeptic about thin concepts might try to stand the preceding argument on its head. Instead of arguing that thin ethical concepts are deficient because they fail to map things along boundaries already charted within the absolute conception, he may charge them with classificatory redundancy. If Williams is right, thick ethical concepts may produce original ways of sorting people and actions. But the thin concept of "best ethical scheme" is applied to something – namely, a particular ethics – that is already clearly distinguishable from all other objects by its particular contents. Williams, however, will surely not wish to endorse this way of denigrating thin concepts. For many perfectly objective concepts have extensions that can be independently specified. And this is true of many or most thick ethical concepts. It is far from obvious, for example, that we cannot find a purely naturalistic description coextensive with "courageous." And it would be odd to think that the actual discovery and publication of such a description could undermine our capacity to go on using the concept of courage objectively. But then it is also odd to think that the redundancy of a thin ethical concept from the point of view of pure classification could tell against its objectivity.

It is, of course, true that if the philosophers had, under the same conditions, agreed to predicate "best" not of the ethical scheme we are supposing that they prefer but of some other scheme, there would have been a different but in some ways similar explanation of that doubly counterfactual agreement. But the same is true of our agreement over colors, the most clearly objective of our perspectival concepts. If under normal conditions of observation we agreed in applying "green" not to grass and leaves but to apples and sunsets, the explanation of our agreement would be different from, but in some ways similar to, the explanation of our actual agreement. It may be objected that, if the physical nature of light and the objects seen were unchanged, "green" would then mean a different color. But if we are inclined to say this about "green," why shouldn't we say the same thing about "best ethical scheme" as applied under ideal conditions of reflection by conscientious philosophers working within a sufficiently rich philosophical culture? If such investigators had applied the term to some quite different ethical scheme, they would have meant something different by it.

IV

I have been arguing that thick and thin ethical concepts may not be as different with respect to objectivity as Williams supposes. I should now like to consider another way in which someone might hope to establish his conclusion – by reference to the manner in which we can explain error. But now I am not addressing Williams himself. For, if I understand him, he holds that we cannot hope to find, for *any* ethical concepts, the kind of empirically respectable theories of error that we find for perceptual concepts (for example, color concepts). In a way this is odd, because someone sympathetic to Williams' general epistemological outlook might naturally suppose that the possibility of the right kind of error theory would go hand in hand with genuine world-guidedness. And he might also naturally suppose that it is because there can be no proper error theory for ethics that ethics fails to be objective. If such a person

146

were persuaded by Williams that the thick ethical qualities were an exception to this – that they could have genuinely objective application – he would expect to find something in the theory of error for these qualities to indicate their privileged status. And conversely, he would expect not to find this in any putative error theory for the thin ethical concepts. Let me conclude, therefore, by briefly considering whether an error theory for the thin concepts would have to be in some way (relevant to the question of objectivity) weaker than an error theory for the thick concepts or, for that matter, for colors.

By an error theory, I simply mean a substantive empirical, and preferably scientific, account of why people sometimes misapply a concept. Such a theory for a perspectival concept C is generally possible, I would argue, only if most of us already know how to identify the proper extension of C. It is, for example, only because most of us already know the colors of things that we can expose the causes of misidentifications of color. And I would also argue that it is only because so many of us are in substantial agreement about color that we can speak of the proper extensions of the various color terms. If we were in some kind of radical disagreement about which things were red or green, we could not hope to have our disagreement resolved by appeal to empirical facts about how various conflicting color judgments arise.

Suppose that in one of Williams' traditional societies most people are in agreement about who deserves and who does not deserve a certain thick term of praise that we might translate "hero." But suppose that a minority within the society awards the term in a somewhat different way. It would surely be wrong to expect a comparison of the best empirical explanation of the majority view and the best empirical explanation of the minority view to show who is right. In this respect, the case of color blindness is quite special. Certain minority reports about colors can be traced to the inability of those reporting to detect real differences in things (differences of wavelength describable in terms of the absolute conception). But not all mistakes about color are like this. Some people get colors wrong out of laziness or inattention, while others have been badly taught. Nor does it seem likely that all or even most mistakes in the application of thick ethical concepts result from some straightforward inability to detect real differences in things. A typical error in the ethical case would lie not in missing a difference, but in thinking some difference relevant when it is not or not relevant when it is. The erring minority might hold, for example, that a certain individual's exploits are sufficient to make him a hero while the majority finds them insufficient. Or the minority might regard special prowess in the hunt as contributing to hero status, while the majority regards only prowess in battle as relevant. Neither side need be any more or less blind to absolute differences than the other.

Let us turn again to the possible future philosophers and their agreement at the higher levels of ethics. But now suppose that their agreement is not quite complete, that some few of them still hold out for other ethical schemes. I think that this case would be no different, with respect to the explanation of error, from the case of minority viewpoints about heroes. A similar kind of empirical explanation might well be available in both cases. It would show why the feature that moves the majority to apply or withhold the concept does not move the minority in the same way. Once we are given that the majority in either case is right, any good empirical account of the minority view will be a good empirical theory of their error. I cannot see how any other kind of error theory would be available in either case. In short, I cannot see that any relevant difference in the objectivity of thick or thin concepts would show up in the empirical theory of error.

To summarize, I have opposed Williams on two fronts. First, I have argued that even where science and the absolute conception are concerned, we should not confuse the question whether a proposition is objectively true with the question whether it appears in the empirical explanation of our believing it. And second, I have tried to show that if we admit thick ethical concepts as objective we cannot, either by reference to explanation or error, exclude the possibility that thin ethical concepts might come to be used just as objectively. I do not claim, of course, to have established either of these points. In matters as dark and difficult as these, it is best to stay somewhat tentative. And even if Williams is wrong in the ways I allege, we clearly remain in his debt for the philosophical power and subtlety he brings to these fascinating questions.

7

Actions, intentions, and consequences: The Doctrine of Doing and Allowing

Sometimes we cannot benefit one person without harming, or failing to help, another; and where the cost to the other would be serious – where, for example, he would die – a substantial moral question is raised: would the benefit justify the harm? Some moralists would answer this question by balancing the good against the evil. But others deny that consequences are the only things of moral relevance. To them it also matters whether the harm comes from action, for example, from killing someone, or from inaction, for example, from not saving someone. They hold that for some good ends we might properly allow a certain evil to befall someone, even though we could not actively bring that evil about. Some people also see moral significance in the distinction between what we intend as a means or an end and what we merely foresee will result incidentally from our choice. They hold that in some situations we might properly bring about a certain evil if it were merely foreseen but not if it were intended.

Those who find these distinctions morally relevant think that a benefit sufficient to justify harmful choices of one sort may fail to justify choices no more harmful, but of the other sort.[1] In the case of the distinction between the intentional and the merely foreseen, this view is central to what is usually called the Doctrine of Double Effect (DDE). In the case of the distinction between action and

From *Philosophical Review* 98 (1989) 287–312. Copyright ©1989 Cornell University. Reprinted by permission of the publisher and author. Thanks to Rogers Albritton, Tyler Burge, Philippa Foot, Matthew Hanser, Thomas Nagel, Michael Thompson, Derek Parfit, T. M. Scanlon, and to the editors of *The Philosophical Review* for valuable suggestions and criticisms.

1 Harm here is meant to include any evil that can be the upshot of choice, for example, the loss of privacy, property, or control. But to keep matters simple, my examples will generally involve physical harm, and the harm in question will generally be death.

inaction, the view has no common name, so for convenience we may call it the Doctrine of Doing and Allowing (DDA). (Because harm resulting from intentional inaction has, typically, been allowed to occur.) Absolutist forms of either doctrine would simply rule out certain choices (for example, murder or torture) no matter what might be gained from them. Nonabsolutist forms would simply demand more offsetting benefit as a minimum justification for choices of one sort than for equally harmful choices of the other sort.

In this paper I shall examine the Doctrine of Doing and Allowing.[2] My aim is twofold: first, to find the formulation of the distinction that best fits our moral intuitions and second, to find a theoretical rationale for thinking the distinction, and the intuitions, morally significant. Both tasks are difficult, but the former will prove especially complex. What we find in the historical and contemporary literature on this topic is not a single clearly drawn distinction, but several rather different distinctions conforming roughly but not exactly to the distinction between what someone does and what he does not do. Special cases of inaction may be treated by an author as belonging, morally speaking, with the doings, and special cases of doing as belonging with the inactions. So in searching for the proper intuitive fit, we shall have to be alert to the possibility that the distinction between action and inaction (or between doing and allowing) is only a first approximation to the distinction we really want.

In evaluating various formulations of the doctrine I shall need special test cases. These will often involve improbable scenarios and repetitive structural elements. This is likely to try the reader's patience (he or she may begin to wonder, for example, whether we are discussing the morality of public transportation). But it may help to recall that such artificialities can hardly be avoided anywhere in philosophy.[3] As in science, the odd sharp focus of the test cases is perfectly compatible with the general importance of the ideas being tested. And the DDA is, I think, of the greatest general significance, both because it enters as a strand into many real moral

---

2 I examine the DDE in "Actions, Intentions, and Consequences: The Doctrine of Double Effect," essay 8 of this volume.
3 Think of Gettier cases, brain transplants, teletransporters, etc.

issues and because it stands in apparent opposition to that most general of all moral theories, consequentialism.

Before beginning, I should emphasize that both the DDE and, especially, the DDA apply more directly to moral justification than to other forms of moral evaluation. It is therefore open to a defender of the DDA to admit that two *unjustified* choices that cause the same degree of harm are equally *bad,* even though one choice is to harm and the other not to save. I note this only because some writers have looked for such pairs in hope of refuting the doctrine.[4] Take the well-known example of an adult who deliberately lets a child cousin drown in order to inherit a family fortune.[5] The act seems so wicked that we understand the point of saying that it is no better than drowning the child. But if so, how can we hold that the difference between killing and letting die matters morally?

This objection seems to presuppose that if letting someone die is ever more acceptable, *ceteris paribus,* than killing someone, it must be because some intrinsic moral disvalue attaches to killing but not to letting die. And if so, this intrinsic difference must show up in all such cases.[6] But the doctrine may, and I shall argue should, be understood in a quite different way. The basic thing is not that killing is intrinsically worse than letting die, or more generally that harming is worse than failing to save from harm, but that these different choices run up against different kinds of rights – one of

---

4 For example, Michael Tooley in "Abortion and Infanticide," *Philosophy and Public Affairs* 2 (1972), 59.

5 From James Rachels, "Active and Passive Euthanasia," *The New England Journal of Medicine* 292 (1975), 79.

6 In "Harming, Not Aiding, and Positive Rights," *Philosophy and Public Affairs* 15 (1986), 5–11, Frances Kamm rightly makes us distinguish between two ways in which killing might be intrinsically worse than letting die: (a) killing might have some bad essential feature that cannot attach to letting die or (b) killing might have some bad essential feature that, while not essential to letting die, can nevertheless be present in cases of letting die. If (b) is true then the moral equivalence of the two cases in which the child drowns would not establish a general moral equivalence between killing and letting die. For letting the child drown might be a special case in which letting die has the bad feature essential to killings but not to lettings die. And even apart from Kamm's point, the idea that intrinsically nonequivalent parts must always make an overall evaluative difference when embedded in identical contexts seems wrong. Consider aesthetics. There may certainly be important intrinsic aesthetic differences between two lampshades even though they create an equally bad overall impression when placed on a certain lamp.

which is stronger than the other in the sense that it is less easily defeated. But its greater strength in this sense does not entail that its *violation* need be noticeably worse.

Such relations between rights are possible because moral blame for the violation of a right depends very much more on motive and expected harm than on the degree to which the right is defeasible. Your right of privacy that the police not enter your home without permission, for example, is more easily defeated than your right that I, an ordinary citizen, not do so. But it seems morally no better, and perhaps even worse, for the police to violate this right than for me to. So there is nothing absurd in saying that the adult acts as badly when he lets the child drown as when he drowns the child, while insisting that there are contexts in which the child would retain the right not to be killed but not the right to be saved.

I

The Doctrine of Doing and Allowing has been most notably defended in recent moral philosophy by Philippa Foot.[7] It will be convenient, therefore, to begin with two of the examples she uses to show the intuitive force of the doctrine.[8] In Rescue I, we can save either five people in danger of drowning at one place or a single person in danger of drowning somewhere else. We cannot save all six. In Rescue II, we can save the five only by driving over and thereby killing someone who (for an unspecified reason) is trapped on the road. If we do not undertake the rescue, the trapped person can later be freed. In Rescue I, we seem perfectly justified in proceeding to save the five even though we thereby fail to save the one. In Rescue II, however, it is far from obvious that we may proceed. The doctrine is meant to capture and explain pairs of cases

7 In "The Problem of Abortion and the Doctrine of the Double Effect," in *Virtues and Vices and Other Essays* (Berkeley, Calif.: University of California Press, 1978), pp. 19–32, Foot argued that the distinction between doing and allowing could do all the work usually credited to the distinction between the intentional and the merely foreseen. In "Killing and Letting Die," Jay Garfield, ed., *Abortion: Moral and Legal Perspectives* (Amherst, Mass.: University of Massachusetts Press, 1984), pp. 178–185 and even later in "Morality, Action and Outcome," in Ted Honderich, ed., *Morality and Objectivity* (London, England: Routledge and Kegan Paul, 1985), pp. 23–38, she withdraws this claim, arguing instead that any intuitively adequate morality must assign an independent moral significance to the distinction between the intentional and the merely foreseen.
8 From "Killing and Letting Die," p. 179.

like these in which consequential considerations are apparently held constant (for example, five lives versus one) but in which we are inclined to sharply divergent moral verdicts.

The first order of business is to get clearer on the crucial distinction that the doctrine invokes. In effect, the DDA discriminates between two kinds of agency in which harm comes to somebody. It discriminates *in favor of* one kind of agency (for example, letting someone drown in Rescue I) and it discriminates *against* the other kind (for example, running over someone in Rescue II).[9] That is, it makes these discriminations in the sense of allowing that the pursuit of certain goods can justify the first kind of harmful agency but not the second. I shall call the favored kind of agency *negative,* since on any plausible account it is usually a matter of what the agent does *not* do. For parallel reasons, I shall call the disfavored kind of agency *positive.* But, as indicated earlier, the distinction between positive and negative agency may or may not line up exactly with the ordinary distinction between doing and allowing or action and inaction. We may discover, as we consider various special circumstances, that certain actions function morally as allowings and certain inactions as doings. So let us begin by sifting various proposals for spelling out the nonmoral difference between the two kinds of agency.

One such proposal comes from some brief passages in the *Summa Theologiae* where Aquinas could be taken to suggest that the difference between the two forms of agency is one of voluntariness.[10] In harmful positive agency, the harm proceeds from the will of the agent while in harmful negative agency it does not.[11] St. Thomas

9 It seems clear than an agent's *not* doing something (for example, not saving someone from drowning) can be morally evaluated as justified, unjustified, right, or wrong, in precisely the sense in which these terms apply to actions. I shall therefore speak of assessing the justification or the rightness of someone's *agency* in some matter, meaning by this an evaluation of his knowingly acting or not acting.

10 *Summa Theologiae* XVII (Cambridge, England: Blackfriars, 1970), 1a2ae Q. 6 article 3, pp. 15–16. The terms "positive agency" and "negative agency" are not, of course, St. Thomas's. This is the interpretation that he might give to them.

11 In speaking of an inaction as harmful or as producing harm (or in speaking of harm as coming from it) I am not begging the question against Aquinas. For I mean these expressions only in the weak sense of connecting the inaction with a harmful upshot, and not in any sense that would imply that the harm was voluntary.

seems to think that foreseeable harm that comes from action is automatically voluntary. But he thinks that foreseeable harm coming from inaction is voluntary only when the agent could and *should* have acted to prevent it. Positive agency would therefore include all foreseeably harmful actions and those foreseeably harmful inactions that could and should have been avoided. And negative agency would include the foreseeably harmful inactions that could not or need not have been avoided.

But what kind of "should" (or "need") is this? If we take it to be moral, the doctrine becomes circular.[12] Inactions falling under positive agency are harder to justify than inactions falling under negative agency. Why? Because by definition the latter need not have been avoided while the former, if possible, should have been.

We could, however, avoid the circularity by taking the "should" to be premoral, reflecting social and legal conventions that assign various tasks to different persons. And we might think that these conventions play a central role in an important premoral, but morally relevant, notion of causality.[13] The helmsman's job is to steer the ship, and this is why we say that it foundered *because* of his careless inaction. The loss of the ship would thus be like the death in Rescue II, which happens because of what we do. And both cases would contrast with the death in Rescue I, which we do not, in the relevant sense, bring about. Voluntariness would thus be seen as a distinctive kind of causal relation linking agency and its harmful upshots in the cases of action and conventionally proscribed inaction (positive agency), but not in the case of conventionally permitted inaction (negative agency). So formulated, the doctrine would not only be clear but would have an obvious rationale. Harmful negative agency is easier to justify because in such cases the harm cannot, in the relevant causal sense, be laid at the agent's door.

I have two objections to this proposal. First, there is little reason

---

12 It may be, of course, that Aquinas's account of the voluntary is not meant as part of the theory of justification and is therefore not directed to the distinction between positive and negative agency. It might instead be part of the theory of praiseworthiness and blameworthiness, which presupposes an independent account of what can and cannot be justified. If so, there could be no charge of circularity. For harmful inaction clearly does deserve blame only if it could and should, morally speaking, have been avoided.

13 I am indebted here to Michael Thompson, who thinks that something like this is suggested in the work of Elizabeth Anscombe.

to treat most instances of the neglect of conventional duty as positive agency. We can usually explain in other ways just why morality takes these tasks so seriously. If human communities are to thrive, people will have to perform their social roles. That is why, in a variant of Rescue I, the private lifeguard of the lone individual might not be morally permitted to go off to save the five, even though a mere bystander would be. To explain this difference, we would not also need to suppose that the private lifeguard and bystander stand in different causal relations to the person's death. There is, moreover, room to think that the special duty of the private lifeguard should be put aside, especially if his employer is a pampered rich man, and the five are too poor to afford personal attendants. But this kind of circumstance would have no justificatory force where death was the upshot of clearly positive agency. In Rescue II, for example, it would not matter that the man trapped on the road was rich and spoiled while the five were poor and worthy.

My second objection is more general. The type of proposal we are examining relationalizes the special moral opprobrium attaching to positive agency by reference to its special causal properties. Since negative agency is not, in the intended sense, the cause of its unfortunate upshots, the moral barriers against it are lower. But this leaves the doctrine open to a serious criticism. For there are other conceptions of causality according to which we are in (the original) Rescue I every bit as much a cause of death as in Rescue II. What matters, according to these conceptions, is whether a nonoccurrence necessary for a given effect was, relative to a certain standard background, surprising or noteworthy. In this sense, we may say that a building burns down because its sprinklers failed to work, even though their failure was traceable to the diversion of water to another more important fire. That the diversion was quite proper is nothing against the claim that the failure of the sprinklers helped cause the loss of the building. And something similar holds for Rescue I. The fact that we did not save the one because we quite properly saved the others would not show that his death was not in part due to our choice.

So even if there is a causal notion that corresponds to Aquinas's idea of the voluntary, it is in competition with other causal notions that may seem better to capture what is empirically important in cientific and ordinary explanation. And it is arguable that the defense of the doctrine should not depend on a causal conception that we would otherwise do without. If the doctrine is sound it ought to remain plausible on an independently plausible theory of causation. In any case, this is what I shall assume here. So I shall grant opponents of the doctrine that the permissible inactions we are considering, no less than the impermissible actions, are partial causes of their harmful upshots. This will force me to try to make sense of the doctrine on other grounds.

But this still leaves the task of stating the nonmoral content of the distinction between harmful positive and harmful negative agency. Perhaps the difference should, after all, be put in the most simple and straightforward way, as the difference between action that produces harm and inaction that produces harm. If we think of action along the lines proposed by Elizabeth Anscombe and taken up by Donald Davidson – a conception whose basic outline I propose to adopt – individual actions are concrete particulars that may be variously described.[14] To say that John hit Bill yesterday is to say that there was a hitting, done by John to Bill, that occurred yesterday. To say that John did not hit Bill, on the other hand, is to say that there was no such hitting. Taking things this way, the distinction between harmful positive agency and harmful negative agency would be the distinction between harm occurring because of what the agent does (because of the existence of one of his actions) and harm occurring because of what the agent did not do but might have done (because of the noninstantiation of some kind of action that he might have performed).[15]

Surprisingly, most moral philosophers who write on these matters reject this way of drawing the distinction. Jonathan Bennett, a severe critic of the DDA, dismisses Davidson's conception of

---

14 G. E. M. Anscombe, *Intention* (2d ed.) (Oxford, England: Blackwell, 1963), especially sec. 26, pp. 45–47. See also Donald Davidson, *Essays on Actions and Events* (Oxford, England: Clarendon Press, 1980). See there "The Logical Form of Action Sentences," pp. 105–122; "Criticism, Comment and Defence," pp. 122–144, esp. pp. 135–137; and "The Individuation of Events," pp. 163–180.

15 What I see as right in the Anscombe-Davidson view is the suggested metaphysics – the claim that action is a matter of the presence of something and inaction a matter of its absence. And I think that our intuitions about whether something is an action or inaction as we think about it morally are metaphysically relevant. So I am not greatly worried that someone pursuing the Anscombe-Davidson line might discover criteria of action and inaction that would radically conflict with our judgments in moral thought.

action without argument.[16] Most likely he minds its failure to provide a clear criterion for distinguishing action from inaction in all cases, one that would tell us, for example, whether observing a boycott (by not buying grapes) or snubbing someone (by not acknowledging his greeting) consists in doing something by way of inaction or simply in deliberately not doing something. Bennett is reluctant to assign moral work to any distinction that leaves some cases unclear, especially where there is no theoretically compelling reductionistic theory for the clear cases. But I am disinclined to adopt such a standard. Almost no familiar distinction that applies to real objects is clear in all cases, and theoretical reducibility is a virtue only where things really are reducible. In any case, the imposition of such a standard would shut down moral theory at once, dependent as it is on the as yet unreduced and potentially vague distinctions between what is and is not a person, a promise, an informed consent, etc.

But Bennett is not simply negative. He proposes an ingenious and, for limited applications, clearly drawn distinction between positive and negative *facts* about agency as a respectable way of formulating the doctrine.[17] (Not of course to save it, but to expose it.) Roughly speaking, an event is brought about by someone's positive instrumentality, as Bennett calls it, when the event is explained by a relatively strong fact about the agent's behavior – for example, that he moved in one of a limited number of ways. Negative instrumentality, on the other hand, explains by reference to relatively weak facts about behavior – for example, that the agent moved in any one of a vast number of ways.

The trouble is that this distinction gets certain cases intuitively wrong. Bennett imagines a situation in which if Henry does nothing, just stays where he is, dust will settle and close a tiny electric circuit which will cause something bad – for example, an explosion that will kill Bill.[18] If Henry does nothing, he is by Bennett's criterion positively instrumental in Bill's death. (For only one of Hen-

---

16 "Morality and Consequences," *The Tanner Lectures on Human Values* II (Salt Lake City, Utah: University of Utah Press, 1981), pp. 54–55.

17 Bennett, pp. 55–69.

18 Bennett, pp. 66–68. If Henry's body were *activating* the device – if he were depressing a trigger or conducting a current – we might see his agency as positive despite his motionlessness. But Bennett doesn't assign any such role to Henry's body.

ry's physical actions, staying still, will cause the death, while indefinitely many will prevent the death.) But suppose Henry could save five only by staying where he is – suppose he is holding a net into which five are falling. Surely he might then properly refuse to move even though it means not saving Bill. For his agency in Bill's death would in that case seem negative, much like that in Rescue I.

Bennett also misses the opposite case. Suppose the device will go off only if Henry makes some move or other. In that case his instrumentality in the death would, for Bennett, be negative. But those who would rule out Rescue II would surely not allow Henry to go to the rescue of five if that meant setting off the device. For his agency in the death of Bill would in that case seem positive.[19] Bennett's distinction, however admirable in other ways, is not the one we seem to want. Perhaps this is already clear when we reflect that, according to him, the instrumentality of someone who intentionally moves his body (in, for example, following the command "Move in some way or other – any way you like!") is negative.

Philippa Foot also rejects the idea that the distinction between positive and negative agency is that between action and inaction.[20] She claims that it would not make any interesting moral difference if respirators (presumably sustaining patients who would otherwise die) had to be turned on again each day. Active turning off and passive not turning on would be morally the same. To be relevant to the present issues, her idea must be that this would not make a difference even in cases where some great good could come about

19 That Bill's death would in this case be a side-effect of the rescue does not distinguish it from Rescue II. For in neither case is the death of the one intended. It might be objected that here but not in Rescue II the killing would not be *part* of the rescue. But if Henry's movement sets off the explosion (for example, by triggering a fuse sensitive to movement) then Henry's killing Bill does seem part of the rescue, at least in the sense that he kills Bill by the very movements that form part of the rescue attempt. Of course there could be circumstances in which Henry's movement would not so much set off the explosion as allow it to be set off. Suppose, for example, Henry's remaining where he is prevents dust from settling on and thereby triggering an explosive device below him. In such a case, I agree that he might go off to save the five. For although he will be active in Bill's death, his agency will involve taking his body from where it would save Bill to where he can make use of it to save the five, a special circumstance that I shall discuss later.
20 "Morality, Action and Outcome," p. 24.

only if a particular respirator were not running. Let us see whether this is right. Suppose there are temporary electrical problems in a hospital such that the five respirators in Ward B can be kept going only if the one in Ward A is off. On Foot's view it should not matter whether a hospital attendant keeps the five going by shutting down the one or, in case it is the kind that needs to be restarted, by simply not restarting it.

It would be very odd to think that if the single respirator were already off, the attendant would be required to restart it even if that meant shutting down the five in Ward B. So Foot's idea must imply that if the single respirator were running, the attendant could just as properly shut it down to keep the others running. Now while there seems something more objectionable about shutting the respirator down, I think that all things considered it might be permitted. One reason is that we could perhaps see it as a matter of the hospital's allocating something that belongs to it, a special kind of circumstance that we shall consider later. But suppose the hospital is an unusual one in which each patient must provide his own equipment and private nursing care. Suppose further that you are an outsider who happens for some reason to be the only person on the scene when the electrical problem arises. In this case, it seems to matter whether you keep the respirators in Ward B going by not restarting the one in Ward A (it being of the type that needs restarting and the private nurse having failed to show up that day) or whether you actually shut it down. The first case seems rather like Rescue I and the second uncomfortably like Rescue II.

Foot goes on to offer what she takes to be a different and better interpretation of the distinction. She thinks what matters is not the difference between action and inaction but the difference between two relations an agent can have to a sequence of events that leads to harm. It is one thing to *initiate* such a sequence or to *keep it going,* but quite another to *allow it to complete itself* when it is already in train.[21] Agency of the first two kinds is positive, while agency that merely allows is negative. One problem with this account arises when we try to explain the difference between allowing a sequence to complete itself and keeping it going when it would otherwise have stopped. We might have thought that the former was a matter

21 Ibid., p. 24, including footnote 2 on p. 37.

of doing nothing to stop it and the latter was a matter of doing something to continue it. But that would seem to take us back to the rejected distinction between action and inaction.

Another problem concerns forms of help and support which do not seem to consist in keeping already existing dangerous sequences at bay. Suppose I have always fired up my aged neighbor's furnace before it runs out of fuel. I haven't promised to do it, but I have always done it and intend to continue. Now suppose that an emergency arises involving five other equally close and needy friends who live far away, and that I can save them only by going off immediately and letting my neighbor freeze. This seems to be more like Rescue I than Rescue II, but it doesn't appear to be a case in which I merely allow an already existing fatal sequence to finish my neighbor off. For he was not already freezing or even, in some familiar sense, in danger of freezing before the emergency arose. Or if we think he was in danger, that danger was partly constituted by what I might fail to do. We might simply stipulate, of course, that any fatal sequence that appears to arise from a *failure* to help someone is really the continuation of a preexisting sequence. But then we seem to be falling back on the notion of inaction as fundamental.

II

I am therefore inclined to reject Bennett's and Foot's positive suggestions, despite their obvious attractions. May we then return to the simple and straightforward way of drawing the distinction, as between harm that comes from action and harm that comes from inaction? I think not. Cases involving the harmful *action of objects or forces* over which we have certain powers of control seem to demand a more complex treatment. Consider, for example, the following variant of Rescue II (call it Rescue III). We are off by special train to save five who are in imminent danger of death. Every second counts. You have just taken over from the driver, who has left the locomotive to attend to something. Since the train is on automatic control you need do nothing to keep it going. But you can stop it by putting on the brakes. You suddenly see someone trapped ahead on the track. Unless you act he will be killed. But if you do stop, and then free the man, the rescue mission will be aborted. So you let the train continue.

In this case it seems to me that you make the wrong choice. You

160

must stop the train. It might seem at first that this is because you occupy, if only temporarily, the role of driver and have therefore assumed a driver's special responsibility to drive the train safely. But, upon reflection, it would not make much moral difference whether you were actually driving the train or merely had access to its brake. Nor would it much matter whether you were in the train or had happened upon a trackside braking device.[22] The important thing from the standpoint of your agency is that you *can* stop the train and thereby prevent it from killing the one.

But this is not the only thing that matters, as can be seen in a different kind of case. Suppose, in a variant of Rescue I (Rescue IV), you are on a train on which there has just been an explosion. You can stop the train, but that is a complicated business that would take time. So you set it on automatic forward and rush back to the five badly wounded passengers. While attending to them, you learn that a man is trapped far ahead on the track. You must decide whether to return to the cabin to save him or stay with the passengers and save them.

May you stay? I think you may.[23] We would be more tolerant of inaction here than in Rescue III. And this is because of your intentions. In Rescue III you intend an action of the train that in fact causes the man's death, its passing over the spot where he is

22 Suppose that you and a friend are off, by car, on a rescue mission that unexpectedly turns into Rescue II. You are sitting in the passenger seat, and your friend is driving. For some reason he hasn't noticed the trapped person, but you have. If you do nothing, your friend will inadvertently run over and kill the man. Can you really think that the end of rescuing the five would *not* justify your friend the driver in deliberately killing the man, but *would* justify you in keeping silent (or in not pulling up the hand brake)? I find this implausible. And it seems equally implausible to suppose that your obligation to yell or pull the brake comes from your having, temporarily, assumed the role of driver. What matters is that the mission has become illicit precisely because, as you can see, it requires that someone be killed. So it has also become illicit to try to *further* the mission, whether by deliberate action or omission.

23 At least if you are not the driver or his designated replacement – that is, someone charged with a special moral responsibility to see to it that the train kills no one. If you have that responsibility but lack a special duty toward the injured people (you are not also their doctor), then there would be something extra on the moral balance in favor of stopping. But we should not build this complication into our account of the difference between positive and negative agency. For the force of this extra factor seems independent of facts about agency. It does not seem to derive from any supposition that, if you stay with the passengers, you will really be taking the train forward or will somehow be party to the fatal action of the train itself.

trapped.[24] Not, of course, because he is trapped there. But because the train must pass that spot if the five are to be saved. In Rescue IV, however, things are different. In that case you intend no action of the train that leads to the man's death. The purposes for which you act would be just as well served if the train's brakes were accidentally to apply themselves.

In Rescue III, but not in Rescue IV, the train kills the man *because* of your intention that it continue forward. This implicates you, I believe, in the fatal action of the train itself. If you had no control, but merely wished that the rescue would continue – or if, as in Rescue IV, you had control but no such wish – you would not be party to the action of the train. But the combination of control and intention in Rescue III makes for a certain kind of complicity. Your choice to let the train continue forward is strategic and deliberate. Since you clearly *would* have it continue for the sake of the five, there is a sense in which, by deliberately not stopping it, you *do* have it continue. For these reasons your agency counts as positive.

The surprise in this is that we must bring the distinction between what is intended and merely foreseen into the DDA. But the two doctrines do not therefore merge. As I shall try to show in another paper, the DDE depends on something different – on whether or not a victim is *himself* an intentional object, someone whose manipulation or elimination will be useful. But the victim is not in that way involved in the special kind of positive agency we find in Rescue III. What is intended there is not something for him – that he be affected in a certain way – but some action of an object that (foreseeably but quite unintentionally) leads to his death.

To the idea of positive agency by action, we must therefore add positive agency by this special kind of inaction. But this is, I think, the only complication we need to build into the doctrine itself. (Other more minor qualifications will be discussed in the next section.) We may now construct the doctrine in stages, starting

24 In Rescue III you intend an action of the train that immediately kills the man. But it would make no difference if, in a variant of the case, you did not intend that the train pass over the spot where the man was trapped, but merely intended that it pass over some nearer part of the track (where that would foreseeably lead to its passing over the fatal spot). Nor would it matter, in a further variant of the case, if the intended action of the train would lead to the man's being killed by some immediate cause other than the train. All that is essential is that you intend some action of the train that you can foresee will cause the man's death.

with some definitions. An agent's *most direct contribution* to a harmful upshot of his agency is the contribution that most directly explains the harm. And one contribution explains harm more directly than another if the explanatory value of the second is exhausted in the way it explains the first.

In the absence of special circumstances involving the actions of objects, an agent's contributions to various effects in the world are those of his voluntary actions and inactions that help produce the effects. So in ordinary cases, his most direct contribution to any effect is the action or inaction that most directly explains the effect. In Rescue I, for example, our most direct contribution to the death of the one is our failure to save him. Our going off to save the five contributes less directly. For it explains the death precisely by explaining the failure to save.[25] In Rescue II, on the other hand, our most direct contribution to the death of the man trapped on the road is our act of running him over.

In special circumstances, that is, where harm comes from an active object or force, an agent may by inaction contribute to the harmful action of the object itself. This, as we have seen, happens just in case the object harms because the agent deliberately fails to control it and he fails to control it because he wants some action of the object that in fact leads to the harm. Having defined this much, the rest is straightforward. Harmful positive agency is that in which an agent's most direct contribution to the harm is an action, whether his own or that of some object. Harmful negative agency is that in which the most direct contribution is an inaction, a failure to prevent the harm.

III

We should now look briefly at certain kinds of cases in which commonsense morality seems to qualify the doctrine as I have just

---

25 We fail to rescue the one *because* we rescue the five instead. But notice that this account implies, in the previously mentioned puzzle cases of boycotting and snubbing (cases where we are unsure whether there is a genuine action by way of an inaction or merely a deliberate inaction), that the agent's most direct contribution to the upshot is an inaction. Grape sales decline because we don't buy grapes, and we don't buy them *because* we are boycotting. Happily, this means that we do not have to decide whether boycotting is a genuine action in order to determine the boycotter's agency in the intended upshot. It will turn out on either hypothesis to be negative.

described it, permitting us to harm or even kill someone in order to help others. I am not thinking here of the avoidance of great catastrophes. The doctrine, as already indicated, need not be absolutist. And even in its nonabsolutist form, it cannot contain everything of moral relevance. Special rights to do that which produces harm and special duties to prevent harm must also be factored in. In this way the doctrine has the force of one important *prima facie* principle among others. Rights of competition, to give a familiar example, legitimate certain kinds of harmful positive agency – such as the shrewd but honest competition in which you take away another person's customers. The right to punish is another familiar example. On the other side, special duties to aid may arise from jobs, contracts, natural relations, or from the fact that someone's present predicament was of your making.[26] These special duties explain why some instances of negative agency seem no easier to justify than active harmings.

These familiar rights and duties do not require that the doctrine be qualified. They merely oppose it in particular cases. But other situations seem either to require special amendments to my definitions of positive and negative agency or to show that in certain situations the doctrine lacks its usual *prima facie* force. Qualifications of the first sort sometimes seem required where harm arises from the active *withdrawal* of aid. In one kind of case you actively abort a project of rescuing or helping that, knowing what you now know, it would have been wrong to undertake. For example, you stop the train in Rescue III, and the five therefore die. In another kind of case, you remove something from where it would help fewer to where it would help more, for example, a raft that is presently within the reach of one drowning victim but that could be moved to the vicinity of several other victims.[27] The object might be your body. You might, for example, cushion the fall of one baby if you stay where you are, but cushion the fall of several others if you

26 If you have advertently or inadvertently poisoned someone who can yet be saved by an antidote that you actually have, then you seem to be in no moral position to go to the rescue of five others rather than staying to save him.
27 It seems important in this kind of case that those who are saved by your action have just as much right to the raft as the one who suffers. Removing it from the reach of its owner would, for example, be very questionable. It also seems important that the person from whom the raft is taken is not already using the raft to save himself. It is one thing to remove it from his reach and quite another to push him off it.

move. In all these cases harm comes to someone because you decide to act rather than to do nothing. But because your action is a certain kind of withdrawing of aid, it naturally enough seems to count as negative agency.

In other cases, harmful positive agency seems to lack some of the *prima facie* opprobrium that usually attaches to it. Sometimes this is because the harm would have been avoided but for some blameable fault of the person harmed. Suppose, for example, that the person in Rescue II who blocks the road had been repeatedly warned not to stray where he might interfere with important rescue efforts. If so, we might feel somewhat more justified in proceeding with the rescue (although never, I think, as justified as we feel in Rescue I). People must, after all, accept some responsibility for the predicaments they stupidly and wrongly bring upon themselves.[28]

In a quite different kind of case, someone may have a special liability to be harmed by a physical or psychological interaction that is generally innocuous and, therefore, of no general moral significance. He might have a rare disease that makes any kind of physical contact very harmful to him. Or he might become dangerously hysterical if we yell in his presence. In such cases we might feel that we could try to save other people from some serious danger even if it would mean brushing up against him or yelling. For, unlike standard instances of harmful positive agency, the attempt would not seem to count as an aggression against the victim, since he does not suffer because of any *general or typical* liability to harm. And this seems sensible. Morality must to some degree reflect the standard human condition. In particular, it must be capable of defining a class of presumptively innocent actions.[29]

28 The responsibility of others also comes in when we know that an action will occasion aggression by a third party – for example, if I know that Jones will murder you if I rescue five of his enemies who are drowning. If it seems that I may proceed with the rescue in this case it is because we shall, quite sensibly, attribute the blame for your death to Jones and not to me. In this kind of situation it is important that the action I undertake is morally pressing. Had Jones threatened to murder you in case I mowed my lawn, my ignoring the threat might well seem a kind of active provocation.

29 But this qualification does not apply to special liabilities created by *external* features of a situation. If driving by Smith's house would set off an explosive device that would blow him up, then driving by, even when it would be necessary to rescue five others, would count as an aggression rather than a failure to help. And this also makes sense. For there seems to be no way in which we can define the class of presumptively innocent actions by prescinding from unusual external

165

Another qualification concerns large public and private projects, like the building of skyscrapers, highways, and dams. We are clearly permitted to help initiate such projects even though we know that in their course some deaths or injuries are practically inevitable. For one thing, the harm is usually remote from what we do. And, more important, the actual harm will generally have been preventable, and its occurrence will be much more directly traceable to the wrongful agency of persons more immediately concerned. It is of course essential that we do not in any way intend the harm that may occur, and take reasonable precautions to prevent it.

In the celebrated Trolley Problem, we seem to find yet another exception to the doctrine's strictures against harmful positive agency.[30] In this case a runaway trolley threatens five who are trapped on the track where it is now moving. If the driver does nothing the five will die. But he can switch to a sidetrack where only one person is trapped. Most people think the driver may switch tracks. But switching is positive agency while doing nothing appears to be negative agency. So the case looks like a counter-example.

But if we look again, we can see that the driver's passive option, letting the train continue on the main track, is really a form of positive agency. This is because the only possibly acceptable reasons for him not to switch would be to prevent the death of the man on the sidetrack or to keep clean hands. But the clean-hands motive begs the question; it presupposes that the doctrine does not also speak against not switching. So in deciding the status of his possible inaction we must put this motive aside. This leaves the aim of

---

circumstances. Removing a ladder is not presumptively innocent when someone is high up on it. And driving down a public road is not presumptively innocent when someone is trapped on it. But entering someone's field of vision (where that sets off no devices, etc.) seems quite different, even where the person will, because of a rare mental illness, be harmed by it.

30 I believe the case was introduced by Foot in "The Problem of Abortion and the Doctrine of the Double Effect," p. 270. See also Judith Jarvis Thomson, "The Trolley Problem," in *Rights, Restitution, and Risk: Essays in Moral Theory* (Cambridge, Mass.: Harvard University Press, 1986), pp. 94–116. And Jonathan Glover discusses a fascinating real-life trolley case in *Causing Death and Saving Lives* (Harmondsworth, England: Penguin Books, 1977), pp. 102–103. During World War II British intelligence apparently had the power to deceive the German command about the accuracy of rocket attacks on London. Had they chosen to do so – and they did not – they could have redirected the rockets to less densely populated areas outside the city.

preventing the death of the man on the sidetrack. But if the driver fails to switch for this reason, it is because he intends that the train continue in a way that will save the man. But then he intends that the train continue forward past the switch, and this leads to the death of the five. So, by my earlier definitions, his choice is really between two different positive options – one passive and one active.[31] And that is why he may pick the alternative that does less harm. Properly understood, Trolley Cases are no exception to the doctrine.

IV

Perhaps we have found the basic form of the doctrine and the natural qualifications that, when combined with other plausible moral principles, accurately map our moral intuitions. But someone will surely object that intuitiveness and correctness are different things and that intuitions about particular kinds of cases may reflect nothing more than conditioning or prejudice. What we need, therefore, is a more philosophical defense of the doctrine, a rationale that can be called upon to support the intuitions. Foot locates a kind of rationale in the distinction, borrowed from the law but applied to morality, between negative and positive rights. Negative rights are claim rights against harmful intervention, interference, assault, aggression, etc. and might therefore naturally seem to proscribe harmful positive agency, whether by action of the agent himself or by action of some object to which, by strategic inaction, he lends a hand. Positive rights, on the other hand, are claim rights to aid or support, and would therefore seem to proscribe harmful negative agency. Foot's idea seems to be that general negative rights are, *ceteris paribus,* harder to override than general positive rights.[32] And while this seems intuitively correct, it is not obvious why it should be so.

The thesis that negative rights are harder to override immediately

---

31 This solution to the trolley problem works equally well for versions in which the choice belongs to someone who happens upon a trackside switch.

32 See "The Problem of Abortion and the Doctrine of the Double Effect," p. 27. Foot does not actually speak of "general" positive and negative rights. But I think that is what she means. For natural or contractually acquired "special" positive rights may sometimes bind as strongly as general negative rights. We saw, for example, that a private lifeguard in Rescue I might not be permitted to leave to save the five.

167

implies that negative rights take precedence over positive rights. And it is the thesis of precedence that matters most to us, since it applies directly to circumstances, such as the ones we have been considering, in which the two kinds of rights compete with each other – situations in which the positive rights of one person or group can be honored just in case the negative rights of another person or group are infringed. In Rescue II, for example, the positive rights of the five to be saved from death compete in this way with the negative right of the trapped person not to be killed.

The weakest thesis of precedence would hold that in such oppositions the negative rights prevail just in case the goods they protect (the goods that would be lost if they were overridden) are at least as great as the goods protected by the positive rights (the goods that would be lost if they were overridden). The goods in question are life, health, freedom from injury, pleasure, de facto liberty, etc. – goods that do not include or presuppose the moral good of respect for any of the rights in conflict.[33] All other things being equal, the weakest thesis of precedence would forbid us to kill one person to save another, but would permit us to kill one in order to save two.

A very strong thesis of precedence, on the other hand, would rule out any infringement of certain very important negative rights (for example the right not to be killed or the right not to be tortured) no matter what positive rights were in competition with them. This would still allow positive rights protecting more important goods to prevail over negative rights protecting less important goods – would permit us, for example, to knock one person down in order to save another from serious injury. But it would not permit us, for example, to kill or torture one to save any number of others even from death or torture.

A perhaps more plausible intermediate thesis would hold that no negative rights are absolute, but would accord to the most important ones considerably more force than they have on the weakest

---

33 In presenting versions of the precedence thesis, I am supposing (*contra* John Taurek in "Should the Numbers Count?" *Philosophy and Public Affairs* 6 (1977)) that the numbers do count – for example, that saving two lives generally does twice as much good as saving one. I am also supposing that goods of different kinds (for example, preservation of life and relief from suffering) can be compared and at least roughly summed up, and that in cases of conflicting rights we can make at least a rough comparison of the overall good protected by the rights on each side of the conflict.

thesis. Such a view might well accommodate the ordinary thought that while someone may not be killed to save five, he might be killed to stave off the kinds of disasters that consequentialists dream up. It might go on to state some kind of criterion for when negative rights must give way; or it might, in Aristotelian fashion, leave the matter to moral perception.[34]

If, on the other hand, negative rights do not take precedence over positive rights then either the reverse is true or neither takes precedence over the other. If positive rights actually take precedence, then we might, as seems absurd, kill two to save one. Suppose one person is drowning and two are trapped on the road. A morality that permitted us to run over and kill the two in order to save the one seems not only odious but incoherent. For once we have decided to kill the two, we have placed them in at least as much danger as the one was in originally. And that would presumably activate their positive rights to be saved from their predicament – rights that would collectively outweigh the positive rights of the one who is drowning.

If there is going to be precedence, it clearly has to be precedence of negative rights. But this leaves open the possibility that neither kind of right takes precedence over the other, that is, that in the competitions we are considering the rights protecting the greater balance of good should, *ceteris paribus,* prevail. In such a moral system the person trapped on the road in Rescue II could not with moral authority object to our running over and killing him. For we shall be saving five others each of whom values his life just as much as he values his. This moral system is perfectly coherent. But it has unappealing aspects.

In such a morality the person trapped on the road has a moral say about whether his body may be destroyed only if what he stands to lose is greater than what others stand to gain. But then surely he has no real say at all. For, in cases where his loss would be greater than the gain to others, the fact that he could not be killed would be sufficiently explained not by his authority in the matter but simply by the balance of overall costs. And if this is how it is in general – if we may rightly injure or kill him whenever

34 Or it might include a criterion that itself requires intuition to apply – by claiming, for example, that a negative right may be justifiably infringed just in case it would be contemptible of its possessor to insist on it. That is the kind of criterion that I find attractive.

others stand to gain more than he stands to lose – then surely his body (one might say his person) is not in any interesting moral sense *his*. It seems rather to belong to the human community, to be dealt with according to its best overall interests.

If it is morally his, then we go wrong if, against his will, we destroy or injure it simply on the ground that his loss will be less than the gains of others. The same is true of his mind. If we may rightly lobotomize or brainwash him whenever others will gain more than he will lose, then his mind seems to belong not to him but to the community. There is an obvious parallel here with his different, and much less important, relation to his property. An object does not belong to him if he may have and use it, and others may not take it from him, only as long as his keeping it would be better for him than his losing it would be for them.[35] Whether we are speaking of ownership or more fundamental forms of possession, something is, morally speaking, his only if his say over what may be done to it (and thereby to him) can override the greater needs of others.[36]

A person is constituted by his body and mind. They are parts or aspects of him. For that very reason, it is fitting that he have primary say over what may be done to them – not because such an arrangement best promotes overall human welfare, but because any arrangement that denied him that say would be a grave indignity. In giving him this authority, morality recognizes his existence as an individual with ends of his own – an independent *being*.[37] Since that is what he is, he deserves this recognition. Were morality to withhold it, were it to allow us to kill or injure him whenever that

35 And something similar holds for damage. You don't own something if others may damage it whenever that is best for all concerned.
36 Reference to the specific moral relation that I have in mind (in saying that someone's body and mind are his and not the community's) is made most naturally by a particular moral use of the possessive pronoun. This makes repeated reference awkward, and tempts me to talk in ways that are potentially misleading. I have spoken of a person's mind as belonging to him and have drawn an analogy with property. But both moves are dangerous. The intended sense of "belong" derives from the special use of the possessive. And the analogy with property is, as indicated, inexact. Both relations ground rights of say in what is to be done, but a person's mind or body are definitely not property – not even his property.
37 I mean here to invoke the ordinary sense of "being," in which human persons, gods, angels, and probably the higher animals – but not plants, cells, rocks, computers, etc. – count as beings.

170

would be collectively best, it would picture him not as a being in his own right but as a cell in the collective whole.[38]

This last point can be illustrated not by thinking of bodies or minds but of lives. The moral sense in which your mind or body is yours seems to be the same as that in which your life is yours. And if your life is yours then there must be decisions concerning it that are yours to make – decisions protected by negative rights. One such matter is the choice of work or vocation. We think there is something morally amiss when people are forced to be farmers or flute players just because the balance of social needs tips in that direction. Barring great emergencies, we think people's lives must be theirs to lead. Not because that makes things go best in some independent sense but because the alternative seems to obliterate them as individuals. This obliteration, and not social inefficiency, is one of the things that strikes us as appalling in totalitarian social projects – for example, in the Great Cultural Revolution.

None of this, of course, denies the legitimate force of positive rights. They too are essential to the status we want as persons who matter, and they must be satisfied when it is morally possible to do so. But negative rights, for the reasons I have been giving, define the terms of moral possibility. Their precedence is essential to the moral fact of our lives, minds, and bodies really being ours.

But it might be objected that the weakest thesis of precedence would give us some degree of moral independence, and at the same time would let us do the maximum good, honoring as many positive rights as possible. On that thesis, it would not be proper to kill one person to save another who is equally happy and useful – it would not be proper, say, to flip a coin. But it could be right to kill one to save two or even five to save six. Why then adopt a stronger thesis? The answer, I think, depends on how important the relevant forms of legitimate control are to us – the extent to which we wish to belong, in the sense under discussion, to our-

---

38 It would make no difference, I think, if the overall good of the whole were thought to be a mere sum of the good of its parts – that is, if the whole were regarded as a mere colony without a morally significant higher-order function of its own. To deny the precedence of negative rights would still be to limit a person's moral protections precisely by this test: whether or not granting the protections would best serve the collective good. It would be to suppose that he may rightly be killed or injured if the cost to him does not outweigh the sum of the benefits to others. And this seems to me a clear enough way in which he would be regarded, morally, as a cell in the collective whole.

selves.[39] And this might depend on the aspect of ourselves in question.

We feel, I believe, most strongly about assaults on our minds. Here most of us are far from minimalists about the precedence of negative rights. The idea that against our will we could justifiably be brainwashed or lobotomized in order to help others cuts deeply against our sense of who and what we are. Here it seems the sense of our own rightful say leads almost to absolutism. We feel less strongly about our persons (at least those parts that do not directly affect our minds) and labor. But even here we wish, I think, to have a kind of defensive say that goes far beyond the weakest thesis of precedence. A system that gave you some authority over what might be done to you but allowed us to kill or injure you whenever that would even slightly maximize the overall good would seem a form of tokenism.

It must be said that something like the precedence of negative rights can be accepted by a certain kind of consequentialist – one who thinks that a person's having an effective say over what is done to him (but not over what is done to others) is, in itself, a kind of good that can be added to the more familiar goods of life or happiness.[40] This kind of consequentialism would grant each of us a kind of special authority against interference. But it is unclear that it would thereby give us the moral image of ourselves we think fitting. For it locates the ultimate ground of proper deference to a person's will in the fact that such deference maximizes the general balance of good. In such a system, it is not so much his right to have his way that really matters as the general goodness of letting him have his way.

A consequentialist might reply that anything other than a consequentially grounded system of rights leads to absurdities, and that in praising the virtues of a rights-based morality I can be saying no more than that there is value in the social influence of such a system – that it is good if people's rights are respected and bad if

39 I am not claiming that any person or persons have actually designed morality with an eye to giving themselves the degree of say they find fitting. But I do think that light can be shed on the (timeless) content of morality by considering the importance to us of what would be realized or unrealized in the design of various moral systems.

40 Amartya Sen makes room for what he calls goal rights in "Rights and Agency," *Philosophy and Public Affairs* 11 (1982), 3–39.

they are violated. But circumstances can arise in which respecting someone's negative rights will lead to an abuse of the negative rights of others. And in at least this kind of case it would be incoherent, the consequentialist will insist, to suppose that negative rights can override their positive counterparts.[41] Suppose B and C will be murdered unless we murder A. A has a negative right against our murdering him, and B and C have positive rights that we help prevent their being murdered. If the ground of the system of rights lies in the value of respect for (or at least nonviolation of) rights, then surely the positive rights of B and C must prevail. For only by murdering A can we maximize the value that the entire system aims at.

But this objection misses the mark. The value that lies at the heart of my argument – the appropriateness of morality's recognizing us as independent beings – is in the first instance a virtue of the moral design *itself*. The fittingness of this recognition is not a goal of action, and therefore not something that we could be tempted to serve by violating or infringing anybody's rights. It is also true, of course, that we think it good if people actually respect each other's rights. But this value depends on the goodness of the moral design that assigns these rights. It is not that we think it fitting to ascribe rights because we think it a good thing that rights be respected. Rather we think respect for rights a good thing precisely because we think people actually have them – and, if my account is correct, that they have them because it is fitting that they should. So there is no way in which the basic rationale of a system of rights rules it out that a person might have a right not to be harmed even when harming him would prevent many others from being harmed in similar ways.

The rationale that I have proposed is anticonsequentialist not only in its assignment of priority to negative rights, but also, and more fundamentally, in its conception of the basic social function of morality. For consequentialism, it seems fair to say, the chief point of morality is to make things go better overall – to increase average

---

41 Samuel Scheffler develops such an argument in *The Rejection of Consequentialism* (Oxford, England: Clarendon Press of Oxford University Press, 1982), pp. 80–114. Sen, in "Rights and Agency," Sec. VI and VII, tries to make room within a consequentialist framework for kinds of agent-relativity that would undermine the argument. But I find these agent-relative features poorly motivated as elements of a possible consequentialism.

or total welfare within the human community. But on the view presented here, an equally basic and urgent moral task is to define our proper powers and immunities with respect to one another, to specify the mutual authority and respect that are the basic terms of voluntary human association. The doctrine we have been discussing addresses this task directly. And this is why it is far more than a casuistical curiosity. Whether we ultimately agree with it or not, we should recognize that, in giving each person substantial authority over what can rightly be done to him, the doctrine conveys an important and attractive idea of what it is to be a citizen rather than a subject in the moral world.

8

Actions, intentions, and consequences: The Doctrine of Double Effect

Situations in which good can be secured for some people only if others suffer harm are of great significance to moral theory.[1] Consequentialists typically hold that the right thing to do in such cases is to maximize overall welfare. But nonconsequentialists think that many other factors matter. Some, for example, think that in situations of conflict it is often more acceptable to let a certain harm befall someone than actively to bring the harm about. I believe that this view, which I call the Doctrine of Doing and Allowing, is correct, and I defend it elsewhere.[2] But there is a different and even better known anticonsequentialist principle in the Doctrine of Double Effect (for short, the DDE).[3] According to one of the common

From *Philosophy and Public Affairs* 18:4 (Fall 1989) 334–351. Copyright © 1989 by Princeton University Press. Reprinted by permission of Princeton University Press.

I am grateful for very helpful suggestions from Rogers Albritton, Philippa Foot, Matthew Hanser, and many others; and for criticism from audiences at New York University, the University of California at Irvine, and Princeton University.

1 Harm is meant in a very broad sense that includes the loss of life, rightful property, privacy, and so on. In my examples, the relevant harm will usually be the loss of life.

2 Warren S. Quinn, "Actions, Intentions, and Consequences: The Doctrine of Doing and Allowing." (Reprinted as essay 7 in this volume.)

3 The doctrine, which is usually traced to Thomas Aquinas, *Summa Theologiae*, II-II, Q. 64, art. 7, is typically put as a set of necessary conditions on morally permissible agency in which a morally questionable bad upshot is foreseen: (a) the intended final end must be good, (b) the intended means to it must be morally acceptable, (c) the foreseen bad upshot must *not* itself be willed (that is, must not be, in some sense, intended), and (d) the good end must be proportionate to the bad upshot (that is, must be important enough to justify the bad upshot). The principle that follows in the text, which I henceforth treat as if it were itself the doctrine, is really what I find most important and plausible in its first three conditions. I ignore the fourth condition both because it is probably best understood in a way that makes it noncontroversial and because I am concerned here not so much with how choices with a "second effect" can be justified as with

readings of this principle, the pursuit of a good tends to be less acceptable where a resulting harm is intended as a means than where it is merely foreseen.[4] It is this controversial idea that I wish to examine here.

There are two major problems with the DDE. First, there is a difficulty in formulating it so that it succeeds in discriminating between cases that, intuitively speaking, should be distinguished. In particular, I will need to find a formulation that escapes the disturbing objection that under a strict enough interpretation the doctrine fails to rule against many or most of the choices commonly taken to illustrate its negative force. Second, there is a question of rationale. What, apart from its agreeing with our particular intuitions, can be said in favor of the doctrine? Indeed, why should we accept the intuitions that support it? In answer, I shall suggest a rationale with clear Kantian echoes.

I

Like the Doctrine of Doing and Allowing, the DDE discriminates between two kinds of morally problematic agency. It discriminates against agency in which there is some kind of intending of an objectionable outcome as conducive to the agent's end, and it discriminates in favor of agency that involves only foreseeing, but not that kind of intending, of an objectionable outcome. That is, it favors and disfavors these forms of agency in allowing that, *ceteris paribus*, the pursuit of a great enough good might justify one but not the other. The doctrine is meant to capture certain kinds of

whether, *ceteris paribus*, the structure of intention makes a justificatory difference. That seems to me the fundamental question.

4 The principle is sometimes put in terms of the difference between a harmful *result* that is "directly" intended and one that is "indirectly" (or "obliquely") intended. But it also might be put in terms of the difference between a directly and an indirectly intended *act* of harming. In either variant, the point of calling the merely foreseen result or action "indirectly *intended*" is to mark a species of linguistic impropriety in an agent's asserting, with a completely straight face, that a clearly foreseen harm or harming is quite *un*intended. If I have no desire to wake you but simply do not care that my fiddling will have that effect, I cannot say that your waking or my waking you is purely unintentional. Whether there is any natural sense in which they are intentional is a debated point. In the final analysis, I shall sidestep this controversy, concerning myself with a species of intention that an agent clearly does not have toward a merely foreseen result of his agency – namely, the intention that the result occur, or that he bring it about, as a means of achieving his purpose.

176

fairly common moral intuitions about pairs of cases which have the *same* consequential profile – in which agents bring about the same good result at the same cost in lives lost and harm suffered – but in which the character of the intention differs in the indicated way.

One such pair of contrasting cases is drawn from modern warfare: In the Case of the Strategic Bomber (SB), a pilot bombs an enemy factory in order to destroy its productive capacity. But in doing this he foresees that he will kill innocent civilians who live nearby. Many of us see this kind of military action as much easier to justify than that in the Case of the Terror Bomber (TB), who deliberately kills innocent civilians in order to demoralize the enemy. Another pair of cases involves medicine: In both there is a shortage of resources for the investigation and proper treatment of a new, life-threatening disease. In the first scenario doctors decide to cope by selectively treating only those who can be cured most easily, leaving the more stubborn cases untreated. Call this the Direction of Resources Case (DR). In the contrasting and intuitively more problematic example, doctors decide on a crash experimental program in which they deliberately leave the stubborn cases untreated in order to learn more about the nature of the disease. By this strategy they reasonably expect to do as much long-term medical good as they would in DR. Call this the Guinea Pig Case (GP). In neither case do the nontreated know about or consent to the decision against treating them.

Another pair of medical examples is found in most discussions of double effect. In the Craniotomy Case (CC) a woman will die unless the head of the fetus she is trying to deliver is crushed. But the fetus may be safely removed if the mother is allowed to die. In the Hysterectomy Case (HC), a pregnant mother's uterus is cancerous and must be removed if she is to be saved. This will, given the limits of available medical technology, kill the fetus. But if no operation is performed the mother will eventually die after giving birth to a healthy infant. Many people see less of a moral difference between these two cases than between the other pairs. This might be for a variety of reasons extraneous to the doctrine: because the fetus is not yet a person and therefore not yet within the moral framework, because the craniotomy is seen as a way of defending the mother against the fetus, because the fetus's position within the mother's body gives her special rights over it, and so

177

on. But the relative weakness of the intuitive contrast here might also signal something important about the doctrine's central distinction. I shall say more about this later. But for the present it will be useful to include this pair of cases under the DDE, if only because it naturally illustrates the objection mentioned earlier.

According to that objection, the doctor in CC does not intend, at least not strictly speaking, that the fetus actually die.[5] On the contrary, we would expect the doctor to be glad if, by some miracle, it survived unharmed. It is not death itself, or even harm itself, that is strictly intended, but rather an immediately physical effect on the fetus that will allow its removal.[6] That effect will of course be fatal to the fetus, but it is not intended *as* fatal. The intentions in CC are therefore really no different from those in HC.

It might seem that this kind of point cannot be made about the bombing and nontreatment cases. In GP the doctors seem to need the disease to continue so that they can observe its effects. And in TB the pilot seems to need the deaths of the civilians to lower enemy morale. But Jonathan Bennett suggests a way of extending the objection to the bombing case.[7] The terror bomber does not, he argues, need the civilians actually to be dead. He only needs them to be as good as dead and to seem dead until the war ends. If by some miracle they "came back to life" after the war was over, he would not object. And something similar might be said about the doctors in GP. While they need the disease to continue its course, they do not need the victims actually to be harmed by it. If by some miracle the victims developed special ways of withstanding

5 See Herbert I. A. Hart, "Intention and Punishment," in *Punishment and Responsibility* (Oxford: Clarendon Press, 1968), p. 123. Hart finds the intentions in CC and HC to be parallel. But he does not argue, and does not seem to think, that a similar point can be made about most other cases that the doctrine might seem to distinguish. Nancy Davis finds more general problems along these lines in "The Doctrine of Double Effect: Problems of Interpretation," *Pacific Philosophical Quarterly* 65 (1984): 107–123.

6 If the miracle happened, and after its removal the fetus were quickly restored to its previous healthy condition, we would say that the craniotomy had done no real harm. In the actual case, the harm done to the fetus by the craniotomy consists in the *combination* of the desired immediate effect on it (which permits its removal) and the further natural effects that flow from that first effect. Since these further effects are not strictly intended, the objection holds that the harm itself is not strictly intended. See Jonathan Bennett, *Morality and Consequences,* The Tanner Lectures on Human Values II (Salt Lake City: University of Utah Press, 1981), pp. 110–111.

7 Ibid., p. 111.

178

the disease so that they remained comfortable and well-functioning despite its progress, the doctors would be glad.[8]

This line of objection clearly threatens to deprive the doctrine of most of its natural applications. One reply is to say that it surely matters how *close* the connection is between that which is, strictly speaking, intended and the resulting foreseen harm. If the connection is close enough, then the doctrine should treat the harm as if it were strictly intended.[9] And, the reply might go on, the connection is close enough in the cases I have used to illustrate the doctrine's negative force. But what does this idea of closeness amount to? H. L. A. Hart suggests a possible answer by way of the example of someone violently striking a glass just in order to hear the sound of the initial impact. In such a case the further outcome, the shattering of the glass, is "so immediately and invariably" connected with the intended impact that the connection seems conceptual rather than contingent.[10] The death of the fetus in CC is, arguably, connected with the intended impact on its skull in just this immediate and invariable way. And the deaths, or at least some harms, in TB and GP seem just as closely connected with what is strictly intended in those cases.

But what of the contrasting cases? Since hysterectomies are rarely performed on pregnant women, they rarely result in the death of a fetus. So we might say that what is strictly intended in HC (that the uterus be removed) is not, in the relevant sense, closely connected with the fetus's death. And we might hope to find something similar to say in SB and DR. But in taking this way of preserving the contrasts, we would be making everything depend on which strictly intended outcomes of the various choices we fasten upon.

This leads to a new problem. For certain things that the doctor in CC strictly intends for the fetus lack an invariable fatal upshot. Indeed, if craniotomies are ever performed on fetuses that are already dead, then a craniotomy is already such a thing. Even more obviously, the doctor in HC might strictly intend something that

8 Perhaps then it would not really be, at least in these people, a disease. But then it might be said that the doctors don't really need it to be a disease in *them*. It would be good enough if, due to their special powers of compensation, it is for them a harmless condition very much like a disease in others.

9 Philippa Foot perhaps suggests this kind of reply in "The Problem of Abortion and the Doctrine of the Double Effect," in *Virtues and Vices and Other Essays* (Berkeley and Los Angeles: University of California Press, 1978), pp. 21–22.

10 Hart, "Intention and Punishment," p. 120.

is invariably fatal to a fetus. Suppose, for example, that hysterectomies performed on patients who are in the early months of pregnancy are distinguished by the use of a special anesthetic that is safer for the patient and, in itself, harmless to the fetus. This peculiarity could hardly make the operation in HC more difficult to justify, but it would imply that the strictly intended medical means were immediately and invariably connected with the death of a fetus.[11] Perhaps similar things can be said about the other cases. A strategic bomber might have as his mission the bombing of automotive factories. This would not make him a terror bomber, for he would still not aim at civilian casualties. But, for obvious reasons, no automobile factories have ever existed completely apart from civilian populations. So the kind of thing the bomber strictly intends immediately and invariably results in some innocent deaths.

Two problems have emerged: First, since more than one thing may be strictly intended in a given choice, the pronouncements of the doctrine may depend on how the choice happens to be described. This relativity is embarrassing. We would like the doctrine to speak with one voice in any given case. Second, if we try to get around this problem by saying that the doctrine discriminates against a choice in which anything that is strictly intended is also closely connected with death or harm, the doctrine will make uninviting moral distinctions. As we have seen, it will speak against HC if hysterectomies performed on pregnant patients have some distinguishing surgical feature. Otherwise it will speak in favor. And it will speak against the strategic bomber's attack on an urban factory if he was looking specifically for an automotive plant but not, perhaps, if he was looking for a strategically important productive facility.[12] Another approach clearly seems called for.

11 Of course this special operation could, however inappropriately, be performed on patients who were not pregnant. And this might lead someone to speculate that the doctrine speaks against a strictly intended and invariably harmful kind of action or omission only if the harm is an empirically necessary consequence. But this cannot be right. Suppose there is some good that will arise immediately upon your being injected with a certain fatal poison. The good does not require that you actually die. But that is what will happen, since the very real and naturally abundant antidote that could save you has not been, and in fact never will be, discovered. In such a case, the doctrine should certainly speak against my poisoning you. But the directly and invariably connected harm would not follow of empirical necessity.
12 If the latter intention sometimes gets fulfilled, for example, by bombing electric power facilities built into remote and isolated dams.

Instead of looking for a way to identify intrinsically bad effects that are "close enough" to what is intended, we might look instead for a way to identify choices that are intended under some intrinsically negative description. We might then find a way to show that the actions in TB and CC, but not in SB or HC, are intentional *as killings* and that the inaction in GP, but not in DR, is intentional *as a letting die*. Elizabeth Anscombe gives us one such criterion.[13] If we ask a man why he is pushing a mower, he will perhaps say "to cut the grass"; if we ask why he is cutting the grass, he may say "to get things spruced up around here," and so on. The "to . . ." answers, or answers that can be understood in terms of them, give further intentions with which the agent acts. If, his choice being described in a certain way, he accepts the "why" question and replies with a "to . . ." answer, then his choice is intentional under that description. But if he rejects the question in a certain familiar way, his choice is unintentional. If asked why he is cutting the grass he replies, for example, "I don't care about that, I'm just out to annoy the neighbors" or "Can't be helped – it goes with this terrific form of exercise," his cutting the grass is not, as such, intentional.

This seems to give the desired result when applied to our cases. If we ask the doctor in CC why he is killing the fetus, he will naturally say "to save the mother." If we ask the pilot in TB why he is killing the civilians, he will say "to help with the war." And if we ask the doctors in GP why they withhold treatment, they will say "to observe the progress of the disease." And it might be thought that if we ask similar questions in the other cases, the "why" question will be rejected in a way that shows the choices to be unintentional. Thus, if asked why he is killing the fetus, the doctor in HC will avoid a "to . . ." answer, saying instead something like "It can't be helped if I am to save the mother."

Actually, this seems not quite right. If the doctors in DR were asked why they weren't treating the group in question, they might naturally reply "*to* save our resources for more easily treated cases." And this, by Anscombe's criterion, would seem to make the non-treatment intentional. But waving this difficulty, there is another

---

13 G. E. M. Anscombe, *Intention*, 2d ed. (Oxford: Blackwell, 1963), sec. 25, pp. 41–45.

worry. What if the agents in the problematic cases (TB, GP, and CC) become philosophically sophisticated? Perhaps they will then come to reject the "why" questions in the manner of their counterparts. The terror bomber, for example, might respond by saying, "The actual deaths can't be helped if I am to create the realistic appearance of death and destruction." By giving such answers, he and the others will be opting for a more demanding criterion of the intentional. All aspects of an action or inaction that do not in the strictest sense contribute to an agent's goal will be trimmed away as unintentional. By this criterion, the action in CC is intentional as a crushing and that in TB is intentional as an apparent killing. But neither is intentional as a killing. And in GP the inaction is intentional as a way of facilitating medical research, but not as a letting die.

Now it would be very natural to object that the ordinary, more relaxed criterion of the intentional is the right one, and that the stricter criterion is specious. But how is this to be made out? We might try to introduce a form of essentialism here, claiming that the surgery in CC and the bombing in TB are essentially killings or harmings, while the surgery in HC and the bombing in SB are not. But surely the ground of this essentialism would be the prior conviction that the killings in CC and TB are intentional while those in HC and SB are not. The issue about intentionality seems to be the basic one. And what would we say about the inaction in GP – that it was essentially a failure to prevent harm? But then this would also seem true of the inaction in DR.

On the one side we have Anscombe's criterion of the intentional, which pretty well maps our ordinary ways of speaking, while on the other we have a criterion that is structurally similar but stricter. The problem here about intention is reminiscent of a problem about causality that arises in connection with the Doctrine of Doing and Allowing. Certain defenses of that doctrine (which discriminates against active harming and in favor of allowing harm) appeal to a familiar conception of causality according to which active harming *causes* harm while inactively allowing harm does not. But opponents counter that according to other, philosophically superior conceptions of causality, inaction can be every bit as much a cause of harm. Now I have argued that if DDA is sound theory, it ought to have

182

force on any plausible conception of causality.[14] And I feel much the same here. If the DDE is sound, its force ought to be capturable on any plausible theory of the intentional, even one that would revise ordinary ways of speaking. So, for purposes of argument, I shall grant opponents of the doctrine the greatest latitude in paring back intentional actions to their indisputably intentional cores.

II

We must therefore find a different reply to the difficulty with which we started. And I think I see a way. For we have been neglecting one striking respect in which members of our contrasting pairs differ. Take TB and SB. In the former case, but not the latter, the bomber undeniably intends in the strictest sense that the civilians be involved in a certain explosion, which he produces, precisely because their involvement in it serves his goal. He may not, if Bennett is right, intend their deaths. But his purpose requires at least this – that they be violently impacted by the explosion of his bombs. That this undeniably intended effect can be specified in a way that does not strictly entail their deaths is, on the view I am proposing, beside the point. What matters is that the effect serves the agent's end precisely because it is an effect *on civilians*. The case with SB is quite different. The bomber in that case intends an explosion, but not in order that any civilians be affected by it. Of course he is well aware that his bombs will kill many of them, and perhaps he cannot honestly say that this effect will be "unintentional" in any standard sense, or that he "does not mean to" kill them. But he can honestly deny that their involvement in the explosion is anything to his purpose.

The same contrast is found in the medical cases. The doctor in CC strictly intends to produce an effect on the fetus so that the mother can be saved by that effect. But the doctor in HC has, as we have seen, no such intention. Even if he cannot deny that, in some ordinary sense, he "intends" the fetus's death, he can rightly insist that the effects on the fetus of his surgery are nothing toward his medical purpose. Similarly, the doctors in GP intend, as some-

---

14 See Quinn, "Actions, Intentions, and Consequences: The Doctrine of Doing and Allowing," pp. 155–156 of this volume.

thing toward their further goal, that the disease in the untreated patients work its course. And this could be true even if, wishing to investigate only the effects of the disease within cells, they had no interest in the pain and loss of function it also causes. But in DR nothing that happens to the untreated patients serves the doctors' further goal.[15]

The important way in which the cases differ should not be obscured by the following complication. We have seen that a doctor in HC might intend to use the special anesthetic "safest for a *pregnant* patient." Would it follow from this allusion to the fetus that the doctor does, after all, strictly intend something for it? No. The medical relevance of the patient's pregnancy does not mean that any of the surgical effects on the fetus are medically useful. Something similar holds in SB. Suppose the bomber wants, for moral reasons, to target factories in the least populated district of a certain city. If so, the formulation of his strictly intended means contains an indirect reference to the civilians whom he may kill. But this hardly turns him into a terror bomber. The impact of his bombs on those civilians is still nothing to his military purpose.

This clear distinction between the intentional structures of the contrasting cases is the key to a new and better formulation of the doctrine. To put things in the most general way, we should say that it distinguishes between agency in which harm comes to some victims, at least in part, from the agent's deliberately involving them in something in order to further his purpose precisely by way of their being so involved (agency in which they figure as *intentional objects*)[16] and harmful agency in which either nothing is in that way

15 Not even, I would argue, the fact of their not receiving the treatment. What really furthers the goal is the treatment received by the other, more tractable cases. The nontreatment of the first group contributes, at most, in an odd and secondary sense. This point applies, I think, to a wide range of intentional expressions. Suppose we decide to combat a disease by spending our limited resources on education rather than on inoculation. Education, and not noninoculation, will then be our *means* of combat; and the *way* we fight the disease will be by educating, not by not inoculating.

16 I might instead have said "agency in which harm comes to victims . . . from the agent's deliberately producing some *effect on them* in order to further his purpose precisely by way of their being so affected." But there is a certain kind of ingenious case, attributed to David Lewis, that such a formulation might seem to miss. Suppose that another terror bomber wishes to demoralize enemy leaders by bombing a major center of population, and suppose he knows that these leaders will be convinced that the city is destroyed by seeing, from afar, the explosion of his bombs over it. The explosion occurs an instant before the fatal

184

intended for the victims or what is so intended does not contribute to their harm.[17] Let us call the first kind of agency in the production of harm *direct* and the second kind *indirect*. According to this version of the doctrine, we need, *ceteris paribus*, a stronger case to justify harmful direct agency than to justify equally harmful indirect agency.[18] Put this way, the doctrine solves the original problem of showing a genuine difference in the intentional structures of our contrasting cases, even under a strict interpretation of what is intended. And it makes no appeal to the problematic notion of "closeness." For direct agency requires neither that harm itself be useful nor that what is useful be causally connected in some especially close way with the harm it helps bring about.[19] There is another, related advantage. With this version of the doctrine, we can sidestep all potentially controversial questions about whether the agents in our various cases kill or harm intentionally. It is enough that we

effects below. So in this case the bomber does not, strictly speaking, intend to blow up the civilians, or produce any *physical* effects on them, as a means to his end. Yet the case seems, morally speaking, to be like TB rather than SB. But notice that while such a strategy does not aim at *physically* affecting its victims, it does strictly aim at exploding bombs in their vicinity. Whether or not this change in their situation could be counted as an effect on them, as I think it could, the bomber strictly intends to involve them in something (to make his bombs explode over them) in order to further his purpose precisely by way of their being involved.

17 This way of drawing the distinction excludes a pair of cases sometimes used to illustrate double effect: in one we give powerful analgesics to lessen the terrible pain of a dying patient, where we foresee that he will die as a side effect. In the other we relieve his suffering by intentionally killing him with the same or other drugs. In both cases we are to suppose that life is no longer a good and that we act with his explicit or correctly presumed consent. So we cannot see ourselves as infringing, justifiably or unjustifiably, any of his moral rights. For this reason I see these cases as really quite different from the others, in which there is conflict between the moral claims of different people. Indeed, I think that the doctrine is misapplied in nonconflict cases. I see, for example, no difference between amputating someone's leg to save him and proceeding with some life-saving treatment that, as a side effect, results in the loss of the limb. And by parity of reasoning it seems to me that if stopping pain is urgent enough from the patient's perspective to make death acceptable as a side effect, it ought to make death acceptable as a means.

18 A terminological point: Something counts as "harmful direct agency" only insofar as harm comes to the very people who are deliberately affected by the agency. Insofar as harm comes to others, the agency also counts as "indirectly harmful." A single act or omission can thus be both directly and indirectly harmful.

19 Nor, of course, does it require that the agent have *particular* victims in mind. It is enough, as in the case of a terrorist's car bomb, that he intends something for someone or other.

185

can identify the things they uncontroversially intend as contributing to their goal.

One further bit of line-drawing remains. We have not yet defined the difference between the more pronounced moral asymmetry of DR and GP, or SB and TB, and the apparently weaker asymmetry of HC and CC. This difference may partly depend on whether the agent, in his strategy, sees the victim as an advantage or as a difficulty. In CC the doctor wants the fetus removed from the birth canal. Its presence there is the problem. In GP and TB, on the other hand, the availability of potential victims presents an opportunity. By bringing it about that certain things are true of them, the agents positively further their goals. Perhaps it would not be surprising if we regarded fatal or harmful exploitation as more difficult to justify than fatal or harmful elimination. If so, we might say that the doctrine strongly discriminates against direct agency that benefits from the presence of the victim (direct *opportunistic* agency) and more weakly discriminates against direct agency that aims to remove an obstacle or difficulty that the victim presents (direct *eliminative* agency).

III

The DDE, of course, has only *prima facie* moral force. Special rights may allow us to harm someone's interests by way of direct (and even direct opportunistic) agency. Various rights of competition and the right to punish seem to be examples. Certain other cases may prompt qualifications or special interpretations of the doctrine. Suppose that the doctor in HC needs to alter, harmlessly, the position of the fetus before the womb can be safely removed. Whether the overall surgical procedure would still count as indirect harming seems a matter of interpretation. If we saw the manipulation of the fetus as a partial cause of its later removal, we would presumably count the harming as direct. If we saw the manipulation as a precondition, but not a partial cause, of the removal, we would count the harming as indirect.

Another problematic kind of case involves innocent hostages or other persons who physically get in the way of our otherwise legitimate targets or projects. Does our shooting through or running over them involve a direct intention to affect them? I think not. It is to our purpose, in the kind of case I am imagining, that a bullet or car move through a certain space, but it is not to our purpose that it in fact move through or over someone occupying that space. The victims in such cases are of no use to us and do not constitute empirical obstacles (since they will not deflect the missile or vehicle in question). If we act despite their presence, we act exactly as we would if they were not there. If, on the other hand, we needed to aim at someone in order to hit a target, that person would clearly figure as an intentional object. Another tricky case is one in which we could, and would if we had to, accomplish our end by harmful indirect agency; but it is better, perhaps safer for those to be benefited, to pursue the end by harmful agency that is direct. It seems clear why we might wish to make this kind of case an exception.

Before we turn to the defense of the doctrine, we should briefly consider the way in which it interacts with the distinction, mentioned in connection with the Doctrine of Doing and Allowing, between what is actively brought about and what is merely allowed to happen. I have claimed that DDE, with the exceptions noted, discriminates against harmful direct agency. But, as we have seen, people may figure as intentional objects not only of a choice to act but also of a choice not to act. DDE therefore cuts across the distinction between harming and allowing harm. Sometimes, as in TB and CC, it discriminates against direct agency in which harm is done. And sometimes, as in GP, it discriminates against direct agency in which harm is allowed.

In all of these cases we seem to find an original negative or positive right that, while opposed by other rights, seems to be strengthened by the fact that harm will come via direct agency.[20] Civilians in wartime have negative rights not to be killed. But if their government is waging an unjust war, these rights may conflict with strong rights of self-defense. A sufficiently developed fetus *in utero* might also have some negative right not to be killed. But this right may not prevail, either because the fetus is not yet fully one of us or because its mother has strong rights over her body. In TB and CC, the directness of the threatening agency apparently serves to strengthen these negative rights, perhaps giving them a power to stand against moral forces to which they would otherwise give

20 Positive rights are rights to aid while negative rights are rights to noninterference. While borrowed originally from the law, these terms are here used in a moral sense.

way. Something similar happens in GP. The untreated people have, presumably, some positive right to medical aid. This right might not be binding if doctors could cure more people by directing aid elsewhere. But it stands against any attempt to maximize medical benefit *by* deliberately letting the people deteriorate. Again, the directness of the intention strengthens the force of the opposing right or claim.

It is interesting to consider whether DDE might also come into play where no independent negative or positive right is present. Suppose, in an act of pure supererogation, I am about to aid you but am checked by the realization that your difficulty can be turned either to my advantage or to that of someone I care more for. Does my change of mind, for that reason, violate any of your rights? I am inclined to think not. It might be bad of me to be checked by such a reason, but its appearance cannot create an obligation where none existed before. Rights not to be caught up, to one's disadvantage, in the direct agency of others seem to exist only where some positive or negative right already applies. Their effect always seems to be that of strengthening some other right.

The effect of the doctrine is therefore to *raise* rather than to lower moral barriers. So we should not expect a proponent of DDE to be more tolerant of harmful indirect agency than those who reject the doctrine but share the rest of his moral outlook. We should rather expect him to be *less* tolerant of harmful direct agency. This point is important. For casual critics of the doctrine sometimes seem to suppose that its defenders must be ready to allow killings or harmings simply on the ground that the agency is indirect. But nothing could be further from the truth. The doctrine in no way lessens the constraining force of any independent moral right or duty.

IV

We must now turn to the question of rationale. At first glance, harmful direct agency might seem harder to justify because it requires that the agent welcome something bad for the victim. The terror bomber, for example, must welcome the news that the innocent civilians are blown up, even if he is not glad that they won't be miraculously resurrected after the war. The trouble is that it also seems the strategic bomber must, in some sense, welcome the same

188

news, since if the civilians had been unharmed the factory would not in fact have been destroyed.[21] Of course the news is good for different reasons. It is good news for the terror bomber because it announces the very thing that he intended, while it is good news for the strategic bomber because it announces the thing that he foresaw would be evidence of what he intended. But this difference does little more than register what we already knew – that the terror bomber strictly intended the deaths while the strategic bomber merely foresaw them as necessary costs. So it is hard to see how it could be used to explain the moral difference between direct and indirect agency.

Nor is it the case that harms of direct agency need be worse than those of indirect agency. If someone threatened by a terror bomber and someone equally threatened by a strategic bomber both needed rescuing, the former would not seem to have the stronger claim to help. Indeed, there would seem to be no reason to rescue either in preference to someone threatened by purely natural causes.[22] And if we sometimes think that the first rescue must have priority, it seems to be only because we are tempted to regard the violation of a special right against harmful direct agency as a distinctive and additional kind of moral evil. But then it would be circular simply to appeal to the evil in order to explain the existence or force of the right.

Perhaps the following rationale is more promising. Someone who unwillingly suffers because of what we intend for him as a way of getting our larger goal seems to fall under our power and control in a distinctive way. And there may be something morally problematic in this special relation – something over and above what is morally objectionable in the simpler relation of bringing about or not preventing harm. If this is right, then harmful direct agency must have two things against it, while equally harmful indirect agency need have only one. This additional negative element can be seen most clearly in the contrast between the doctors' attitudes in GP and DR. In the former, but not the latter, they show a shocking failure of respect for the persons who are harmed; they treat their victims as they would treat laboratory animals. DDE

21 See Bennett, *Morality and Consequences,* pp. 102–103.
22 Samuel Scheffler makes a similar point in *The Rejection of Consequentialism* (Oxford: Clarendon Press, 1982), p. 109.

might therefore seem to rest on special duties of respect for persons, duties over and above any duty not to harm or to prevent harm.

While this is surely on the right track, we must proceed with caution. For there is also a kind of disrespect in typical cases of wrongful indirect agency. A strategic bomber who ought to have refrained from destroying a rather unimportant target because of likely civilian casualties has failed to treat his victims with the consideration that they and their interests deserve. So we must look for a kind of disrespect that is peculiar to wrongful direct agency – a kind different from that shown in wrongly giving a victim's interests too little weight.

What seems specifically amiss in relations of direct harmful agency is the particular way in which victims enter into an agent's strategic thinking. An indirect agent may be certain that his pursuit of a goal will leave victims in its wake. But this is not because their involvement in what he does or does not do will be useful to his end. The agent of direct harm, on the other hand, has something in mind for his victims – he proposes to involve them in some circumstance that will be useful to him precisely because it involves them. He sees them as material to be strategically shaped or framed by his agency.

Someone who harms by direct agency must therefore take up a distinctive attitude toward his victims. He must treat them as if they were then and there *for* his purposes. But indirect harming is different. Those who simply stand unwillingly to be harmed by a strategy – those who will be incidentally rather than usefully affected – are not viewed strategically at all and therefore not treated as for the agent's purposes rather than their own. They may, it is true, be treated as beings whose harm or death does not much matter – at least not as much as the achievement of the agent's goals. And that presumption is morally questionable. But in a counterpart case of direct agency there is the *additional* presumption that the victim may be cast in some role that serves the agent's goal.

The civilians in TB serve the bomber's goal by becoming casualties, and the infected people in GP serve the doctors' goal by becoming guinea pigs. If things were different, the victims might become these things only voluntarily. Suppose, for example, the civilians had effective bomb shelters and the sick people medicines of their own. Then the bomber or doctors could succeed only with the cooperation of the victims. The service exacted would then be

190

voluntary. But in cases of indirect agency the victims make *no* contribution. If the civilians in SB had shelters and if the sick people in DR had medicines, the bomber and the doctors would see no point in their refusing to use them.

The DDE rests on the strong moral presumption that those who can be usefully involved in the promotion of a goal only at the cost of something protected by their independent moral rights (such as their life, their bodily integrity, or their freedom) ought, *prima facie*, to serve the goal only voluntarily.[23] The chief exceptions to this strong presumption are cases in which people have or would have strong moral obligations to give themselves to the service of a goal even at such personal costs – especially cases in which it would be indecent of them to refuse. But surely there is not, or may not be, any such obligation in the cases we have been considering: non-combatants (even those on the wrong side) are not morally obligated to serve the right side by accepting the role of demoralizing civilian casualties, victims of dangerous diseases are not typically obligated to become guinea pigs for the sake of others, and I suppose it is at least open to question whether the fetus in CC, if it could grasp its predicament, would have to accept, for the sake of its mother, the sacrifice of its life.

In these cases, but not in their indirect counterparts, the victims are made to play a role in the service of the agent's goal that is not (or may not be) morally required of them. And this aspect of direct agency adds its own negative moral force – a force over and above that provided by the fact of harming or failing to prevent harm.[24] This additional force seems intuitively clearest in direct opportunistic agency, such as TB and GP, where unwilling victims are not only harmed but, in some sense, used. And this must be why the doctrine seems most plausible when it discriminates against opportunistic direct agency. It must also help explain why some of the most perverse forms of opportunistic agency, like torture, can seem absolutely unjustifiable.

23 I am deliberately not considering cases where the sacrifice is financial. What to think in such cases partly depends on the sorts of moral rights people really have to keep money or property that is legally or conventionally theirs when others have more pressing material needs. It is quite consistent with everything I say here to deny that the doctrine speaks against liberal schemes of redistributing wealth.
24 Although it is, as we have seen, a kind of negative moral force that is activated only when other rights are present.

It is less plausible, on the other hand, to think of the victims of direct eliminative agency as used. This may be why the doctrine seems to discriminate against eliminative agency less forcefully. And it may therefore help explain why some people feel that the direct agency of CC is not much harder to justify than the indirect agency of HC. But something of the questionable character of direct opportunistic agency also seems present in direct eliminative agency. Someone who gets in your way presents a strategic problem – a causal obstacle whose removal will be a service to your goals. And this is quite unlike what we find in harmful indirect agency, where victims can be obstacles only in a moral sense.

In discriminating to some extent against both forms of direct agency, the doctrine reflects a Kantian ideal of human community and interaction.[25] Each person is to be treated, so far as possible, as existing only for purposes that he can share. This ideal is given one natural expression in the language of rights. People have a strong *prima facie* right not to be sacrificed in strategic roles over which they have no say. They have a right not to be pressed, in apparent violation of their prior rights, into the service of other people's purposes. Sometimes these additional rights may be justifiably infringed, especially when the prior right is not terribly important and the harm is limited, but in all cases they add their own burden to the opposing moral argument.

The Doctrine of Double Effect thus gives each person some veto power over a certain kind of attempt to make the world a better

---

25 But there is a way in which the rationale I have provided is not Kantian. For it draws a sharp moral line between adversely affecting someone in the pursuit of an end that he does not share (not treating him as an end in itself) and adversely affecting someone because his being so affected is strategically important to achieving an end that he does not share (very roughly, treating him as a means). Neither the terror nor the strategic bomber treats his victims as ends in themselves, but only the former treats them as something like means. And I have argued that this difference is significant – that morality erects an extra barrier against the strategic posture of harmful direct agency. Kant might disagree, focused as he is on the alleged status of people as ends in themselves. But I have difficulty attaching any sense to that idea except via intuitions that certain forms of treatment are unacceptably disrespectful of rational beings. And the intuition that it is more disrespectful, all other things being equal, to treat someone as if he existed for purposes he does not share than simply not to be constrained by his purposes, seems to me plausible enough to be worth incorporating in a proper idea of what it means for persons to be ends in themselves. On this conception, one aspect of being an end in itself would be to have, *ceteris paribus*, a stronger right against directly harmful agency than against indirectly harmful agency.

place at his expense. This would be absurd if the entire point of morality were to maximize overall happiness or welfare. But that is not its entire point. An equally urgent basic task is to define the forms of respect that we owe to one another, and the resulting limits that we may not presume to exceed. The doctrine embodies our sense that certain forms of forced strategic subordination are especially inappropriate among free and equal agents.

9

Reply to Boyle's "Who is entitled to Double Effect?"

I have only minor quibbles with Boyle's presentation of my version of the Doctrine of Double Effect (DDE).[1] On my view, the extra morally problematic element in cases of direct intention is the subordination of a victim to purposes that he or she either rightfully rejects or (and this is something that I should now wish to add in light of Boyle's criticisms) cannot rightfully accept. In cases of indirect intention the victim is incidentally affected by an agent's strategy, but in cases of direct intention the victim is made part of the strategy. Boyle suggests at one point that this amounts to using the person.[2] But I do not think the "using" metaphor is always apt in these cases, although it is perhaps helpful in pointing to the objectionable element in direct intention, which in its perfectly general form can be put only more abstractly.[3]

My only other concern with Boyle's exposition of my view involves his use of the expression "intentionally harming."[4] The discussion there tends to suggest, in contrast to what Boyle has said earlier, that I represent DDE as discriminating between cases of incidental and intentional harming. But this is precisely what I tried to avoid. For some cases of harming that the doctrine intuitively speaks against are arguably *not* cases of *intentional* harming, precisely because neither the harm itself (nor anything itself causally very close to it) is intended. Deciding whether this arguable point

From *The Journal of Medicine and Philosophy* 16 (1991) 511–514. Copyright © 1991 by Kluwer Academic Publishers. Reprinted by permission of Kluwer Academic Publishers.

1 J. Boyle, "Who is entitled to Double Effect?" *The Journal of Medicine and Philosophy* 16 (1991): pp. 475–494.
2 *Ibid.*, p. 484.
3 Warren Quinn, "Actions, intentions, and consequences: The Doctrine of Double Effect" (reprinted as essay 8 in this volume), pp 188–193 (of this volume).
4 Boyle, "Who is entitled to Double Effect?" p. 484.

is in fact correct is something I wished to avoid in my presentation of the doctrine. I therefore constructed it so as to be neutral with respect to the question.

Boyle has two main criticisms of my view. The first[5] concerns the possibility that indirect harming might be worse than direct harming (where, presumably, the harms are of the same magnitude). He does not give an example, but he might be thinking of cases of direct harming in which an agent deeply regrets the harm and takes every opportunity to make it up, and contrasting them with cases of indirect harming in which an agent is wantonly indifferent to, or even pleased by, the harm he brings about. In such comparisons we might easily say that the indirect harming was more vicious, or even that is showed less respect for its victim. I agree.

But this seems to me fully compatible with my justification of DDE, which regards it as *one moral factor among others*. On my view, there is an offensive element (a kind of disrespect) intrinsic to direct harming that is not present in indirect harming. From this it follows that there is a standing objection to direct harming that does not apply to indirect harming. *Ceteris paribus*, direct harming is harder (perhaps much harder) to justify. It is perfectly consistent with this to say that in particular cases of direct harming there may be various *other* features of the agent's attitude that speak in his or her favor (e.g., sincere regret) or that in particular cases of indirect harming there may be special features that speak in the agent's disfavor (e.g., wanton indifference or sadistic enjoyment). And it may be that these features sometimes have more weight in the overall assessment of the agent and his action than do the factors proper to the distinction between direct and indirect harming.

Boyle's second objection concerns the way my account of DDE, being rights based, excludes cases in which harm is voluntarily accepted. Boyle thinks it might, for example, be wrong to kill someone who was ever so willing, indeed eager, to be killed. And if so, it might be worse to kill him directly than indirectly. Given the not implausible assumption that some rights cannot be validly waived, my view can accommodate this kind of case. If you have some such unwaivable right that I not kill you under certain conditions, then according to my conception of DDE you may well

5 *Ibid.*, p. 484.

195

have an additional unwaivable right under those conditions that I not kill you directly. So here it seems that there is no serious conflict between the general lines of my conception and the idea that DDE can function where harm or death are voluntarily accepted.

The other respect in which traditional views of DDE and my conception seem to part company is typified by the famous medical cases in which, e.g., a terminal and suffering cancer patient is, in one case, given very potent analgesics that foreseeably lead to his death and, in the other case, actively euthanatized. While traditional defenders of the doctrine see the former as more acceptable than the latter, on my view the doctrine does not apply. For not only is the patient presumably able validly to waive his right to life when life has become so unbearable but, more important, both actions kill by way of treating him as an intentional object. I tend to think that the sound moral core of DDE has been misapplied in these cases. But I should like to note that there is room within my conception of DDE to distinguish direct killings (killings in which death foreseeably comes from deliberately affecting someone) in which death is *itself* intended from those in which it is not. And it may be possible to refine the doctrine by holding that there is a still further objection to direct killings (or harmings) of the first sort. If this wrinkle were adopted, and if it were combined with the view that this patient could not waive his right to life, even in his dire circumstances, then it would be possible to use the amended doctrine in the traditional way: that is, to show that it is harder to justify actively and deliberately euthanatizing the patient than to justify relieving his pain with a predictably fatal dose of pain killers. I myself would have little taste for such a move, which would seem to me to reflect the kind of casuistry that has given DDE a bad name. But perhaps I am wrong.

This leads me to a final reflection on absolutism. It is quite compatible with my view of DDE that no direct harmings, however final or terrible, are absolutely forbidden. It is also quite compatible with my view of DDE that some direct harmings *are* absolutely forbidden. I think the latter must be true of certain cruel punishments and acts of torture. But it seems to me important to see that the absolutism of the prohibition in these cases flows not from the fact of direct intention alone, but from that plus the final or terrible character of the evil inflicted. For where less serious harms are involved, direct harming can be permitted. One may, for example,

196

injuriously knock someone down in order to clear an exit in a dangerous emergency.

If I am right, the DDE has so wide an application in so diverse a set of circumstances with such a wide range of evils at stake that it could not plausibly issue an absolute prohibition against every form of direct harming. There may be special and sometimes terrifying cases in which a specific absolute prohibition is warranted. But we should not allow these admittedly riveting cases to lead us away from the essential character and justification of the doctrine.[6]

---

6 In her article "The doctrine of double effect: Reflections on theoretical and practical issues," (*The Journal of Medicine and Philosophy* 16 [1991]), Frances M. Kamm raises an objection to a brief solution I put forward to the famous Trolley Problem in my paper, "Actions, intentions, and consequences: The doctrine of doing and allowing" (*The Philosophical Review* 98, 287–312). I thought, and still think, that the key to that Problem is not the Doctrine of Double Effect but what I call the Doctrine of Doing and Allowing with its distinction between agency that is akin to doing (positive agency) and agency that is akin to allowing (negative agency). I argued that the choice not to switch the trolley from the track with five to a sidetrack with one was, surprisingly, a special form of positive agency (pp. 298–302 and pp. 304–305), and for that reason one might, exercising ordinary positive agency, switch. And I treated this special form as morally equivalent to ordinary action. Kamm claims on p. 576 that this makes the case in which one chooses not to switch from five to one morally equivalent to a different case in which one switches from a track with one to a sidetrack with five. Since the latter switching is obviously forbidden and may be violently prevented, she regards the equivalence as having two "incredible" implications: (a) that one has a *duty* in the Trolley Case to switch from the five to the one, *and* (b) that one *may* in that case shoot someone to make them switch. Now while (a) – which does follow from my stated views – may be false, it does not seem to me incredible. Surely many nonconsequentialists hold it. And if (a) is true, then someone who wantonly or benightedly refused to switch might, arguably, be shot to make him switch. The whole matter is complicated by the fact that the Trolley Problem (the case of switching from five to one) is a "hard case," while the case of switching from one to five is not. So even if my "solution" to the Problem were correct, someone might blamelessly disagree with it and refuse to switch for that reason. If (b) is meant to include such a person, it is compatible with my view that he could not properly be subjected to the same violence as someone switching from five to one. And if (b) further includes someone who (unintentionally and without fault), will fail to switch from five to one, my views in no way imply that he may be treated like someone who (unintentionally and without fault) will switch from one to five. For the latter is about to kill the five, while the former (lacking what I regard as the intention necessary to convert inaction into positive agency) is merely about to fail to save them. And surely the five have certain rights of self-defense, which we may exercise on their behalf, against innocent potential killers that they do not have against innocent potential nonsavers.

10

The puzzle of the self-torturer

Suppose there is a medical device that enables doctors to apply electric current to the body in increments so tiny that the patient cannot feel them. The device has 1001 settings: 0 (off) and 1 . . . 1000.[1] Suppose someone (call him the self-torturer) agrees to have the device, in some conveniently portable form, attached to him in return for the following conditions: The device is initially set at 0. At the start of each week he is allowed a period of free experimentation in which he may try out and compare different settings, after which the dial is returned to its previous position. At any other time, he has only two options – to stay put or to advance the dial one setting. But he may advance only one step each week, and he may *never* retreat. *At each advance he gets $10,000.*

Since the self-torturer cannot feel any difference in comfort between adjacent settings, he appears to have a clear and repeatable reason to increase the voltage each week. The trouble is that there *are* noticeable differences in comfort between settings that are sufficiently far apart. Indeed, if he keeps advancing, he can see that he will eventually reach settings that will be so painful that he would then gladly relinquish his fortune and return to 0.[2]

From *Philosophical Studies* 59 (1990) 79–90. Copyright © 1990 by Kluwer Academic Publishers. Reprinted by permission of Kluwer Academic Publishers.

I've profited from discussions with Alan Nelson, David Erikson, Yoram Gutgelt, Tony Martin, members of a seminar at New York University, and, especially, Kit Fine.

1 The device derives from Derek Parfit's case of the Harmless Torturers in *Reasons and Persons,* Clarendon Press, Oxford, 1984, pp. 80–82. Parfit uses the devices to present, as he puts it, a puzzle in moral mathematics. I have appropriated them in order to present a puzzle of rational choice. The idea was provoked by Parfit's denial that the self-interest theory of rationality could be, as he puts it, directly self-defeating. See p. 55.
2 But I am supposing that even at 999 he will want things that an extra $10,000 can buy. Suppose he is a devoted philatelist who, even in severe pain, would

The self-torturer is not alone in his predicament. Most of us are like him in one way or another. We like to eat but also care about our appearance. Just one more bite will give us pleasure and won't make us look fatter; but very many bites will. And there may be similar connections between puffs of pleasant smoking and lung cancer, or between pleasurable moments of idleness and wasted lives.

In all these cases, we find a mix of transitive and intransitive preferences. The self-torturer's *stepwise* preferences are intransitive. All things considered, he prefers 1 to 0, 2 to 1, 3 to 2, etc. . . . but certainly not 1000 to 1. This is why he cannot say that any setting is *better than* the previous one. "Better than" is, while his stepwise preferences are not, transitive. But when he compares settings so far apart that he prefers the earlier setting, his preferences are transitive. If he prefers 500 to 1000 and 0 to 500, then he prefers 0 to 1000. This seems to permit us to say that 1000 is worse for him than 0.

The self-torturer's preferences are considered and well-informed. Before forming them, he freely experiments with all the relevant settings. And he is well-informed about the pleasures and advantages that different amounts of money can buy. Despite this, many theorists would condemn his intransitive preferences as irrational.[3] But this response may be too hard on the self-torturer and too easy on the theorist. The self-torturer's intransitive preferences seem perfectly natural and appropriate given his circumstances. They are

value important new acquisitions – or a philanthropist who would still care about helping others. And if it seems too hard to believe that the marginal attractiveness of each new dollar would remain the same, imagine the payments compensatingly increased as he grows richer and more uncomfortable.

3 For a classic discussion of some difficulties arising in other cases of intransitive preferences see Donald Davidson, J. C. C. McKinsey, and Patrick Suppes, "Outlines of a Formal Theory of Value, I," *Philosophy of Science* 22 (1955), 146. Prominent among these difficulties is the way someone with intransitive preferences can become a "money pump." The self-torturer is quite different in this regard: he is more of a money vacuum. Amos Tversky, in "Intransitivity of Preferences," *Psychological Review* 76 (1969), 45, introduced cases in which intransitive preferences seem natural because the subject is understandably indifferent to very small differences in some variable even though he cares very much about larger differences. Our case is certainly of this sort. Note that other writers have suggested various ways of ruling out various allegedly offensive aspects of intransitive preferences. See, for example, Thomas Schwartz, "Rationality and the Myth of the Maximum," *Nous* 6 (May 1972), 97–117; and Dennis Packard, "Cyclical Preference Structures," *Theory and Decision* 14 (1982), 415–466.

the very ones most of us would have in his place (and *do* have in structurally similar, everyday situations). To insist that he get new, more "rational" preferences might well invite bad faith. He wants to know how he should act on the ones he actually has. Intuitively, this question does not seem to be one that must lack a satisfactory answer. So the theoretical convenience of rejecting the question must be weighed against the failure to address what seems to be a genuine problem. In any case, I shall assume provisionally that the self-torturer has, as he is, a real problem of rational choice: How to take reasonable advantage of what the device offers him without ending up the worse for it.

I

Let's begin by considering some objections to my description of the case – objections that would point the way to some familiar way of solving the puzzle or some further grounds for rejecting it.

(1) *The self-torturer's preferences are changing*: On this objection, he is like an addict. At 0, the thought of 1000 appalls him, but at 999 it looks good. The changes wrought in him between 0 and 999 affect his outlook. Since he now (at 0) prefers not to change, he should resist any advance that has that effect.

But his preferences do not change. Even at 0 he prefers 1000 to 999. The same holds for plans of sequential choice. He always prefers a plan that would take him to setting s to one that would take him only to $s-1$. This is why he finds it so hard to set an initial overall plan.

(2) *We are neglecting behavioral evidence*: Someone might not be able to notice introspectively that his comfort had declined in a single step, even though his demeanor or behavior indicated otherwise – he might look less comfortable, or be grouchier. But while this is a possibility, it is also possible that the individual increments of current are too small even to have these effects. And this is the case I want us to consider.

(3) *We are ignoring the measures of his discomfort*: If we assign the self-torturer a discomfort index, quantifying his discomfort at each setting, the numbers will have to change as he advances. Since he starts, we may suppose, at 0 discomfort and ends in great pain, there must be some *first* setting s with a positive discomfort index.

200

So, whether he knows it or not, his comfort would decline in stepping from $s-1$ to s.

But the measure of the self-torturer's discomfort is *indeterminate*. There is no fact of the matter about *exactly* how bad he feels at any setting. And if so, we cannot argue that the measure of his discomfort must increase in some single step.[4]

(4) *We are ignoring the effects of "triangulation"*: The self-torturer can triangulate a difference between s and $s+1$ if he can find some third setting s' that feels the same as s but better than $s+1$. And if he can use 0 to triangulate such a difference, then it is obvious that his comfort, at least compared to 0, declines in stepping from s to $s+1$.

But surely it ought to be an open empirical question whether such triangulations are possible. If there are increments of voltage just small enough to be directly undetectable, it seems there might be even smaller increments that cannot be detected by triangulation. And I want such a case.[5] The self-torturer (and his observers) try to triangulate differences between adjacent settings but honestly cannot – not because they are inattentive, but because we have made the increments of current too small to make *any* difference in comfort, even one that can be detected only by triangulation.

(5) *We are ignoring the reversal of his preferences*: The self-torturer starts out preferring early settings to 0 but ends up preferring 0 to late settings. At some intermediate setting his preferences must reverse. There must be some s such that he prefers s to 0 but 0 to $s+1$. And that must mean that the added money at $s+1$ isn't worth the extra discomfort.

This argument goes wrong, I think, in presupposing that for any positive setting s, the self-torturer (counting both pain and gain)

---

4 The objection could not be met by assigning determinate measures *with determinate margins of error* – saying, for example, that his comfort index at setting s was n plus or minus m. For it would still seem arbitrary to say that the range in which his comfort index lies has n as its precise center and $n-m$ and $n+m$ as its precise outer limits.

5 Remember that, technology aside, we can make the increments as small as we like. We might, for example, have 100,000 settings with each increment reduced to 1/100th its original size. Then we might offer the self-torturer $100 for each advance and allow him to make 100 advances every week. And so on. Also note that, strictly speaking, I need claim only that the increment is too small to make a subjective difference *for the worse*. For it seems possible that a barely noticeable change might be completely unobjectionable in itself even though wholes composed of many such changes are very bad.

determinately prefers s to 0 or 0 to s. But, empirically speaking, his preferences as between s and 0 can exhibit various kinds of *indeterminacy*. Not only is there no empirically determinable *first* setting that he disprefers to 0, there is no empirically determinable *first* setting at which these preferences become indeterminate. There is simply nothing in the way a single increment of current affects him to warrant such precise line drawing. This is implicit in the failure of triangulation. A first setting at which his overall preferences (as between 0 and s) reversed or went indeterminate, would have to be a setting at which his comfort (relative to 0) suddenly declined.[6] There could be no other explanation. But then the self-torturer himself, or observers, could detect the decline, if only by the evidence provided by his reversing preferences. And we are considering a case in which the increments of current are too small to have any such effect.

(6) *Because the self-torturer's preferences are paradoxical, they cannot present genuine problems of rational choice*: He feels no worse at 1 than at 0, and the comfort comparison between 1 and 0 is the same for him as the comparison between 2 and 0. From this it seems to follow that he feels no worse at 2 than at 0. Reiterated enough, the argument implies that he feels no worse at 1000 than at 0. Here we find a kind of *sorites puzzle*. Some of his clear and immediate judgments about his comparative comfort are true only if others are false. Surely preferences based on such paradoxical discriminations are not to be taken seriously. The self-torturer must either change his preferences or give up the mix of vague and precise terms that generates the puzzle.

It would be fair enough to discard a practical puzzle that *depended on* the empirically false conclusions of a sorites argument. But the self-torturer's problem doesn't depend on any such conclusion. What naturally matters to him is that the comfort status of s and $s + 1$ are, introspectively and behaviorally, no different – either in direct comparison to each other or in oblique comparison with any third setting. It is enough for him that the empirical data give him *no* reason to suppose that his comfort declines, either directly or relative to some fixed point, in any single step. His predicament in

6 Sharply enough to make it questionable whether an initial plan to stop at s was really worth $10,000 more than a plan to stop at $s-1$!

no way depends on his supposing something that he can see to be empirically false or dubious.

And to say that the self-torturer should give up thinking in the vague terms that give rise to the sorites puzzle (terms such as "more painful than," "no less comfortable than," etc.) is to say that he should give up thinking about his real predicament. Whether something will or will not be less comfortable than something else is precisely what matters to him. It might be barely plausible to recommend that he purge such terms from his scientific psychology. But it seems bizarre to advise him to remove them from his practical deliberations.

II

The self-torturer's situation seems to defy conventional solutions. Let's look at a couple. It has been suggested that he can solve his problem in something of the style of a utility maximizer. Since "just as comfortable" is intransitive, he cannot infer from the fact that 1 is just as comfortable as 0 and that 2 is just as comfortable as 1, that 2 will be just as comfortable as 0. So he cannot infer that his comfort won't decline in the overall move from 0 to 2. To make things simple, we may imagine an ultra-conservative self-torturer who is always eager to collect $10,000 so long as he remains *just as comfortable* as he was at 0, but regards $10,000 as too little to justify *any* increase of discomfort relative to 0 (i.e., any entry into the discomfort zone). This gives him a reason to move from 0 to 1. But the next move is a different matter. Then he must reckon with the probability that in moving one more step he may in fact begin to experience a decline relative to 0. And as he continues to advance, that probability must rise, until it cancels the expected advantage of the next payment. At that point a rational self-torturer would stop, well short of any disaster.

Of course, there is no solution here for a less conservative self-torturer who feels, as most of us might, that a minimal decline relative to 0 would be worth $10,000. But it is far from clear that even the ultra-conservative self-torturer's problem is solved. The alleged solution asserts that there is some chance that in taking a further step (e.g., from 1 to 2, or from 2 to 3), he will suddenly feel slightly worse than he did at 0; and this seems to presuppose that, for all we know, there is a step at which this actually happens. In the case we are imagining, however, there is simply no evidence of any such change. This is implicit in the failure of triangulation. The increments of current have been made so small that not only is there absolutely no indication of a subjective change from s to $s+1$, there is absolutely no indication that any third point p has a different subjective relation to s than to $s+1$.[7]

To press the alleged solution in the face of this is to suppose that there can be subjective contrasts that the self-torturer, and those observing him, cannot identify. But if this is true, the "solution" is needlessly subtle. Why suppose that the self-torturer's ability to identify these contrasts breaks down only when he tries to triangulate? Why not say that it already breaks down in his direct comparisons of adjacent settings? Indeed, why not say that he immediately feels worse whenever there is *any* undetectable increase in current, no matter how small? But this line of thought threatens to undermine the distinction between the physically objective and the experientially subjective. For given the possibility of an undetectable subjective contrast, that distinction would surely presuppose exactly what we seem to lack: a principled way of distinguishing stimuli differences that are too slight to be felt at all from those just strong enough to be felt undetectably.

Another possible risk-based solution might seem to sidestep this problem. When deciding whether to advance a step, any self-torturer must take into account not just the danger of encountering unacceptable discomfort at the next setting, but also the danger that, if he takes the step, he will *eventually* find himself (as a result of further moves) in some unacceptable discomfort. At some point short of disaster, this latter danger may be too great to justify taking even one more step.

The trouble with this solution is that it cannot work for a self-torturer who assumes that he will always act rationally. If such an agent supposes that the risk of eventually finding himself in unacceptable discomfort is too great to warrant taking the next step, it must be because he thinks it will be rational for him to go on

7 Nor are they able to find subjective differences in more complex contexts that vary only by the substitution of $s+1$ for s. And this is not because the self-torturer or his observers are rushed or distracted. There is no reason not to allow the self-torturer and his observers to make their comparisons and observations with all due care and concentration.

taking enough more steps to get himself into trouble.[8] But this means the next step is irrational only if *no subsequent step* that would occur before he found himself in unacceptable discomfort is irrational in the same way. For if some such future step would be irrational, he could foresee that he wouldn't take it and hence wouldn't be risking trouble by taking the next step. So there is a good objection to the next step (from s to $s+1$) only if there won't be a good objection to, say, the step after that (from $s+1$ to $s+2$). But how could this be, given that both steps are intrinsically innocuous and that stopping at $s+1$ is just as sure to prevent disaster as stopping at s.

Perhaps risk-based solutions won't work. But if so, what is to prevent the self-torturer from adopting an even simpler solution? Why not pick a reasonable looking stopping point, proceed to it, and then *really stop?* If he could execute such a strategy, he could enjoy his material gains at a cost in discomfort that would seem to him well worth it. The trouble is that, even if we waive the theoretical difficulty of determining such a stopping point, he would be tempted to formulate a *new* forward-looking strategy once he reached it. And it is far from clear how conventional accounts of rational choice could oppose this temptation. For they see as irrelevant everything about a present choice except the way it serves the agent's preferences for outcomes. They are therefore ready to dismiss any past strategy that now requires him to forgo something that he would in fact prefer to get, all things considered. Strategies continue to have authority only if they continue to offer him what he prefers overall. Otherwise, they should be changed. We might call this natural idea the *Principle of Strategic Readjustment.*

This principle is compatible with all familiar desiderata of rational choice. It in no way speaks against long-term planning or temporally extended policies.[9] Policies need to be monitored to see

---

8 Or if he sets mixed strategies for advancing, he thinks it will be rational for him to adopt mixed strategies for future decisions whose combined effect will be an unacceptably high chance that he will get into trouble.

9 And it is in no way incompatible with the familiar idea that an overall policy or plan (in which there must be a succession of choices) is best regarded as a *single* decision. See, for example, Leonard J. Savage, *The Foundations of Statistics,* John Wiley and Sons, New York, 1954, pp. 15–16. Savage's "look before you leap" advice is, as I understand it, directed not at all to the special kind of case we are considering here but to the altogether familiar situation in which long-term

whether they are still serving our preferences. And when they are not, they need to be adjusted. But it is precisely this familiar and seemingly innocuous idea of strategic readjustment that leads to trouble in the kind of case we are considering.

III

How then should the self-torturer proceed? There are, I think, two different kinds of cases. To distinguish them we need a new notion. Suppose that instead of moving one step at a time (which is, in fact, his only way of advancing), the self-torturer could move from 0 to 1000 in roughly equal-sized hops. At each landing point he would collect all the money attaching to the settings he had traversed. Call the sequence of positions he would occupy in such hops *a filtered series* of the original 1001 positions. Over some of these series the self-torturer's preferences would be transitive. In one kind of self-torturer case, some of these transitive series would have a position better than 0. Let's consider such a case first.

The self-torturer must begin by setting an initial strategy. This will consist in selecting a *reasonable* stopping point – a final goal. But this is not an easy task. For if s looks like a reasonable goal, won't $s + 1$ look better? And won't he then be on the slippery slope? Yes, but since he can see this, he can see that this is no way to select a reasonable goal. Instead, he might imaginatively restructure his problem. He could look for some orderly way of constructing a set of increasingly refined filtered series (each new series in the set containing more positions than the preceding one) such that one of them is identifiable as the most refined series in the set that clearly preserves transitivity of preference *and* contains a position better than 0. One natural way to try to do this would be to divide the overall range into two steps as nearly equal in size as possible (giving in our case the filtered series 0, 500, 1000), then into four smaller such steps (0, 250, 500, 750, and 1000), then into eight, and so forth.[10] If the most refined transitive series containing a member

planning is required by the fact that the utility of a present option depends on the utility of the future options it makes possible.

10 When the steps have to be slightly unequal, there will be alternative subdivisions that are equally eligible. For example, in the series with sixteen steps, the first step could be either to 62 or 63. In such cases, it won't matter which series is chosen. Intuitively, there are many positions that represent acceptable compromises between wealth and comfort.

better than 0 contains only one such member, that should be his goal. If the series contains more than one best member, then either would be an equally reasonable goal. Suppose, for example, that the most refined such series was (0, 250, 500, 1000). If 250 is best, it should be his goal. If 250 and 500 are tied for best, then either (or perhaps any setting in between) will serve.[11]

Of course, this is only a sketch of a possible solution for setting a reasonable goal. But suppose we press ahead to a second problem. Suppose he has chosen a reasonable goal by this procedure, and has finally reached it. How can he now rationalize adhering to his original strategy? As we have seen, the idea of adopting a new strategy of continuing, say, only one more step has this in its favor: it will take him to a setting he prefers, all things considered, to the setting he is at.

But of course he could foresee all this when he chose his original goal. And it is not that he now sees something wrong with that choice. It was, let us suppose, as good as any he could have made. Intuitively, his recognition of these facts should keep him from abandoning his original strategy. He should be stopped by the principle that a reasonable strategy that correctly anticipated all later facts (including facts about preferences) still binds. On such a theory of rationality some contexts of choice fall under the authority of past decisions. In these contexts, the Principle of Strategic Readjustment is suspended. *An agent is not rationally permitted to change course even if doing so would better serve his preferences.*

The other kind of self-torturer case offers a more radical challenge at the very outset. Since in these cases there is *no* transitive filtered series with a member better than 0, the procedure cannot be used to set a goal. But if the self-torturer simply picks some setting that

11 Will there always be a clearly identifiable most refined series that preserves transitivity? That seems to be an empirical question. The intransitivity in these cases results, as we have seen, from the original steps being so small. As we increase the size of the steps (by progressively coarser filters on the original problem) we eventually reach steps that are clearly big enough for the discomfort to be registered and to be taken account of. In such series preferences will be transitive. In between, there is an (indeterminately limited) range of step sizes for which the self-torturer's preferences are neither determinately transitive nor intransitive. Call this the cross-over range. If one or more of the filtered series have steps whose sizes fall within the cross-over range, then it may be indeterminate which progressively more refined series is the last to preserve transitivity of preference. In such a case, the self-torturer will simply have to pick some clearly transitive filtered series as refined enough for his purposes.

he prefers to 0 as a reasonable goal, e.g., 1, he will find himself in trouble. For when he reaches 1, his preferences will importune him to change strategy and pick a *new* goal, e.g., 2. And so on.

It therefore seems that there is no way for him to take advantage of the opportunities that confront him at the start. If he could proceed, for example, to 1 and then stop, he would get a $10,000 cost-free gift. Surely a plausible theory of rationality would give him a way of seizing that or some even more attractive prize. But, again, it could do this only by setting aside the Principle of Strategic Readjustment – by giving his choice of a reasonable strategy that makes no mistakes about later developments binding authority over later choices. The self-torturer's predicament thus reveals a quasi-deontological aspect to a fully adequate theory of rational choice. It is this aspect that provides the theoretical "brake."

IV

Such a conception may remind one of David Gauthier's idea that it can be rational for an agent to honor a past agreement (in which the other party has performed his part) even though it would be disadvantageous for him overall to do so.[12] Gauthier has cases in mind that, simplifying somewhat, satisfy two conditions: First, the agent benefited more from securing the agreement than he would now lose by honoring it. And second, since he was unable to deceive the other party, he secured the agreement only by having the sincere intention to honor it. Since it is doubtful that rational agents can intend to do what they think it will in fact be irrational to do, either they cannot enter into such advantageous agreements or they are fully rational in honoring them. Gauthier is loathe to think that reason might stand in the way of these important advantages and therefore chooses the second alternative.

But perhaps it is not intolerable to suppose that rationality might get in the way of someone burdened with certain *inabilities* to maximize advantage. Gauthier's type of agent is unable to hide his true character. If he were a better actor, he could secure advantageous

---

12 *Morals by Agreement,* Clarendon Press, Oxford, 1986. See Chapter 6, pp. 157–189. The case we are considering is one in which noncompliance will have no bad further effects on the agent's ability to reach agreements. The obligation might, for example, have been assumed in secret and the promisee might now be dead.

agreements by seeming to be transparently faithful while actually being opaquely faithless. So perhaps we should simply say that his inability to dissemble combines with his rationality to create a problem for him. That is unfortunate (from his point of view), but his misfortune might seem a doubtful reason to qualify the theory of rationality.[13]

The problems of the self-torturer are different. No inability stands in his way. It isn't that he lacks the willpower to stop at some reasonable initial goal. It is that a certain specious ideal of rational choice drives him onward – by advising him always to bring about some preferred outcome. It is the Principle of Strategic Readjustment itself that prevents him from getting and keeping the real advantages that his situation offers him. The self-torturer's predicament therefore invites, not a compromise theoretical accommodation to a standard human limitation, but a real revision of the theory of what it is for the best-positioned kind of agent to act rationally. His problem warns us that it would be a bad mistake for even the most advantageously endowed to see every moment as a possible new beginning in their practical lives.

---

13 Of course I am thinking of rationality (as I have been throughout) as *instrumental* – as something that is and ought to be the slave of the agent's preferences. On a more comprehensive *moral* picture of rationality, the disposition to comply with a fair agreement would no doubt count as a virtue and therefore something desirable to possess and, derivatively, to act upon. This is the kind of moral solution to Gauthier's problem I favor. But note that there is no moral question raised by the case of the self-torturer.

11

Rationality and the human good

In this essay I want to look at some questions concerning the relation between morality and rationality in the recommendations they make about the best way to live our lives and achieve our good. Specifically, I want to examine ways in which the virtue of practical rationality (conceived in neo-Humean terms as the most authoritative practical excellence) and the various moral virtues might be thought to part company, giving an agent conflicting directives regarding how best to live her life. In conducting this enquiry, I shall at some crucial points be presupposing something of an Aristotelian perspective, but only in the most general way.[1]

I

In what follows, I shall distinguish *reason*, the faculty or power, from *rationality*, the excellence or virtue (taken in the broadest sense) of that faculty. By *practical reason* I mean that part of reason that tells us what to do and how to live. By *practical rationality* (or, henceforth, *rationality*) I mean the excellence of that part of reason in virtue of which an agent is practically rational as opposed to irrational. By a *neo-Humean* conception of rationality I mean one that makes the goal of practical reason the maximal satisfaction of an agent's desires and preferences, suitably corrected for the effects of misinformation, wishful thinking, and the like. There are various versions of neo-Humean theory, and I shall not here be concerned

From *Social Philosophy and Policy* 9:2 (Summer 1992) 81–95. Reprinted by permission of the publisher and author.
1 I will also be indebted to Philippa Foot's recent unpublished development of that perspective in *The Princeton Lectures* ("Human Desires," "Miklukho-Maklay and His Servant," and a third, untitled lecture), and also in her later "Virtue and Happiness," and "Happiness II."

with their specific differences. Their common essence lies in an appeal (1) to a notion of *basic* desires or preferences, which are not subject to intrinsic criticism as irrational and are subject to extrinsic criticism only by ways in which their joint satisfaction may not be possible, and (2) to a notion of *derived* desires or preferences, which are criticizable only instrumentally. The kind of neo-Humean theory I want to consider allows that basic or derived desires and preferences may be intrinsically criticized as *immoral*. But it does not regard that assessment as automatically relevant to the question of whether it is rational to act on them or aim at their objects.

Questions of human rationality are conceptually connected in complex ways to questions about human good. Hume himself seemed to be something of a hedonist about both our motivations and our good. But most modern-day Humeans would disagree, casting their net more broadly to include desired items other than pleasure and the avoidance of pain. It would be possible to adopt a neo-Humean view on which the distinctive aim of rationality, the maximization of an agent's desires and preferences, just is his good, however little he desires things that bring him joy and fulfillment or however little he prefers things that make his life richer, more interesting, and so forth. But it might be more plausible to look for some subset of these desires and preferences that are *self-regarding* in the ways just suggested and to see his good as constructed out of the maximization of these. It would, of course, be no easy task to come up with a suitable sense of the self-regarding, and indeed it might prove impossible. But it might be within the spirit of contemporary Humeanism to try, and in what follows I shall suppose that we have both a neo-Humean conception of rationality and a companion, similarly spirited, neo-Humean conception of an agent's good, with the latter sharing the moral indifference of the former. While basic items that an agent wants *for himself* will be subject to various kinds of serious moral criticism, they will not thereby be excluded from contributing to the intrinsic goodness of his life. Neo-Humean theories of rationality and the good, thus conceived, are not only conceptually linked, they also reinforce each other. In particular, the conception of rationality can be seen as supporting the conception of the good. A possible end, considered in the abstract, is part of my good only because rationality gives it to me as one of my goals; and an end would, in these particular circumstances, be part of the best life available to me only because it could, in these circumstances, be rational for me to pursue it. This means that if the moral indifference of the neo-Humean conception of rationality undermined its credentials as a theory of rational choice, it would also tend to undermine the corresponding neo-Humean conception of the good.[2] Part of my argument will take this route: I will begin by trying to show how hard it is for neo-Humean rationality to maintain its attitude of moral indifference to our choices and ends and still be all the things we want rationality to be.

I spoke earlier of rationality as authoritative. By the *authority* of one excellence over another I mean the ability of the former to prevail over the latter in determining what the agent should, in some unqualified and unrelativized sense, do. Suppose, along with Thrasymachus, that injustice is a form of rationality (if we may thus translate "*sophia*") which can oppose justice in directing an agent toward his good.[3] The question then arises as to which, if either, takes precedence. Thrasymachus thought that *sophia*, the more genuine *arete* (excellence), should trump justice, the mere "noble simplicity and goodness of heart."[4] But it would be possible for someone to counter with the observation that, given Thrasymachus's unpalatable assumptions about rationality, the preference should go the other way. Perhaps on those assumptions, or those of the neo-Humean, we should even wonder whether rationality might not be a minor virtue, or no virtue at all, that is, whether its preoccupation with calculation and maximization might not put the most important human goods out of reach.

What blocks this line of thought is the idea, implicit in almost all philosophical accounts of reason (including neo-Humean ones), that there not only *is* such a thing as practical rationality but that it is very important – indeed, so important that it deserves center stage in normative treatments of action and choice.[5] When David

2 Although the latter could perhaps be defended on other grounds.
3 Plato, *Republic*, 348C–349A.
4 Ibid., 348D.
5 Hume is the maverick here, denying that there is any such thing as practical reason or rationality – any way in which actions or desires can, "except in a figurative and improper way of speaking," be reasonable or unreasonable and, therefore, any way in which reason can pronounce them to be so. See David Hume, *A Treatise of Human Nature*, ed. L. A. Selby-Bigge (Oxford: Clarendon Press, 1888), p. 459. The neo-Humeans I have in mind do *not* follow Hume in this radical conclusion, supposing instead (and rightly, I think) that there is a proper and

212

Gauthier, Richard Jeffrey, Leonard J. Savage, and other (partial or complete) neo-Humean instrumentalists write about rationality of preference and choice, we do not take them to be writing about what they consider a minor virtue, like neatness.[6] We take them to be making their own modern, metaphysically minimalist, and elegantly mathematicized contributions to the grand philosophical tradition in which some form of rationality ("*sophia*") is the authoritative perfection of man *qua* agent. The neo-Humean simply takes the perfection to be coherentist and instrumentalist in character. Thus, on all familiar accounts, the pronouncements of perfected practical reason are seen, in one way or another, as having normative authority; and rationality, as that perfection, is seen as *the* excellence of human beings *qua* agents. As already indicated, I shall rely on this assumption in arguing that there is something in the moral indifference of neo-Humean rationality that keeps it from shining forth in this role.

Another of my major assumptions concerns morality. I shall assume that judgments about what is good and bad, or more precisely, judgments about what is shameful, contemptible, petty, unworthy, and so forth can sometimes be objectively true.[7] The conflict I am interested in examining is not between neo-

important way of speaking of actions, and at least derivative preferences, as reasonable or unreasonable.

6 Different neo-Humeans have different ways of indicating the way in which they take their theories of rationality to be normatively central. The clearest and least technical recent statement of neo-Humean rationality is by David Gauthier in *Morals by Agreement* (Oxford: Clarendon Press, 1986), chap. 2. Gauthier shows the significance he attaches to the theory in his defense of a neo-Humean theory of *value* which, in accordance with his theory of rationality, is subjective, relative, and dependent on preferences that can be criticized only in respect of their mathematical coherence and the extent to which they are well informed. It must be noted that Gauthier is not a complete neo-Humean, since he argues (in chap. 6) that in situations involving the keeping of agreements, instrumental rationality may be constrained. In *The Foundations of Statistics* (New York: John Wiley & Sons, 1954), Leonard J. Savage, after putting "rational" in quotes, as if it were too hot to handle, immediately explains that the suggested criteria and maxims of rationality will have to be judged by the reader according to whether the latter would *try* to behave in accordance with them. Richard Jeffrey, in *The Logic of Decision*, 2d ed. (Chicago: University of Chicago Press, 1983), presents his theory of rational choice as a theory about *desirabilities* of choice. And what could be more important than the most desirable choice?

7 That is, I assume that someone who denies a judgment of this sort could simply be mistaken, in the way that someone who denied that Hume was intelligent would simply be mistaken.

Humeanism and morality conceived as a mere projection of feelings and attitudes. I am interested, instead, in the more resounding clash between neo-Humeanism and morality conceived as a system of evaluative truths about our actions and lives. That is, I am assuming that sometimes we are ashamed *because* we correctly see that we have done something shameful, and that sometimes we have contempt for someone *because* we see that he has acted contemptibly.

II

Neo-Humean rationality and morality can seem irreconcilable in a variety of situations that raise different problems and demand different solutions. In one kind of case, discussed by Philippa Foot in her recent work, someone takes great pleasure, and may even (in some sense) find great "fulfillment," in some intrinsically evil end such as killing innocent people in the name of "purifying mankind."[8] Other, less ideological examples come to mind: the intense pleasures of arsonists and rapists, for example, or the pleasure some may find in the very act of taking dishonest "shortcuts."[9]

These objects of desire cause trouble because, as we have seen, a neo-Humean rationality, in its indifference to the moral, tolerates, or even recommends, aiming at them. (Remember Hume's claim that "'tis not contrary to reason to prefer the destruction of the whole world to the scratching of my finger.")[10] And while an agent who does aim at them may face dangers from neighbors or police, he may also find that the expected satisfaction to be gained from braving the dangers outweighs the risks.

Suppose, for example, that someone enjoys, and therefore basically desires, forms of quite *nasty* interaction with his fellow human beings (for instance, spreading lies that put his "friends" at odds with each other). Let us also suppose that he has good reason to think that he can safely have this pleasure – that his nasty machinations will not be finally exposed, as in a Molière farce. What are

---

8 Foot's example in "Virtue and Happiness" is Gustav Wagner, a Nazi deputy commander of one of Hitler's death camps. According to Foot (p. 2), Wagner "said when he was finally apprehended at the age of 68, that whatever happened next he would not be 'the real loser'." He is reported to have added: "I thoroughly enjoyed Brazil, and I didn't think about the past."

9 Naturally, I am assuming in all these cases that the pleasures are objects of basic desire and preference.

10 Hume, *Treatise of Human Nature*, Book II, part III, section III, p. 416.

we to say of rationality if it gives him a green light, recommending the activity as a fit object of pursuit?

Before answering this question it is important to step back and raise another. What *kind* of thing is the excellence of practical rationality, whether we adopt a moralized or amoralized version of it? I think it is first and foremost a quality of character, taken in a broad but recognizable sense (as in: "What was the character of the woman ... what was she like?" "She was an aesthete," or "She was devoted to religion," or "She was a meticulous planner of her career," or "She was a coward," and so forth). Rationality, no less than aestheticism or bravery, is a quality whose actualization gives shape to the personal character of our choices and lives. The prudent woman is a woman of a certain character, no less than her opposite, the reckless woman. So, too, is the man who conceives his good as the maximal satisfaction of his self-regarding desires even though they are nasty. He is a man whose ideas and choices have a certain spin, quite different from that of others, even if the spin is sanctioned by the supreme practical virtue.

If it is right to treat rationality as a quality of character, then what can we say of the character of this man's rationality? The moralist might be tempted to conclude straight away that such a rationality is nasty. But this inference would be too swift. For the agent must have many other desires for himself, including desires for things that he likes, that are in perfect moral order – desires that his rationality also counsels him to maximally satisfy. Moreover, it is not the nastiness of what he wants for himself that makes his rationality speak in its behalf. It is simply that his rationality is *indifferent* to the nastiness.

But what can we say of this indifference, which seems so essential to the rational life constructed on neo-Humean lines? Suppose the end in question were a perverted one. Would not a quality that was indifferent to that fact show the same fault? I am inclined to think so. And something similar seems to follow in the case of the nasty, odious, offensive, disgusting, etc. Personification may be a helpful exercise here. Suppose you aim at something nasty, and I, seeing that you do, advise you to go ahead. Surely my indifference to the nastiness of your goal implicates me in that nastiness – makes me, to that extent, a nasty person. I cannot see why the same should not be true of the qualities of our own character that advise and direct us. To the extent that such qualities do not turn us away from the negative moral features of our ends, they are subject to the corresponding negative charges. A rationality that is indifferent to the nastiness of our pleasures is to that extent a nasty form of rationality.

We can conclude from this, I think, that neo-Humean rationality, in its indifference to the shameful character of our ends, is shameless. Its shameless side will not, of course, be manifest in someone without shameful desires, but it will be latent. This latency must now be placed against the idea that neo-Humean rationality can be the most perfect expression of our practical reason – the *summa virtus* of our practical selves.

III

Of course, I have been presupposing in all this that the neo-Humean agent *sees* as nasty, and hence shameful, the proposed pleasures and activities that he basically desires. But what if, as is often true, he does not? Does practical reason then fail to be implicated in the opprobrium attaching to the activities? I do not think it is thereby off the hook. Indifference to what is in fact clearly nasty, but is not recognized to be so, seems just as nasty.[11] If practical rationality is authoritative, it must be sensitive to all knowable aspects of its agent's ends, which if known, would bear on its status as a real virtue. It must, therefore, be sensitive on pain of a negative moral charge to the various modes in which its ends might be shameful.

Suppose, seeing that you delight in spreading lies that put people at odds with each other, I advise you, without noticing the nastiness of that desire, to go ahead and spread the lies. This makes me, I would have thought, a pretty nasty person. For my very ignorance of the moral fact is, as Aristotle would have pointed out, culpable.[12] Similarly, a practical reason, cast in its essential role as our internal advisor, that was ignorant of the nastiness of our ends would be, to that extent, nasty. Moral ignorance does not, therefore, seem to provide an escape from the *modus tollens* argument that I am trying to construct.

11 Of course, I am thinking of sane adults here.
12 Aristotle, *Nicomachean Ethics*, 1110b27–32.

216

But now we must face a new problem. There is no getting around the nastiness of an intrinsically nasty end. But what about situations in which morality blocks a choice not because the end is bad considered in itself but because the morally unobjectionable end can be obtained only by a shameful means? Here there is something that morality and neo-Humean rationality must agree upon as good to be put in the balance against the immoral choice needed to bring it about. The desire, for example, is not for sadistic pleasure, but for a lovely fling. The trouble is that having such a fling would mean cheating on someone who deserves better.

One strategy for dealing with these cases is to argue – although it would take some sophisticated and speculative psychologizing to do so – that the willingness to gain the good by the wrongful means makes it impossible to get what is *really* wanted in the end. Foot has suggested in unpublished material that a deeply dedicated Nazi cannot really have, in his personal life, what he seems to want, for example, the love of family and friends.[13] There is a great deal of plausibility in this. How could I really cherish a friend, or love my children, if I would wish them dead were I to come to believe them Jewish, or Gypsy, or gay?

It is perhaps surprising how far this strategy can be extended. The point underlying it is that many of the good things that we want essentially (if obscurely) involve friendly or respectful relations to human beings as such. The love of art, it might be argued, is the love of something whose essential function is to widen and deepen our appreciation of the feelings that bind us together as human. To sacrifice others in the name of art may therefore be to reveal in oneself an incapacity to appreciate those feelings and, therefore, to get the good that lies concealed at the center of art. Similarly, the love of fame, a powerful motive in human affairs, is something one could reasonably make a central aim only on condition of having some considerable respect for those in whose eyes one hopes to seem important. Thus, a contemptuous readiness to step on others in the pursuit of fame might seem to put the true object out of reach.

13 Foot, "Virtue and Happiness" and "Happiness II."

How far this line could be pushed is unclear to me. It is certainly a very important part of the proper response to the idea that rationality might recommend immoral means, but I am inclined to think that it cannot be the whole story. Perhaps what I want is scientific knowledge of something important – say, the basic physical structure of the universe. What I need is money for instruction and research. I can get the money only by cheating or stealing – or by violating some fair principles of distribution for educational funding. It might be possible to argue that the proper object of scientific research is the intellectual and material betterment of mankind, and thus that someone with little regard for the rights of others cannot enter into the proper spirit of the scientific enterprise. But even if this is partly true, there is surely an important solipsistic residue to the love of knowledge – a simple desire to understand, for oneself alone, how things are. It seems hard to deny that someone might strongly desire such knowledge even though it could, in the circumstances, be gotten only by shameful means.

V

A neo-Humean who agrees with me that there is a conceptual tension in the very idea that our first excellence as agents might be shameless could perhaps make the following argument: There are certainly some, and perhaps many, situations in which one basically desires a morally acceptable end that can be obtained only by shameful means. In such cases, the shamefulness of the action must, if it is given negative weight, be balanced against the strength of the desire for the end. If that desire is strong enough, then rationality may declare the end to be *worth* the cost of the shameful action and so recommend its pursuit. It could be argued that in so recommending, rationality would not be subject to the charge of shamelessness that it sustained in the case where it was indifferent to shameless ends.

Such an argument might be modeled on other familiar cases in which negative features of action do not rub off on an agent or his qualities. Someone might have to make an *aesthetically awkward* reach for some badly needed medicine perched high up on a shelf. It would be ludicrous to conclude that her decision to reach for it showed any aesthetic fault. It would be equally absurd to conclude that she showed any *trait* of physical awkwardness in making the movement. Here we see that the person and her aesthetic qualities are insulated from the aesthetically negative character of her physical movement. In another case, poised between the aesthetic and the moral, one might have to destroy something good – for example, a finely wrought door – to escape from a fire. The act, considered narrowly, is destructive. But because the escape is *worth* the damage, one does not show oneself in making it to be in any degree an aesthetic or moral barbarian.

It might seem that the situation with morality is like these. Something immoral must be done to get something that reason says to be nevertheless worth it. Because it is worth it, the agent shows no shamelessness in going ahead. Thus, there need be nothing shameless in his rationality insofar as it gives him this advice.

But surely there is something wrong in assimilating this case to the others. If a generally shameful action remains so *in the situation*, it is because the good at which the action aims cannot cancel or outweigh the negative moral charge. I do not mean to be considering cases in which an act that is generally shameful (for example, stealing) is not shameful here and now because it is done for such and such an obligatory end (for example, to feed one's family). These cases do not present a conflict between neo–Humean rationality and the moral virtues. I mean to be speaking instead about readily recognizable cases in which it remains shameful to do something even though such and such desired good will come of it (for example, the case of falsifying experimental results in order to get more funding for one's otherwise legitimate and important research).

The difference between the shameful act and the aesthetically awkward or physically destructive act is that the shamefulness, unlike the awkwardness or destructiveness, is already something internal to the agent. One expresses a shameless side to one's character in performing a shameful act, and, similarly, a shameless side in recommending one. This is how the concept of the shameful works. Even if reason judged an end to be *worth* a shameful act, then, reason would show itself as shameless in recommending the act. The concepts of the aesthetically awkward and the physically destructive are quite different. One need not express an awkward or destructive side to one's character in performing an awkward or physically destructive act. It would first need to be established that the act was incompatible with the relevant virtue (for example, of physical grace, or of a due regard for aesthetically valuable property). In the cases we considered, there was no such incompatibility.

In the case of the shameful choice, however, nothing insulates the shamefulness of the action from the shamelessness of the agent in doing it or – and this is the important point – the shamelessness of his reason in recommending it. The same holds true, I believe, of all moral qualities that specify the shameful. A rationality that would recommend a nasty choice is to that extent a nasty quality; a rationality that would recommend a cowardly choice is therefore a cowardly quality; and so on. This ought to give a neo-Humean pause. For whatever else we may be prepared to say of human reason at its most excellent, it seems that we must shrink from saying that it could be nasty or cowardly.

VI

Before proceeding with some of the implications of this argument, I would like to consider two objections. First, one might reply that there is no single, supremely authoritative virtue of reason: There is moral rationality (the moral perfection of reason), preference-governed rationality (the instrumentalist perfection of reason), prudential rationality (the prudential perfection of reason), and possibly other forms. The most my argument shows is that moral rationality could not be shameless. It leaves open the possibility that other forms of rationality might be.

Part of my reply to this is *ad hominem*. Such an objection will not appeal to a neo-Humean, who wants to co-opt rationality for his own instrumentalist view. Nor, to my knowledge, has it had much appeal in other theoretical quarters. Some philosophers (for example, Plato, Aristotle, and Kant) think that rationality is essentially moral in its incapacity to deliver any immoral advice. Others (for example, such neo-Humeans as Frank Plumpton Ramsey) think that rationality is essentially amoral in its exclusive attachment to the agent's mathematically coherent preference orderings.[14] But while many wonder what perfected reason would in the end demand when morality and advantage seem to conflict, few would suppose that there are two or more rationalities in the sense of two

14 Frank Plumpton Ramsey, "Truth and Probability," in *The Foundations of Mathematics* (London: Routledge & Kegan Paul, 1931), p. 174.

or more equally authoritative and supreme excellences of practical reason that can give conflicting advice.

The other objection is this: One may say that in the situations I am imagining the conflicts are merely between the rational and the *morally* shameless. It should not bother us that rationality is wanting when assessed from some external viewpoint. What matters is whether rationality is all right in its own terms – whether it is stupid, unimaginative, uninformed, etc. In the cases we have been considering, it was not accused of any of these faults.

I have two replies. First, we must reject any suggestion that there is some specific, moral use of terms such as "shameful" to be contrasted with other uses. It might seem at first that something might be intellectually or aesthetically shameful without being morally so, and that defenders of neo-Humean rationality need only be worried about cases in which rationality would be cognitively shameful. But on closer examination we will find that all uses of the range of terms I have in mind are moral. Something can be called intellectually shameful only when it is the product of something like laziness or fraud. Simple failures of intelligence, for example, are not shameful.

Second, and more important, accusations of shamelessness or its specific varieties do not get their force because morality is assigned some antecedent importance. On the contrary, morality commands our attention precisely because these accusations are so gripping. They constitute rather than draw upon the force of morality. This gives them their clout in the present argument. No neo-Humean who wants to preserve the supremely authoritative status of rationality as our chief excellence as agents should be entirely undisturbed if his rationality turns out in whole or part to be a proper object of shame. Therefore, no neo-Humean can draw upon such a rationality to support the claim that an agent's good might sometimes consist in taking shameful means to otherwise acceptable ends.

VII

It might be asked at this point why I have not conducted the argument in terms of the wrongful or unjust, rather than the shameful. I might have argued in the following way: Suppose some intrinsically good end can be reached only by performing an act that is, even considering the end, morally wrong. Could rationality as the supreme virtue recommend such a choice and still retain its luster? It might seem that it could do so *if* we place emphasis on the fact that the act is *morally* wrong. For "wrong" has other, perhaps more pertinent, uses. An answer can be wrong without being immoral (whatever that would mean), and even a practical choice can be wrong aesthetically, or from the point of view of etiquette, without being morally wrong.

The proper understanding of these various uses of "wrong" is, of course, very complicated. As I see it, "X-ly wrong" has at least three different senses. On the reading just suggested, there is *no* absolute sense of "wrong." Different senses are created by the various points of view which we may, without being right or wrong in any more basic sense, adopt or reject in evaluating things. "Wrong from the X point of view" is often used in modern moral philosophy to express this deeply relativistic conception.

Against this, we may see "wrong" as having an absolute sense such that different factors may weigh for and against the ultimate wrongness of a choice. Some of these factors may be moral, but others may not. Something might have nothing against it morally speaking but be a bad tactic in bringing something about, for example, getting an appointment approved by the dean. Or, again, it might be wrong to dress in a certain way for the opera, but, unless one were trying to give offense, not morally wrong. On this reading, the various considerations feed together to determine the basic character of the choice as right or wrong in the circumstances. Many who accept such a core sense will suppose that moral factors typically override, for example, tactical or sartorial factors (but perhaps not when the moral considerations are very weak and the others very strong).

"Morally wrong," in this sense, might have two sub-readings. First, it might mean "wrong, considering moral factors alone," which would allow something to be morally wrong but not wrong overall. Second, it might mean "wrong for moral reasons," a reading on which its moral defects are claimed to be decisive. Thus, everything depends on which use of "morally wrong" we have in mind when we imagine reason knowingly advising in favor of morally wrong actions. If we mean it in the last sense, then the neo-Humean is faced with the paradoxical possibility of perfected practical reason knowingly telling us to make the wrong choice, which seems just as absurdly unacceptable as perfected theoretical reason knowingly telling us to make the wrong inference. The neo-Humean is also faced with the equally paradoxical idea that an agent's life might be better by virtue of her going wrong in the way she lives it.

I have not made the argument in terms of "wrong" because to do so would have required me to argue that morality feeds into (and indeed can dominate) an absolute sense of "wrong" that transcends the moral. While I believe both these things, I could not defend them here. I have conducted the argument in terms of the shameful and its specific varieties, first, because it is so much less plausible to see these terms as relativized to "different points of view," and second, because, unlike "wrong" taken even in an absolute core sense, these terms do not appear to admit of nonmoral grounds. Something shameful cannot, I think, be shown otherwise by reference to nonmoral reasons that point the other way, for example, reasons of tactics or etiquette. This is in large part why it is so difficult to slide out from under a charge of shamefulness.

VIII

The argument of Sections IV and V tried to convict a neo-Humean rationality that is prepared to advocate shameful means to morally unobjectionable ends as to that extent shameless, and therefore unworthy of its status as the supremely authoritative practical virtue. But what if one goes ahead with the shameful deed and is successful, getting the end that one desires for oneself? Has one then gotten something good? Well, by hypothesis, one has gotten what one wanted and judged worth the cost. For we have put to one side the interesting cases in which a readiness to do the shameful act betrays an incapacity to enjoy or profit from the desired end.

But there is a problem that we have not yet touched upon. In choosing means to an end, one is choosing a larger object that includes both: living in such a way as to obtain the end by way of the means. A question must therefore arise about that larger whole. Is it something that someone who accepts the argument so far can see as part of the agent's good?

Someone who accepts the argument shrinks from the idea that rationality might be shameless, and must therefore count the fact that the means in such a case is shameful as showing that it could not be recommended. In that case, the whole comprised of getting the end by that means could not be recommended either, since recommending the means as a way of getting the end and recommending getting the end by way of the means seem to be equivalent. But in the cases we are considering, the attractions of such a whole are for the agent, and therefore would have to belong, if they fitted into the neo-Humean conception of welfare sketched earlier, to the agent's good. Thus, to the extent that we were right in supposing that the neo-Humean identifies something as good only because she thinks that rationality could *recommend* it in the circumstances, she could not see the whole as part of the agent's good.

But could she hold it to be such on other grounds? Let me try, tentatively, to construct an argument that she could not. First let us raise the question of whether the whole is something the agent ought to be *ashamed* of, containing as it does a shameful act. Remember that we have set aside cases in which what would ordinarily be shameful is not in the special moral circumstances. In the cases before us, the general shamefulness of the act is not canceled or outweighed by any morally redeeming feature. Its shamefulness stands.

Is there anything to be ashamed of in these cases other than the action under a description that gives nothing more than its generally shameful feature, for example, that it is lying, stealing, betraying, or the like? It seems to me that there is this in addition: that one is trying to get a certain end by such an action, an end that does not, *ex hypothesi*, cancel its shamefulness. But if an agent should be ashamed of trying to get the end at such a cost, then surely he should also be ashamed, after the fact, of having gotten it at that cost. And having gotten it at the cost is precisely the means–end whole that we are evaluating.

The next step is a variation of my earlier argument. If the interconnected means–end whole is something that the agent ought to be ashamed of, then there must be a problem for someone who accepts my line of argument in seeing it as the best the agent could have brought about for himself. For while most of us would deny that the relevant sense of "best" is straightforwardly moral, it does go with the idea of that which, given our available options, makes our lives most worth living. However much pleasure, love, or friendship a life contained, it would be hard to see it as worth living if the totality of those items in connection with the acts that brought them about did not add up to something worthwhile or meaningful. But these notions import a certain kind of *dignity* that properly belongs to the prudential. The dignity that our lives can achieve as goods for us, no less than the dignity of our perfected faculties, is something serious – something that sets us far above the other animals. Thus, it is uninviting to suppose that something could be part of our good, that is, could dignify our lives by making them more worth living, and yet be something of which we ought to be thoroughly ashamed.[15]

IX

The neo-Humean, who wants to allow for the victory of rationality over morality in the kinds of cases we are considering, might try to disarm my argument by simply accepting the idea that our perfected reasons and lives might, after all, be shameless. Perhaps, in accordance with some Nietzschean conception of the soul, we are at our most vigorous and unfettered, and in closest contact with our deepest and most ineliminable drives, when we are prepared to be shameless in the way we live. Perhaps there is honesty and truth (and even a kind of nobility) in shamelessness, so long as it knows itself.

There are some species of the shameful which might make this

---

15 Some – including most notably James Griffin, who has written with uncommon insight and good sense about human good in *Well-Being: Its Meaning, Measurement, and Moral Importance* (Oxford: Oxford University Press, 1986) – find this line of argument particularly implausible in cases where the shameful deed is done to preserve one's life, which then goes on to contain many prudentially good things (see *ibid.*, chap. 4, esp. p. 69). Perhaps many will agree that a life-segment composed of, say, stealing a car and then enjoying its use cannot, because of its shamefulness, make the life to which it belongs more worth living. Perhaps the same is true of the life of the wrongful usurper, despite its prizes of power and control. It is often possible to restore the worthwhile status of such lives by simply giving up the illicit gain, but this may not be a morally acceptable option where life itself was wrongly purchased. And this may make our thinking about these cases special. For in all cases where we have brought shame upon ourselves, including these, we want there to be some way of restoring our lives (or some particular element of them) as worth having. Where the ill-gotten gain is life itself, most of us think that this restoration can be brought about by a combination of sincere regret (which seems, by the way, compatible with the disturbing thought that we would again succumb to the temptation), good works expressive of that regret, and, finally, the simple passage of time prudentially well spent.

response barely plausible. But let me close by pointing to other species that could scarcely be seen in this light. Consider first the *petty*, taken in the pejorative sense it almost always now has. We are used to thinking of the adoption of certain ends as petty (for example, setting too much store by small honors), but there are also petty means to certain small, but perfectly sensible and therefore in no way pejoratively petty, ends. Everyone needs pencils and stamps, but it would be petty to save oneself inconvenience and expense by stealing them from the office. Suppose, however, one could easily conceal the theft and enjoy its benefits. If rationality would therefore recommend the pilferage it would, in accordance with our earlier assumptions, show itself to be a petty excellence. If our life would thereby be more worth living, its betterness would be a petty perfection.

The tension is even clearer in the case of the contemptible. Suppose the only way in the circumstances to achieve the support of influential people is to join in their cruel criticisms of a good friend. To go ahead with this kind of opportunistic infidelity would be contemptible in the extreme. To recommend it to others as an acceptable strategy of personal advancement would be just as bad. Thus, again, rationality would, in giving it the nod, be exerting a contemptible influence on the will. Similarly, the worthwhileness of the part of the agent's life in which the advancement was achieved by the betrayal of friendship would show itself to be a contemptible worthwhileness. But surely it is doubtful whether either the excellent or the worthwhile *can* be contemptible. The ideas do not seem to cohabit comfortably in the same logical space.

X

There is more than one possible moral to be gathered from this argument. First, of course, there is the moral I prefer: that a neo-Humean conception of rationality and the good should be given up in the face of the objectivity of the moral and a proper respect for human life and practical reason. But other responses are possible. One is to retain the neo-Humean accounts but give up the idea that the powerful moral terms we have been deploying can be used objectively. If some things that we most want as ends or need as means can be shameful, nasty, petty, contemptible, and so forth,

226

then perhaps we should say that the use of such epithets is just so much emotive name-calling.

This might not be Hume's own response. While morality for him is rooted in the passions, it is also considerably objectified: by being universal,[16] by attaching itself to objective distinctions of character and action,[17] and by having the means to correct various biases of private connection.[18] Hume's response would surely be more radical, falling back on his rejection of the idea that there really is such a thing as *practical* reason or rationality − a rejection most sharply epitomized in his famous claim that reason (by which he clearly means theoretical reason in both its a priori and a posteriori forms) "is, and ought only to be, the slave of the passions."[19]

In any case, it is good to see what pressures the argument has placed upon us. If we are, as most of us seem to be, inclined to accept the objectivity of the shameful and the concepts that fall under it, and if we are also inclined to embrace a neo-Humean conception of practical rationality and the good life, then it will be hard for us to retain a certain form of self-respect as it applies to our reasons and lives. I think many of us will want to have it both ways. But perhaps we cannot.

16 Hume, *Treatise of Human Nature*, Book III, part I, section II, p. 474.
17 See, for example, Hume, *An Enquiry Concerning the Principles of Morals*, section IX, in *Hume's Ethical Writings*, ed. Alasdair MacIntyre (London: Collier-Macmillan Ltd.), p. 109.
18 Hume, *Treatise of Human Nature*, Book III, part I, section II, p. 472.
19 Ibid., Book II, part III, sections III, p. 415.

12

Putting rationality in its place

One kind of metaethical debate between realists and antirealists is about the character of ethical truth, with realists asserting and antirealists denying that truth in moral thought transcends our capacity to find reasons in support of our moral judgments. The antirealist in this kind of debate, no less than the realist, thinks that there is objective moral truth and knowledge. And the truth in question is not merely disquotational. Both parties think that a true moral claim corresponds, in some way or other, to the way the world is. Their disagreement, like that of their counterparts in mathematics, is about the nature of this correspondence. The antirealist sees it as a relation between the claim and the publicly available facts that could be adduced as good reasons to accept it, while the realist sees it as a relation to what he thinks of as the truth condition of the claim – a state of the world that may transcend our ability to detect its presence by way of reasoned argument. This issue is surely an important one, but it is posterior to the more fundamental question that has dominated metaethics in the last half-century. This is the question whether what lies at the heart of moral thought are beliefs capable of genuine truth or noncognitive attitudes that cannot be so assessed: feelings, emotions, desires, preferences, prescriptions, decisions, and the like.

Let's use J. L. Mackie's terms "subjectivism" and "objectivism"

Frey and Morris (eds.), *Value, Welfare, and Morality*, pp. 26–50. Copyright 1993. Reprinted by permission of Cambridge University Press. This essay was written during 1987 and delivered in the fall of that year at the University of Washington and the University of Rochester. It was revised in 1988 with the very helpful comments of Tyler Burge, Bob Adams, and Philippa Foot. It was delivered in that form to the conference at Bowling Green State University. It benefited later from elaborate comments by Joseph Raz and interesting criticisms from Chris Morris, Mark Greenberg, and Ruth Chang.

to name the opposing camps in this older debate.[1] In this essay (in Section II) I will argue against a certain common and influential version of subjectivism as it bears on the nature of reasons for action and practical rationality, and then (in Sections III and IV) try to sketch out part of the defense of a vaguely neo-Aristotelian version of objectivism. But first I will try to bring out some important features of the contrasting conceptions.

I

The earlier subjectivists, notably Charles Stevenson and R. M. Hare, argued that the primary function of ethical thought and language is emotive or prescriptive rather than descriptive. Stevenson thought that the job of ethical language is to express moral feeling and so to influence the feelings and behavior of others.[2] Hare thought that a person's morality consists in the universalized principles he decides to try to live by and therefore prescribes to himself and others.[3] These authors were, in short, noncognitivists about ethical judgment. To say or think that an act is good or bad might, in a secondary way, imply certain facts about it, but its goodness or badness could never consist in such facts. Ethical concepts and judgments are on this view quite special. The concepts do not have the function of picking out properties or relations, and the judgments do not have the function of ascribing them. Their job is rather to enable us to express to ourselves or others the noncognitive attitudes mentioned above.

J. L. Mackie himself rejects this noncognitivist version of subjectivism in favor of an "error theory."[4] According to him, our

1 J. L. Mackie, *Ethics: Inventing Right and Wrong* (Harmondsworth, England: Penguin Books, 1977), chap. 1. Mackie's introduction of "objectivism" (p. 15) as the view asserting that (intrinsic or categorical) moral values are "part of the fabric of the world" could at first suggest evaluative realism. And if so, subjectivism, which is introduced as the denial of objectivism, would be compatible with moral antirealism of the truth–admitting kind. But as Mackie gives content to the notions in the following discussion, it turns out that his subjectivism denies that moral evaluations of the relevant kind *can* be true. So the salient contrast turns out, after all, to be over truth.
2 The nub of the theory is clearly presented in Charles Stevenson, "The Emotive Meaning of Ethical Terms," reprinted in *Facts and Values* (New Haven: Yale University Press, 1963), pp. 10–31.
3 R. M. Hare, *The Language of Morals* (Oxford: Clarendon Press, 1952) pp. 69ff.
4 Mackie, *Ethics*, p. 35.

ethical concepts and judgments have the same descriptive function as their empirical counterparts. The trouble is that there are no moral properties or relations answering to the concepts and no moral truths answering to the judgments.[5] For such properties and truths would be unacceptably "queer." They seem real only because we mistakenly project our own attitudes onto the world. But Mackie wishes not simply to do away with morality, but to reconstruct it. And if this reconstruction is to be done along metaphysically respectable lines, it will have to avoid the vulgar projective error. This is what he must have in mind when, speaking of the honest ethics that is "not to be discovered but to be made," he says that "the morality to which someone subscribed would be whatever body of principles he *allowed* ultimately to guide or determine his choice of action."[6] So Mackie's reconstructed morality looks something like Hare's version of noncognitivism.

This is not surprising. The subjectivists I want to consider are not, in Mackie's terms, "first order" moral skeptics.[7] They want to be able to make and "defend" moral claims. So given that the point of *belief* has so much to do with the acquisition of truth, morality – conceived as a set of false beliefs, or beliefs that can be neither true nor false – seems needlessly defective. The natural remedy is to reconceive, or remake it along expressivist lines. So, following this line of thought, I will treat all error theorists who think, like Mackie, that what lies behind and animates each sincere moral belief is a corresponding noncognitive attitude as potential noncognitivists.

But there is another aspect to typical subjectivist thought that is as essential as its noncognitivism. *It is the idea that an agent's moral judgments can and must, despite their noncognitive character, rationalize the moral choices that he makes in accordance with them.*[8] The objectivist agrees, at least when the moral judgments are reasonable. But the agreement is superficial. For we find two very different conceptions

5 Mackie admits that certain claims of instrumental value can be true, but only because those claims are naturalistically reducible (ibid., pp. 50–59). Judgments of instrumental value that presuppose judgments of intrinsic value must be just as badly off as the judgments of intrinsic value they presuppose.
6 Ibid., p. 106. The emphasis of "allowed" is mine.
7 Ibid., p. 16.
8 This use of "rationalize" is an old one that completely lacks the modern psychoanalytical idea of finding false but self-comforting reasons for what one does or feels.

of how the rationalization comes about. The subjectivist of the kind I am imagining adopts a broadly instrumentalist (or derivitivist) theory of practical rationality that includes finding suitable means to one's determinate ends, suitable determinations of one's inde-terminate ends, and suitable applications of one's chosen principles.[9] If, for example, an agent has a moral pro-attitude toward helping the poor and believes that something he can now do will relieve someone's poverty, he then has a perfectly objective instrumental *prima facie* reason to do it. And if he subscribes to the principle of keeping his promises, then he has a perfectly objective *prima facie* reason to keep this particular promise.[10]

Moral pro- and con-attitudes, whether directed to goals or to principles, thus have the power to rationalize choice. And this power is essential. For it is extremely uninviting to suppose that an agent's moral judgments – or on cognitivist accounts, an agent's reasonably correct moral judgments – could fail to provide reasons for action. For subjectivists, these reasons are provided only with the help of the noncognitive attitudes that moral judgments express. In this respect modern subjectivists have extended Hume's idea that morality produces motives only through its noncognitive content to the idea that it produces reasons only in the same way.[11]

9 For an example of a very broad conception of instrumental rationality see Bernard Williams' "sub-Humean model" in "Internal and External Reasons," *Moral Luck* (Cambridge: Cambridge University Press, 1981), p. 102.

10 David Gauthier, who certainly holds that moral preferences and self-prescriptions give instrumental reasons, also accepts a kind of reason applying to certain important moral situations that cannot be counted as instrumental. On his view, if it is instrumentally rational for me to be disposed to honor personally advan-tageous agreements (as it might be if enough people could see through any insincerity) then I thereby have a special moral reason to comply with the terms of one that I made with the honorable intention to comply. See *Morals by Agreement* (Oxford: Clarendon Press, 1988), chap. 6. Of course, if I retain my earlier honorable disposition then I have, in my broad sense, an instrumental reason that flows simply from that. For complying instantiates a pattern of behavior that I personally value. This is a typical subjectivist reason that pre-sumably remains present in Gauthier's system. But, given the other parts of his complex view, I would still have a reason even if I had lost the disposition. This latter reason does not fall under the present discussion of subjectivism.

11 Stevenson was, admittedly, strangely silent about reasons for action. But Hare makes it clear that moral reasons come from preferences, which he certainly regards as noncognitive dispositions to choose, exposed to facts and logic. See, for example, R. M. Hare, "Another's Sorrow," in *Moral Thinking: Its Levels, Methods and Points* (Oxford: Clarendon Press, 1981), pp. 104–105. Something similar holds, I believe, for Mackie, although his discussion of reasons in chap. 3 of *Ethics* makes things a bit tricky. He there distinguishes three categories of

This shows up in Bernard Williams' "Internal and External Reasons," where he includes *"dispositions of evaluation"* in an agent's "subjective motivational set" (S-set), the set from which all the agent's reasons for action derive through various acts of deliberating.[12] The evaluations that an agent's S-set disposes him to make presumably include the moral evaluations that he has internalized and made part of his way of life. But the practical reasons afforded by these moral evaluations do not derive from his recognizing them to be true. Even if he could come to see that they were false and others not flowing from his S-set true, he would not, on Williams' view, have any reason to follow the latter. For he would have no rational method of transferring the motivation present in his existing dispositions to the better ones.[13] Indeed he would be caught in such a bizarre dilemma (forced to accept his self-acknowledged false evaluations as reasons and unable to act on their true alternatives) that the overall position can be saved, I think, only by denying that the evaluations that flow from his motivational set can be rationally assessed as true or false. And, by our criterion, this not only makes Williams, at least in "Internal and External Reasons," a subjectivist about what must be an important class of moral evaluations, but also one who thinks that reasons follow from their noncognitive force.

Objectivists – at least of the kind I am considering – see things very differently. They agree that moral thought, at least when it is correct, provides reasons for action. But they think it does so only because of its cognitive content. What rationalizes or makes sense of the pursuit of a goal, they assert, is some way in which the goal in question seems *good*. And what rationalizes or makes sense of strict conformity to a principle is some way in which it seems that one can act *well* only by following it.

According to this kind of objectivism, practical rationality is not

reasons or requirements: merely external and conventional ones (like the rules of a game or social practice seen from the outside), those that spuriously purport to bind categorically and intrinsically, and those that, depending on an agent's own attitudes, bind hypothetically. The latter might be called natural reasons. And it is these that, on his account, a properly "made" morality would give the agent whose morality it was.

12 Bernard Williams, *Moral Luck* (Cambridge: Cambridge University Press 1981), pp. 101–113.

13 According to Williams, deliberation is always *from* existing motivations, bringing *them* to bear on the possibilities of action. See *Moral Luck*, p. 109.

as different from theoretical rationality as the subjectivist supposes. Practical thought, like any other kind of thought, requires a subject matter. And for human beings the subject matter that distinguishes thought as practical is, in the first instance, human ends and action insofar as they are good or bad in themselves. The branch of practical thought that is usually called practical reasoning is the determination of how something desired as good can be obtained. In practical reasoning, thus defined, one does not critically examine the desired good to see if it is genuine or, if it is, to question whether something in the special circumstances forbids its pursuit.

These important questions belong to a more fundamental kind of practical thought that might be called ethical. Here one tries to determine what, given the circumstances, it would be good or bad in itself to do or to aim at. These questions are referred to larger ones: what kind of life it would be best to lead and what kind of person it would be best to be. The sense of "good" and "best" presupposed in this noncalculative form of practical thought is very general. In an Aristotelian version of objectivism these notions attach to actions, lives, and individuals as belonging to our biological species.

The object of this kind of thought is not in the first instance morality or prudence as these are commonly understood. For most people think that a human being may be prudent without being good, and many think that there is room for Nietzschean or Thrasymachean skepticism, according to which the best kind of human life might be immoral in one or another way. An objectivist of the kind I wish to defend sees practical thought as deploying a master set of noninstrumental evaluative notions: that of a good or bad human end, a good or bad human life, a good or bad human agent, and a good or bad human action. Practical reason is, on this view, the faculty that applies these fundamental evaluative concepts. If there is no truth to be found in their application, then there is no point to practical reason and no such thing as practical rationality.

I have already indicated a way in which subjectivists who hold an instrumentalist conception of practical rationality can be objectivists about practical reason and rationality. While they deny that ends, principles, and actions are objectively good or bad in themselves, they hold that a person acts rationally in trying to realize his own ends or maximize conformity to his own principles. On the plausible assumption that acting rationally is a natural and not

233

merely conventional form of acting well (and acting irrationally a natural form of acting badly), and in the apparent absence of grounds for other not merely conventional forms, instrumental rationality thus becomes the one objective virtue and instrumental irrationality the one objective vice.[14] In contrast, my objectivist regards instrumental rationality, in this sense, as mere cleverness – something that may or may not be a good to its possessor or make her a better agent. If, on the other hand, someone's practical reasoning is necessarily constrained by appropriate ends and principles, and a sense of the fine and the shameful, then his cleverness constitutes a real virtue – part of his overall practical rationality.[15]

According to the objectivism I will defend, the primary job of practical reason is the correct evaluation of ends, actions, and qualities as good and bad in themselves. And what it is for something to be a reason for action follows from this. *On this view, a reason to act in a certain way is nothing more than something good in itself that it realizes or serves, or, short of that, something bad in itself that it avoids.*

14 Note, however, that some subjectivists have backed away from this theoretically odd hybrid – either, like Richard Brandt (in *A Theory of the Good and the Right* [Oxford: Clarendon Press, 1979], pp. 10–16) by adopting a descriptive account of practical rationality that does not require it to be regarded as an objective excellence or, like Allan Gibbard (in *Wise Choices, Apt Feelings: A Theory of Normative Judgment* [Cambridge, Mass.: Harvard University Press, 1990], for example, pp. 45–46) by applying an expressivist-prescriptivist account of rationality itself. For Gibbard there is no fact of the matter whether maximizing the satisfaction of one's preferences is rational, and argument can break down about fundamental questions of rationality in much the way Stevenson thought it could about fundamental questions of goodness. That such argument breaks down as rarely as it does (that there is mutual argumentative influence over even such basic matters) is a result of the fact that we have been biologically selected to be conversationally cooperative creatures. While I suspect that the substance of my antisubjectivist argument could be applied to these authors, I must postpone the complexities of that discussion for another occasion.

15 A review and minor elaboration of this quasi-Aristotelian vocabulary might be helpful. *Practical reason* is the generic faculty of which *practical thought* is the characteristic generic activity and practical rationality the generic virtue. *Practical reasoning* (that is, *instrumental reasoning* in my broad sense) and *ethical thought* are the two main species of practical thought. If practical reasoning does not presuppose a correct evaluation of the ultimate suitability, whether in general or in the circumstances, of the desired goal or chosen principle, then its virtue is *cleverness*. For the neo-Humean, cleverness exhausts the virtue of practical rationality. If practical reasoning does rest on a correct assessment of the present suitability of the goal or principle, its virtue is, let us say, *real instrumental rationality*. And *wisdom* is the virtue of ethical thought. *Prudence* and so-called *moral goodness* are conspicuous but controversial candidate characteristics that wise ethical thought may deem the chief virtues of action.

234

To the extent that one realizes or serves some such good one acts well. To the extent that one realizes or serves some such bad one acts badly. An objectivist therefore sees moral obligation as giving an agent reason to act only because, and only to the extent that, the agent will act well in discharging it or badly in neglecting it. Moral skepticism therefore comes to nothing more than the doubt that acting morally is a genuine form of acting well.[16] This is the kind of doubt with which moral philosophy began. And, on this view, it is the most important doubt for moral philosophy to resolve.

The subjectivist has a very different account of how moral judgment provides reasons for action. He obviously wishes to avoid bringing in any of these allegedly grounding concepts of actions, lives, ends, and agents as good or bad in themselves. He proposes instead an appeal to basic and therefore cognitively uncriticizable *attitudes*. And this is what, as I shall now try to argue, he cannot do. As unpromising (or even "queer") as the objectivist picture may seem (and I shall be examining some objections to it later), I wonder if it is not our only hope of retaining the idea of practical rationality that we want.

II

The problem lies, I think, in what the subjectivist must take these noncognitive pro- and con-attitudes – these emotions, desires, aversions, preferences, approvals, disapprovals, decisions of principle, and so on – to be.[17] So far as I can see, a reasonably up-to-date subjectivist would present them as functional states that, *inter alia*, tend to move an agent in various practical directions and therefore help explain why his having certain beliefs and perceptions makes him choose, or feel inclined to choose, one course rather than another. They underlie his *tendencies* or *dispositions* to form and express feelings and to choose certain practical actions in the presence of various perceptions and beliefs. To say in the intended sense that someone has a pro-attitude toward world peace is to say, among

16 Alternatively, that the so-called moral virtues are real human virtues.
17 I use the term "noncognitive attitude" here broadly to cover all of these mental states. A decision of principle includes a pro-attitude toward the standard of behavior one has chosen and a con-attitude toward behavior that violates the standard.

other things, that his psychological setup disposes him to do that which he believes will make world peace more likely. And to say that keeping his promises is one of his principles is to say that, among other things, he is set up to do that which he sees as required by the promises he has made.

But how can a noncognitive functional state whose central significance in this context is to help explain our tendency to act toward a certain end, or in accordance with a certain principle, *rationalize* our pursuit of the end or our deference to the principle? How can the fact that we are set up to go in a certain direction make it (even *prima facie*) rational to decide to go in that direction? How can it even contribute to its rationality? Even if a past decision is part of the cause of the psychological setup, there still remains the question whether to continue to abide by it. It is not, according to the view we are considering, the specifically moral aspect of the noncognitive attitude that gives *it* the power to rationalize. Moral attitudes, whatever their special moral earmarks, rationalize because they are dispositive functional states and not because they are moral. The underlying neo-Humean theory of rationalization is completely general. So in testing its plausibility we are free to turn to nonmoral examples. Such examples also free us from the distracting worry whether a given functional-dispositional state rationalizes in a distinctively moral way. *The basic issue here is more fundamental: whether pro- and con-attitudes conceived as functional states that dispose us to act have any power to rationalize those acts.*[18]

Suppose I am in a strange functional state that disposes me to turn on radios that I see to be turned off. Given the perception that a radio in my vicinity is off, I try, all other things being equal, to get it turned on. Does this state rationalize my choices? Told nothing more than this, one may certainly doubt that it does. But in the case I am imagining, this is all there is to the state. I do not turn the radios on in order to hear music or get news. It is not that I have an inordinate appetite for entertainment or information. Indeed, I do not turn them on in order to *hear* anything.[19] My

---

18 My skepticism about this and related matters is shared by others in recent ethics, perhaps most thoroughly by E. J. Bond in *Reason and Value* (Cambridge: Cambridge University Press, 1983), esp. p. 56.

19 There are several variations on what the object of my pro-attitude might be: (a) the *act* of my turning on radios, (b) the *state of affairs* in which I turn them on, (c) the state of affairs in which they are turned on (by anyone), and so forth.

disposition is, I am supposing, basic rather than instrumental. In this respect it is like the much more familiar basic dispositions to do philosophy or listen to music.

I cannot see how this bizarre functional state in itself gives me even a *prima facie* reason to turn on radios, even those I can see to be available for cost-free on-turning. It may help explain, causally, why I turn on a particular radio, but it does not make the act sensible, except insofar as resisting the attendant disposition is painful and giving in pleasant. But in that case it is not the present state that is the reason but the future prospect of relief.[20] Now at this point someone might object that the instrumentalist subjectivist does not or need not regard basic noncognitive pro-attitudes as rationalizing their *objects*, but rather as rationalizing actions that are the *means* to them. So, of course, my odd pro-attitude gives me no reason to turn on radios.

The picture here is of practical reason as a cognitively criticizable mechanism for transferring motivation from the objects of attitudes to that which is "toward" them.[21] Since the ultimate objects are rationally uncriticizable, no reasons are produced for them – no reasons to have those ends or principles or to do those things that are wanted or chosen for their own sakes. But since it is possible to reason well or badly about what will enable one to have or do those objects, reasons are produced for ancillary actions. So if, for example, one loves to listen to music – a contingent taste unassessable by reason – one's attitude does not give a reason actually to listen, but only, in the context of further intentions, to get a record down from the shelf and put it on the turntable.

I find this construction of instrumentalism, while possible, unattractive. If my basic love of listening to music doesn't give me a reason to listen, then it doesn't, I think, give me a reason to take the record down. The appeal of the view, apart from suggesting a line of escape from my argument, may come from conflating two

For my purposes it doesn't matter how my state is conceived, although I will tend to use (a) for simplicity. Note that on all three interpretations, hearing something coming from a radio may be evidence that the object of my proattitude has been achieved, even though hearing something is not in itself the object of that attitude.

20 We will be coming back to the question of rationalization by the prospect of pleasure or pain.
21 This possible objection, to whose subtleties I may not be doing complete justice in the following remarks, was raised by Joseph Raz.

distinct points: (a) that, on an instrumentalist view, a person's ultimate preferences are uncriticizable (except by reference to their compatibility), and (b) that a person's ultimate preferences do not mark off their objects as, given that he has those preferences, rationally appropriate for him. The first point is essential to instrumentalism, but the second does not follow from it. Nor is it a particularly plausible part of that view. But even if it were, my counterexample still works. For my basic noncognitive pro-attitude (conceived as a dispositive functional state) toward turning on radios seems not only to give me no reason to turn on radios but also no reason to take the necessary steps, such as plugging them in. Both seem equally senseless.[22]

But surely my disposition must strike me as odd, if only because it must strike others as odd. Perhaps then I regard it as an embarrassment and wish to be rid of it. And this might seem to make a difference that the subjectivist can exploit. It is not any old functional-dispositional state that rationalizes action, but only one that an agent is ready to stand behind or is at least not alienated from. A second-order endorsement (or the absence of a second-order rejection) is the missing ingredient.

It will be admitted, of course, that an unwelcome first-order attitude can provide the actual point of someone's doing something. A pyromaniac may hate it that he takes pleasure in setting fires, yet set another fire for that very pleasure. But perhaps the subjectivist will say that in such a case the pyromaniac's pleasure fails to give him a genuine reason to set the fire. For that he would need to approve it, or at least not disapprove it, at some higher level.

Now I think it very doubtful that a subjectivist can legitimately attach this significance to the existence or nonexistence of opposing higher-level attitudes. Here, as elsewhere, he is presupposing a significance that depends not on level but on content. An objectivist would take the pyromaniac's higher-level disapproval seriously because he would see in it an evaluation of the pleasure as bad – for example, perverse or shameful. And this would be relevant simply because someone who thinks that an attraction is bad in some such

22 Since turning on radios and taking the steps thereto (for example, plugging them in) seem to me to stand or fall together, I will continue, for reasons of economy, to apply the question of rationalization to the former. If the reader disagrees, he may, whenever I speak of turning radios on, substitute some mere means to that end.

way can scarcely think that he will act well by giving in to it. So the higher-level disapproval shows that the *positive evaluation* that would normally attach to an action as pleasure-producing is canceled. The self-disapproving pyromaniac would not see the prospective pleasure as something that tends to make the torching choice-worthy. But the subjectivist, in rejecting the idea of choice-worthiness as the subject matter of practical reason, can see nothing in the higher-level disapproval except more complexly structured psychological *opposition,* and such opposition would seem to leave the lower-level attitude securely in place with its own proper force.

This point is perhaps worth emphasis. Higher-order attitudes pro and con lower-order attitudes will presumably be treated by the subjectivist as further noncognitive states of the same generic functional type – states grounding, among other things, dispositions to choose one thing rather than another in the face of certain percepts and beliefs. Rather than grounding dispositions to seek certain first-order ends such as pleasure or health, they ground dispositions to seek to be or not to be a person who has or acts toward those ends. What this picture does not explain, however, is the *authority* of the higher-level attitudes.

If the pyromaniac regards his fascination as sick and reprehensible, then he will not see it as giving him a reason to set fires. He may succumb to it as a temptation, but as he looks back on his choice he will not regard the pleasure he took as at least something positive to be credited to his choice. But on the subjectivist's view, it is hard to see why he shouldn't be consoled in just this way. For the subjectivist sees the pyromaniac as having two practical attitudes at odds with each other. His lower-level attraction moves him toward the act of pouring the kerosene, and his higher-level aversion moves him away from it. If he goes ahead he satisfies one of these attitudes, if he refrains he satisfies the other. There is therefore something to be said for and against each alternative. Without the thought that the appetite for fires is bad and therefore *without power to rationalize choice,* there seems no way to keep it from counting.[23]

Even setting this point aside, I cannot see how the subjectivist

---

23 In case one is tempted to think that the force of the higher-order attitude derives from its taking account of the lower-order attitude, note that in typical cases the lower-order attitude also takes account of the higher. That is, it remains in existence despite its recognition of opposition from above. Even though the pyromaniac may hate himself, he still wants to set fires.

can insist that I *must* have some higher-level disapproval of my odd disposition to turn on radios. Perhaps, upbeat person that I am, I positively like my first-order attitude. But even if I do, this still doesn't seem to help rationalize my behavior. Turning on radios still seems perfectly senseless.

Perhaps a subjectivist should simply reject the example as too bizarre. According to this objection, we can make sense of someone's behavior as revealing pro- and con-attitudes only if the attitudes are ones we share to some considerable extent. So if my allegedly basic pro-attitude toward turning on radios is not rendered in one way or other familiar, it may have to be rejected. Attempts to undermine the neo-Humean theory by way of outlandish examples are thus doomed to failure.

Subjectivists may hope by means of some such argument to bring the actual implications of their theory of rational action more in line with those of objectivists who think that we make sense of an action only when we find something that seems good about it – some advantage, pleasure, boost to the ego, or the like. For the objectivist, the state disposing me to turn on radios fails for want of a point. Neither acts of turning on radios nor the state of affairs in which radios are on can intelligibly be seen as goods in themselves. But since the pro-attitude is stipulated to be basic, it cannot be rationalized by being referred to any further good, such as entertainment or knowledge.

Perhaps subjectivists can rule out motivational interpretations that are very strange. But it is difficult to see how. For I do not see how they could rule it out that I might actually engage in the odd behavior in question and that the best functional explanation would be that I had a correspondingly odd pro-attitude understood in their favorite functionalist terms. Indeed, I do not see how they could rule it out that someone might have basic pro-attitudes (conceived as such favored functional states) toward very many bizarre things (disease, pain, poverty, or the like). This is easiest to imagine in someone who desires to communicate reasonably truthfully,[24] is aware of her own eccentricity, has a reasonably accurate picture of the world, deliberates well about means toward and constituents of her largely bizarre ends, and acts accordingly. Such a person

---

24 That and other familiar pro-attitudes (about communication and learning) are certainly necessary when so many others are lacking.

would be intelligible as desiring these strange things *if* desires were the things subjectivists took them to be.[25] And she would not be incapable of recognizing her odd ends and counterends for what they were, and for their oddity. A person does not have to be set up to strive for health to know what health is, a gloomy ascetic temperament does not rule out the knowledge of pleasure, perverse drives frequently recognize (indeed revel in) their own perversity, and so on. Such odd psychologies might, of course, be determined by an anomalous brain state. We might even come to recognize the neurological causal factors. But then the rest of us could imagine that we too might (unhappily) come to have these attitudes.

So I do not think that subjectivists can rule out the possibility of my radio case. Nor can they rule it out that, if I perform my odd routine cheerfully and without regret, my first-order attitude is unopposed by higher-order attitudes of disapproval. So they ought to see it as having the power to rationalize. But that is exactly what it seems to me not to have. It may in some way explain the fact that I turn on another radio, but it does not, in my view, go one step toward showing it to be sensible.

I have chosen a bizarre example to make my point as sharply as possible. But the argument applies, I think, with complete generality. No noncognitive, dispositive functional state of the kind under consideration can, by itself, make the contribution to rationalizing action that subjectivist instrumentalists suppose it to make. This is true even if the state points toward something good like pleasure or health. For pleasure or heath provide a point to their pursuit that does not consist in the fact that they are pursued.

25 It is sometimes said that some interpretations of preferences, conceived along subjectivist lines, will simply be ineligible on the ground that neither we nor the subject will be able to justify the interpretation. For example, that while the subject might, on perhaps frivolous aesthetic grounds, prefer normal oranges to red apples but green apples to normal oranges, she could not, for example, be understood to prefer normal oranges to red apples on high shelves but red apples on low shelves to normal oranges (at least not unless there was something more to the story – highness and lowness of shelf could simply not be an ultimate object of attachment). But again this seems to confuse the question of causation and justification. If preference is conceived along subjectivist lines as a preevaluative functional state causing one to feel and act in various ways under various conditions of belief and recognition, then there is no reason why this odd "preference" could not emerge. Indeed, the person might be bemused by her own highly unusual internal psychological economy. And to say this in no way implies that either the subject or anyone else is infallible about her "preferences" – we might come to see that it was something other than shelf height after all.

A noncognitive pro-attitude, conceived as a psychological state whose salient function is to dispose an agent to act, is just not the kind of thing that can rationalize. That I am psychologically set up to head in a certain way, cannot by itself rationalize my Will's going along with the setup. For that I need the *thought* that the direction in which I am psychologically pointed leads to something good (either in act or result) or takes me away from something bad.

Someone might object that I am imputing to the subjectivist too narrow a conception of desire, aversion, preference, approval, disapproval, commitment, and the like – that I am focusing too exclusively on their role in explaining tendencies to *act*. These states may have other characteristic noncognitive features that better account for their rational force. Chief among these would be the pleasing light that positive attitudes, and the unflattering light that negative attitudes, cast on their objects.[26] These hedonic colors may also be lent to the idea of doing that which will make the pleasant or painful prospect more likely. And perhaps it is here that we find the rationalizing force of pro- and con-attitudes.

But how is this to be spelled out? It might be said that pleasure or pain in the prospect of having or doing something makes pleasure or pain in the reality more likely. So a person with a basic pro-attitude can expect pleasure in achieving his object and frustration in failing to achieve it, just as someone with a basic con-attitude can expect unpleasantness in getting his. And it is this that rationalizes pursuit or avoidance.

There are at least two problems that stand in the way of this solution. To the extent that a present basic pro-attitude rationalizes by virtue of a promised pleasure, then rationalization should also be present – and just as strong – in the case where the agent expects the pleasure but oddly lacks the present motivation. If I believe that I will get just as much pleasure from this piece of candy, which tempts me, as from that piece, which oddly does not, then it is hard to see, at least as far as gustatory pleasure is concerned (the typical reason for buying candy), how I could have more reason to choose the first. That I now find pleasure in the *thought* of eating

---

26 Here I return to a point that I explicitly put aside earlier. It may be more plausible with respect to desire and aversion than to commitment to principle. But it might also be thought that commitments (whether moral or personal) lend the prospect of their fulfillment a pleasing aspect of self-consistency and personal integrity, and their violation a disturbing aspect of incoherence and failure.

or buying the first piece but not the second seems irrelevant. Or if I believe that I will feel as much psychic pain in violating a rule (in the sense of a possible rule) that I have deliberately not subscribed to (perhaps because I feel its pull on me is irrational) as in violating a rule that I have adopted, it is hard to see how the prospect of pain can give me more reason to observe the second than the first.

But there is an even more serious problem with supposing that a basic pro-attitude rationalizes by reference to the pleasure its fulfillment promises or the pain its frustration threatens. For the objects of many basic desires do not include the subject's pleasure or pain at all. Suppose, for example, I want to see famine ended in Ethiopia. I therefore take pleasure in the very idea of famine relief (and perhaps also in the idea of working toward it) and feel pained when politics stands in the way. But if I attach basic value to the end to famine, then it is the thought that doing such and such will help feed people that gives me my basic reason to do it – not the thought that doing it will bring me pleasure or save me pain. These might give me *additional* reasons, but they cannot be my basic ones.

It seems, moreover, that the pleasure one expects in getting (or working toward) what one basically wants and the displeasure in failing to get it are themselves rationally assessable. It generally *makes sense* to be pleased or frustrated in these circumstances. What more sensible thing to be pleased or displeased about? But surely the subjectivist will want to say that this good sense depends entirely on the attitude. It is rationally appropriate to be pleased at getting what one wants or displeased at failing to get it *because* one wants it. So, again, the pleasure or displeasure cannot provide the basic reason to pursue the object.

In any case, it seems to me a mistake to think of the concepts of pleasure and displeasure as purely descriptive, psychological concepts. To call an experience pleasant or unpleasant is already to bring it under an evaluative concept.[27] That is why purely psychological accounts of pleasure seem to leave it utterly mysterious *why* we should pursue the pleasant and shun the unpleasant. On one such account, a pleasant experience is, roughly speaking, one whose intrinsic character makes an agent want to prolong it. When we

27 In *The Varieties of Goodness* (London: Routledge and Kegan Paul, 1963), pp. 63–85, Georg Henrik von Wright argued that pleasure is not merely good but is itself a kind of goodness.

combine this with a subjectivist account of wanting, we conclude that a pleasant experience is one whose intrinsic character creates a functional state grounding, among other things, the disposition to prolong it. But why should anybody want to be in such a state? Suppose I tell you that if you start scratching your ear the experience will strongly dispose you to keep on scratching. Does this by itself give you reason to want to scratch? Conceived as a kind of psychological inertial force, pleasure takes on a somewhat sinister aspect. This is because the account leaves out the salient thing: that an agent wants to prolong a pleasant experience precisely because it is pleasant – because it feels good. Pleasantness is not merely that which brings about a prolonging disposition, it is what makes sense of it.

So far, I have urged that neither the dispositional nor the hedonic aspect of pro-attitudes can provide what we want in the way of reasons for action. The subjectivist might respond by taking a somewhat different tack. He might claim that noncognitive attitudes may be formed in a rational or irrational way, and that *rationally formed* attitudes can provide reasons. This might, of course, mark a considerable retreat from the familiar subjectivist position that *any* pro- or con-attitude can give a reason for action. But if the requirements of rational attitude formation turn out to be weak, the retreat may be limited. If the requirement were merely one of reasonably adequate information, then many noncognitive attitudes would provide reasons. If, on the other hand, the requirement were as demanding as Kant's generalization test, far fewer would qualify.

My response to this strategy is to deny that the kinds of non-cognitive states the subjectivist means to be talking about can be made rational or irrational by the way in which they are formed. This is because I cannot see how, in the absence of objective prior standards for evaluating ends or actions as good or bad in themselves, a state disposing one to act can be any more rationally criticizable than a state disposing one to sneeze. Any factor (like having a perfectly regular character or being caused by true rather than false beliefs or valid rather than invalid reasoning) could be just as true of sneezing as acting. It's true that the disposition to sneeze can be irresistible, while dispositions to turn on radios or read philosophy papers typically are not. But space for the voluntary seems to me in itself devoid of rational significance unless it is in the service of an agent's values.

244

It is often said that an attitude formed in light of true beliefs has more power to rationalize than one formed in error. And while there is something right about this, it is not something that the subjectivist can obviously make use of. Suppose, liking canned chop suey and believing it to be a typical Chinese dish, I am moved to seek more Chinese food, and in particular to try out my local Szechwan restaurant (where my bland tastes are likely to be shocked). Such examples are often taken to show the need for some informational constraint on rational desire and preference.

But surely what is ultimately bad about my motivation here is not that it is based on false belief, but that it is a very uncertain guide to food that I will find good tasting. To the objectivist, information is relevant because without it I won't be pointed in the direction of good things, like innocent pleasure. But the subjectivist must reject the cognitive claim that pleasure is a good. For him, liking something is just another noncognitive pro-attitude. And his account of pleasure, in omitting the idea that what is liked is found experientially good, removes the sting from the criticism of my motivation to patronize the Szechwan restaurant. For if we ask the subjectivist why it's too bad that my desire for Chinese food was rooted in error, he can say only that it is because the functional state in which my desire consists will probably extinguish itself once I get real Chinese food. But this seems to miss the point. Why should cultivating a functional state that will extinguish itself be less rational than cultivating one that won't? What is so important about resistance to extinguishability?

One might agree that an informational constraint is not enough, but think that adding some other conditions will do the trick. Hare, for example, has argued that if we are going to give ourself certain kinds of prescriptions, we must give ourselves perfectly universal ones.[28] (He thinks that moral language is analytically cut out to express just such universal commands or norms.) Yet why should someone who sees himself as choosing in a cognitive void where there is no prior truth about good or bad action, insist on giving himself universal commands? Of course *we* wish to give ourselves such commands, because we think there is a subject matter of good and bad action that, like all genuine subject matters, is to some considerable extent regular. Since we think that certain *kinds* of

28 Hare, *Moral Thinking*, pp. 1–24.

actions are bad – for example, sticking one's hand in a fire – we tell ourselves not to do actions *of that kind*.[29] But if we thought there were no such knowledge of good and bad action to be had, I do not see why we should want our self-prescriptions, or some set of them, to be universal. And it would make no difference if there were, which I think there is not, some special vocabulary exclusively dedicated to making such commands. Why should we use this vocabulary? Or why shouldn't we subvert it?

Of course it may be said, plausibly, that we need to cooperate and coordinate, and so need to find common norms.[30] But I do not see it as a point of subjectivists. For on their reading, this need must consist in something like the fact that with the cooperation bred of common norms we will get more of what our pro-attitudes – either independent, norm-permitted ones (for example, my morally innocuous pro-attitude toward turning on radios) or new, norm-generated ones – point us toward. And if the preceding argument is correct, we have no reason to care about *this*. I suspect that the theoretical appeal to the importance of coordination works because we think that without common norms (or serviceable and just common norms) life with each other would be pretty bad – indecent, painful, suspiciously on guard, and too short to be meaningful. We need good common norms to live well together. If human beings didn't need to be thus coordinated, the selection of such norms would be pointless. Since they do need it, norms that make it possible, especially those that help us make the most of our human potential, have something objective in their favor.

III

But am I really claiming that desire and preference can't rationalize choice? Not at all. I am claiming instead that the subjectivist's account of desire is impoverished, leaving out precisely that element of desire that does the rationalizing. I have been careful not to raise the question whether my odd functional state is in fact a basic desire to turn on radios. That is, I have been careful not to raise the question whether the existence of a noncognitive dispositive functional state of the kind subjectivists would take desire to be is

29 With perhaps an escape clause for very unusual situations.
30 A point stressed by Gibbard, *Wise Choices*; see, for example, pages 26–27.

sufficient for desire. I have not raised it because I am not at all sure of the answer. What I feel sure of, and what I have argued, is that, whether or not the mere functional state is sufficient, it cannot ground reasons for action. What does that is another element (of necessity) typically present in basic desire, namely, some kind of evaluation of the desired object as good – for example, pleasant, interesting, advantageous, stature-enhancing, as decent. I am not saying, however, that desire is in general nothing more than positive evaluation. In some cases we would not speak of desire if the implicit positive evaluation did not provoke or were not accompanied by some kind of appetite that prods the will toward the object for the good that it seems to offer.[31] What seems amiss in standard neo-Humean subjectivism is the way it runs together the ideas of explanation and rationalization. The noncognitive attitude present in many cases of desire may sometimes be part of the causal account of why the desired object is pursued, but the pursuit is rationalized not by the attitude but by the apparent value that attaches to its object or to the pursuit of it. Without the appearance of the value, the attraction would be empty, as it is in my counterexample.

It might seem, however, that the view that desires and preferences rationalize only because of the value judgments they involve can scarcely be correct. Aren't there rationalizing desires and preferences that point to no real or apparent good? To answer this question I need to make some distinctions between different types of goods to be attained in action and the different types of rationalization that they involve. First and most obviously, an action may promote goods that speak in its favor *as a good action* and therefore

---

31 This kind of motivating state – one that has influence *on* the will – must be distinguished from dispositive states *of* the will, forms of executive rationality (steadfastness, courage, prudence, and the like) or irrationality (distraction, cowardice, weakness, and the like) that enable or disable the will in its natural pursuit of the best course of action. On my anti-Humean conception, which has been greatly influenced by discussion with Philippa Foot and by Thomas Nagel's *The Possibility of Altruism* (Oxford: Clarendon Press, 1970), chap. 5, much rational human action comes about without the influence of motivational pushes and pulls. I see that it is a convenient time to get needed service for my car and I simply proceed to do it. All that is required is the perception of overall advantage (the safety and comfort of having a well-running car and the convenience of present service) and a reasonable degree of executive rationality. In such a case we may also speak of my desire for the advantage, but this desire is nothing more than my will's healthy recognition of its availability. Such a desire is not something the will *takes account of* in determining a rational choice.

one that ought to be done. It is in this way that considerations of health and pleasure typically support visits to the supermarket and doctor. A good such as this – one that in the circumstances tends to make its pursuit good – may be called *choice-worthy*. Some choice-worthy goods are in particular circumstances *conclusive* – they provide decisive reasons for acts that would bring them about – while others are *contributory*, providing reasons that may be overruled. Choice-worthy goods give full-fledged reasons for action. So here we may speak of rationalization in the fullest sense.

But we must also consider goods that are *not* choice-worthy. These are goods that do not ever, or at least in some particular circumstances, speak in favor of their pursuit. A plausible example is the pyromaniac's pleasure in watching a building burn. The pleasure of parent–child incest is another. No right-minded person who is capable of these pleasures would suppose that he had good reason to seek them. They are clearly not goods in the full-fledged sense, for they do not contribute to the goodness of action or life. Yet, contra Plato and Aristotle, these pleasures do seem genuine. We can imagine a prospect that has nothing in it to attract us but that, oddly, sets up in us a strong impulse to seek it. But the prospect of these pleasures, to one who can experience them, is not like that. They present such a person with a real temptation. It therefore seems plausible to regard them as some kind of experiential good. We might say that they *make intelligible,* but do not rationalize, a choice to pursue them.

Perhaps we should also briefly consider goods that are *merely apparent*. These are objects that appear good in some choice-worthy or nonchoice-worthy way, but are not. Some present simple illusions, like vanilla, which smells delicious but tastes bad. Some involve symbolic connections with real goods, as in the case of someone who anxiously avoids stepping on cracks. Other cases are less psychiatric. At some emotional level all of us invest certain minor successes and failures with a significance they really lack. Such "goods" and "evils" cannot, when they fail to take us in, rationalize pursuit or avoidance. Nor can they make pursuit or avoidance intelligible, at least not in the way in which the special class of goods and evils just considered can. Yet to the extent that we are taken in, they can, in a sense, do both.

With these distinctions in mind, we may consider cases in which an inclination unadorned by any prospect of objective value might seem to rationalize or make sense of action. What about whims, for example? Can't people have whims to do that which serves not even an apparent value? I think we should not assume that they can. Philosophers' examples might, in this regard, be misleading. What we would do on whim is usually something whose value (or apparent value) can either be discerned or made the object of intelligent speculation. In some cases only the timing or means is capricious. One flies off to London for a haircut. One gets up at midnight, dresses, and goes out to seek pie à la mode. Anscombe's example of wanting to touch a spot on the wall or Davidson's example of wanting to drink a can of paint may not, I think, be all that typical. But they do count, so what can I say about them?

It seems to me a mistake to say that your wanting to drink paint counts as a whim only if there is no answer to the question what you see in it. We often, of course, put off that question by saying that it's just a whim. But putting off the question and there being no answer are different. The smooth and creamy paint might, after all, look delicious. And the allure of this appearance might be reinforced by a perverse curiosity. You might wonder what the paint tastes like.[32] The whim might have other explanations. It might be an odd desire to do something really, if trivially, original – to break the fetters of convention if only in some silly way. Adolescents are famous for this kind of desire, and there are outbreaks of adolescence even in the apparently mature. It might have a related but even more primitive significance. Children are continually performing actions that might at first glance seem pointless but that may well aim at the demonstration, however symbolically, of what they wish to be unlimited powers of independent agency in the physical world. They empty out drawers, pick up sticks and run them along fences, skim stones on the water, and so forth. Given the vicissitudes of the human predicament, all this makes a certain sense. And adult whims might sometimes be like this. They might reflect a curiously displaced need to demonstrate the power to act outside our rutted ways.

There are other diagnoses of very odd whims that have a more exclusively psychiatric significance. The odd desire to drink the

32 When one is curious about something, the knowledge one seeks seems interesting and perhaps even important, even if at some level one knows that it is not. And it is this impression of significance (or urgency) that makes the curious behavior intelligible.

paint might focus some unconscious need of rebellion. Perhaps you drank some paint as a child and were severely reprimanded by your frightened parents. Or perhaps the drinking has a hidden sexual significance. Doesn't everything?

I think we are very reluctant to rest content with the whim as a state that merely disposes you to drink the paint. This is because we wish to treat the whimsical urge as at least marginally intelligible. And to do this we need to see the whim as pointing to something that might be or at least seem attractive from your point of view. If we can find no such value – if there is nothing that you see or seem to see, consciously or unconsciously, in drinking the paint – then however effective its causal influence, the dispositive state gives no support to your choice to drink the paint.[33] Perhaps we should treat such a disposition as a limiting and degenerate case of desire. Or perhaps we should treat it as merely resembling genuine desire and preference. But on either view, I am inclined to see whims as no exception to the general rule that desires can rationalize only by reference to the conscious or unconscious evaluation that is (typically) at their core.

But here another, perhaps more difficult, objection arises. Even if some kind of value judgment is always, or almost always, present in desire and preference, a desire or preference is often, as I have indicated, more than a value judgment. We may see the availability of certain good things but be unmoved by them, and if we are unmoved then surely we may lack at least a certain kind of reason to seek them. Some good things that leave us cold (for example, our future health) still give us strong reasons for action, but in other cases an absence of felt attraction may affect our reasons. Both X and Y may offer the prospect of equally witty and intelligent conversation, but you may be much more attracted to the kind offered by X than to the kind offered by Y. Surely then you have much better reason to spend time with X.

According to this objection, at least some good things are rationally pursued only to the extent that they attract us. But then contrary to what I have been urging, our being moved must itself be part of our reason for pursuing them. If mere pro-attitudes are not sufficient to rationalize, they are in some cases necessary. But

33 Unless of course it is unpleasant to resist.

if so, then surely some doubt is thrown on the claim that they lack any kind of rationalizing force.

I cannot here try to consider all the kinds of cases in which reasons might seem to depend partly on attraction as well as on expected value. In cases that involve personal taste, such as taste in company, the significance of attraction might lie in its containing a foretaste of pleasure or satisfaction. Attraction to people, or for that matter to novels and paintings, promises a kind of personal pleasure in our future interactions with them. And that anticipated pleasure can give a perfectly respectable reason to seek them out.

Someone might object that such pleasure is nothing more than the consciousness of having gotten that to which one's noncognitive pro-attitude propelled one. If so, the pleasure would be a mere logical reflection of the earlier pro-attitude. But this picture seems wrong to me, although it may be encouraged by an easily missed ambiguity. An inclination might, in one sense, be said to be satisfied when its object is obtained. But it is a sad truth that this kind of technical satisfaction may lack any element of real pleasure or fulfillment. The anticipated pleasure that is part of ordinary attractions to people or art is, however, real pleasure. It might, as a matter of empirical fact, be pleasure partly caused by the previous inclination. And if it were, the existence of the inclination could be evidence for it. But even so, it is only the pleasure itself that makes sense of acting on the inclination.

There are many other cases in which we would have to look closely to see whether noncognitive attitudes were themselves providing reasons. Let me just mention one of the most puzzling. Two people may be equally supportive, kind, admirable, beautiful, pleasant to be with, and so on, but we may, because of some other difference of quality that in no way reflects well or badly on either, be fonder of the first than of the second. And when this happens most of us suppose, at least in practice, that we have greater reason to pursue the good of the first. Why? Someone might say that the greater fondness is simply constituted by a stronger altruistic disposition. But I think the answer must be more complicated. Human beings can thrive only in various private connections of concern and identification – as with family, friends, colleagues, or acquaintances. Some of these connections are thrust upon us, but many are not. And some people simply fit better than others into the

251

highly personal sympathetic world we have already created for ourselves. These people belong in our story and so their good is especially important to us. I cannot claim to fully understand the nature and operation of such judgments of importance. But I feel it would be a travesty to interpret them as nothing more than functionally grounded tendencies to go for some people's good over that of others.

IV

My claim has been that noncognitive analyses of desire, preference, commitment, and the like cannot capture their reason-giving force. In depriving pro-attitudes of any evaluative thought, noncognitivism reduces them to functional states that, upon reflection, may show what we will do under certain conditions but not what we should do. Practical rationality, I have argued, requires a subject matter of the values to be achieved or realized in human action – a subject matter that only cognitivism can provide.

Even if I am right about this, there remains room for evaluative skepticism, which if correct, might remove actions altogether from the authority of reason. As noted earlier, Mackie and others have argued that certain evaluative judgments, while genuinely cognitive, cannot be true. There are in evaluative thought the concepts appropriate to a genuine subject matter, but the world does not, indeed cannot, furnish the corresponding properties and relations. Evaluative facts would be unacceptably queer in two ways: first, in providing motivation – in effect exercising a power over the will – and second, in providing reasons for action that do not depend on subjective inclinations. Mackie objects to the idea of motivation or rationalization (he speaks of the latter as prescriptive authority) that is not wholly explained in a neo-Humean manner. Like Hume, he thinks that genuine thought is by itself powerless to cause or make good sense of action.

Now I think an objectivist should be more or less unperturbed by the part of the argument that concerns motivation. To say that someone recognizes a value (say a moral value) that can be achieved in action is not to say that the recognition must be a spur to his will. To recognize that justice or decency requires us to do something is, in my view, to recognize that we shall act badly if we do not do it. The connection with motivation is indirect and conditional. To be unresponsive to the genuine badness of an action is to have a will that is unmoved by a conclusive reason for not doing something – a will that is, to that extent, irrational or unreasonable. If we were more reasonable, we would care more about the quality of our actions. And since most of us are not wholly unreasonable, we do to some extent care. That, I think, is what the motivational force of unconditioned value comes to. And that does not require value facts to have any "queer" power over the will. It requires instead a conception of the will as the part of human reason whose function is to choose for the best.

The other skeptical argument questions whether objective value could have rational authority. Let's begin with the objective value of ends. Why, it will be asked, should we care whether or not our ends have objective value? Why is such a concern rational? If, as I think, practical rationality chiefly consists in correctness of thought about human good and evil, a concern is rational just in case reason determines that it is a good concern for us to have. And if a concern belongs to real human virtue – the qualities that make us and our actions good – then it can hardly be denied that it is a good concern. So, on this conception of rationality, to show that we have reason to be concerned with the objective goodness of our ends it is enough to show that such concern is essential to human excellence. And while showing this may present many difficulties, it does not seem to be ruled out in advance as an unacceptably "queer" task. Something similar can be said about reasons given by the objective goodness of action itself. If, as I think, the reasons for doing an action just *are* the good-making features that it has either in itself[34] or that it derives from the good ends it serves, then the mystery of how the goodness of action can provide reasons seems to disappear. Mackie's problem depends on supposing that we start with an idea of practical rationalization or prescriptive authority that is prior to our idea of good and bad action. If that were true, and if goodness weren't in some way reducible to rationality, then we could raise the question, and so make it seem mysterious, how the mere recognition of something good about an action could give us a reason to do it. But I am skeptical of this prior conception of reasons, and therefore suspect that the real mystery that Mackie and others are

34 Either directly (for example, its pleasantness) or because of the virtue or right principles to which it conforms (for example, its fidelity).

circling around is how actions can have objective goodness in the first place. They suggest that the problem is how, if there were such a thing, it could give reasons. But, if I am right, the problem must be more fundamental.

In much of contemporary moral thought, rationality seems to be regarded as the basic virtue of action or motivation, one that grounds all the other virtues. This, I have been arguing, is a mistake. Practical rationality is a virtue of a very special kind. But it is not special in being the most fundamental merit of action or motivation. It is special by being the virtue *of* reason as it thinks about human good. A virtue isn't a virtue because it's rational to have it. A good action isn't good because it's rational to do. On my view, the only proper ground for claiming that a quality is rational to have or an action rational to do is that the quality or action is, on the whole, good. It is human good and bad that stand at the center of practical thought and not any independent ideas of rationality or reasons for action. Indeed, even in its proper place as a quality of practical reason, rationality is validated only by the fact that it is the *excellence*, that is, the *good* condition of practical thought. Even here the notion of good has the primary say.

But note that I have not here argued against the possibility that practical rationality makes demands on practical thought that should be understood antirealistically as requirements on the *construction* of a picture of human good and bad.[35] On such a constructivist view, we might have to begin practical philosophy with a critique of practical reason as it thinks about human good. Here I have been arguing only that the primary questions are not what it

35 The evaluative realist thinks that every constraint on practical reason has the function of maximizing the likelihood of correspondence to a transcendent, and therefore possibly unapproachable, reality. The constructivist, in the perhaps special sense I have in mind, thinks that there are constraints that, coming from the nature of practical thought itself, must set limits on where the truth can lie and how much truth there can be. The method of reflective equilibrium as discussed by John Rawls in *A Theory of Justice* can be given a constructivist interpretation not as the best method for descrying an external or internal moral reality, but as the only systematically acceptable method of moral thought, the applications of which determine, insofar as such determination is possible, where the moral truth is to lie. Such constructivism might come, however, in two varieties. In one, the rational constraints would lead first to the identification of actions and ends as rational and therefore good. In the other, the constraints would be from the very start constraints on rational thought about the good. It is only the first kind of constructivism that I have been attacking.

254

is rational or irrational, but what it is good or bad to be, seek, or do – that is, protesting the confusion that arises when the notions of rationality escape their proper place and become themselves the primary objects of practical thought.